I0128239

Migration and Health
Theories, Policies, and Experiences

Migration and Health
Theories, Policies, and Experiences

Edited by
Michela C. Pellicani and Gül Ince-Beqo

TRANSNATIONAL PRESS LONDON
2024

MIGRATION SERIES: 55

Migration and Health

Theories, Policies, and Experiences

Edited by Michela C. Pellicani and Gül Ince-Beqo

Copyright © 2024 Transnational Press London

All rights reserved. This book or any portion thereof may not be reproduced or used in any manner whatsoever without the express written permission of the publisher except for the use of brief quotations in a book review or scholarly journal.

First Published in 2024 by Transnational Press London in the United Kingdom, 13 Stamford Place, Sale, M33 3BT, UK.
www.tplondon.com

Transnational Press London® and the logo and its affiliated brands are registered trademarks.

Requests for permission to reproduce material from this work should be sent to: sales@tplondon.com

Paperback
ISBN: 978-1-80135-024-2
Digital
ISBN: 978-1-80135-025-9

Cover Design: Nihal Yazgan
Cover Photo by Krzysztof Hepner on unsplash.com

Transnational Press London Ltd. is a company registered in England and Wales No. 8771684.

CONTENTS

ABOUT EDITORS

Michela C. Pellicani

Associate professor of Demography at the Department of Political Science - University of Bari (Italy), PhD in Economics of Population and Development.

Research expertise: Population Ageing; International migrations; Integration of immigrants particularly focused on the European Union and the Mediterranean area. Main research partnerships with: La Documentation Française - Paris; Institut National d'Etudes Démographiques (INED) – Paris; l'Institute for Employment Research (IER) University of Warwick; Centre d'étude de Gestion Démographique pour les Administrations Publiques (GéDAP) – University of Louvain-la-Neuve; Department of Social Policy and Social Work - University of Oxford; Institut de Recherche sur le Maghreb Contemporain (IRMC-CNRS) – Tunis; Groupe International de Recherche: Economie de la Méditerranée et du Monde Arabe (GDRI-EMMA-CNRS); Réseau International de Recherche DémoBalk; Association Marocaine d'Etudes et de Recherches sur les Migrations (AMERM); Mediterranean Universities Union (UNIMED), Centre d'Etudes sur le Développement International et les Mouvements Economiques et Sociaux (CEDIMES).

Responsible for many research programmes financed by the Italian Ministry of University and Research (MIUR), the Italian National Council of Research (CNR), and the European Asylum, Migration and Integration Fund (AMIF). Over 50 publications (as author or editor) on both national and international scientific reviews and volumes. Referee for several scientific reviews.

Coordinator/President of numerous national and international institutional or scientific committees. Delegate of the University of Bari for the Migration Policies and Integration. Director of the II level Master "Management del Fenomeno Migratorio e del Processo di Integrazione" of the University of Bari and Co-director of the Master in "Migration and Diversity Management" integrating Level 7 Diploma in "Strategic management and Leadership" of the International Business School, Manchester, UK and the University of Bari, Italy.

Gül Ince-Beqo

Gül Ince-Beqo is a postdoctoral researcher at the University of Milan. She received her co-tutelle Ph.D. at the Catholic University of Milan and the Regent's University London. Her research focuses mainly on the intersection of migration, gender, and family. She has published in a number of international and national peer-reviewed journals, including *International Review of Sociology*, *Migration Letters*, *Italian Political Sciences*, *Mondi Migranti*, and *De Europa*. Prior to her current postdoc position at Milan University, she was involved in various EU-funded projects at Bari University and Urbino University. In May-June 2023, she was a visiting researcher at the Department of Sociology, Lund University.

INTRODUCTION

In this volume, we have collected several contributions to offer a broad overview of distant and different approaches in the conceptualisation and implementation of migration-related social services in general, and health services in particular. Due to the extreme heterogeneity of the socioeconomic, political, and cultural conditions of migrant-receiving societies, we have identified some significant contexts in terms of geographical location, categories of migrants, and integration policies. We have enriched the theoretical and empirical contributions with case studies reporting on the first-hand experiences of doctors who are dealing with migrants. All chapters present original results obtained from analyses of national and international sources as well as field studies. Indeed, different research methods have been adopted to capture both qualitative and quantitative aspects of the multiple facets of the migration-health nexus.

Below is a brief description of the chapters.

Ince-Beqo and Pellicani examine how the relationship between health and migration is conceptualised and reproduced at different levels based on in-depth literature and policy analysis. The paper also analyses how some specific diseases are shaped by migration both in the country of origin and in the country of arrival. Furthermore, by examining the role of two key actors in health care provision and access, the general practitioner and the intercultural mediator, the authors also analyse the barriers and obstacles to accessing health services according to the legal status and classification of migrants. The results highlight that a proper analysis of the inequalities perpetuated at various levels in access to services is crucial. Also, encouraging migrant-sensitive health policies enforced with an effective intervention of intercultural mediators is crucial to ensuring the right to health for all, regardless of legal status.

The chapter by Schubert and Ringeisen summarise research results on refugees' mental health in relation to negative attitudes that members of receiving societies might have towards refugees. To highlight the underlying mechanisms, the authors describe theoretical approaches that explain the intergroup dynamics leading to these attitudes and further severe health consequences for refugees. Complementarily, they consider refugees' prevalence of psychological diagnoses and introduce a taxonomy of accompanying relevant resources and stressors, hereby dissecting the stress process as it unfolds from fleeing to arrival and resettling in the receiving society. As integrated threat theory outlines, negative behavioural responses from receiving society members to refugees can be triggered by perceiving different types of threats, namely intergroup anxiety, symbolic and realistic threat, and negative stereotypes. In contrast, positive intercultural interactions as well as empathy towards refugees, have been shown to improve attitudes of the receiving society and to raise awareness for refugees' struggles and socio-emotional/informational needs. The chapter shows how fostering these protective factors in the host countries could improve refugees' access to health care and well-being, ultimately raising the chances of a successful inclusion into society.

Lane and Vatanparast analyse the health-migration relationship from a food insecurity perspective in Canada, with a particular focus on Syrian refugees. Based primarily on a thorough literature review, this paper examines how food insecurity among Syrian refugees has been linked to low income and higher levels of education, indicating that poor integration into the labour market, coupled with limited coping skills on low incomes, probably play a role. This widespread food insecurity could be putting refugee families at risk of consuming suboptimal diets and developing chronic diseases. Efforts to improve food security among Syrian refugees should involve a review of minimum income requirements to meet basic needs, as well as programming that builds on Syrian refugees' agricultural and cooking skills.

Pellicani and Ince-Beqo investigate the health and migration nexus regarding service provision and migration governance, particularly asylum seekers' health access in the Apulia Region, one of the main Mediterranean routes for asylum seekers heading for Europe and representing an exception in the Italian national territory, extending the medical treatments and services provided for Italians and regular migrants to those irregular ones. The analysis relies on the data collected within a research project that aims to create an integrated system of prevention, diagnosis, treatment, and rehabilitation of asylum seekers and holders of international protection on the regional territory. It is mixed-method research based on (1) quantitative data from an ad hoc field survey organised in the reception centres and drafted to retrieve information unavailable in other databases and distributed to, and (2) qualitative data collected through semi-structured interviews with local policymakers, representatives of reception centres, and NGOs. The results highlight that in the reception process, the medical service appears decisive, and the absence of constant control of health status can cause the worsening of not visible symptoms, creating further psycho-physical

4

problems. Another essential aspect is the importance of the communication: the diffusion of the information and the role of competent intercultural mediators in the outpatient visits in the first-level reception centres, especially during the certification and treatment of violence, torture, or other severe forms of physical, psychological, or sexual violence. Some best practises are presented and some suggestions for further implementations of health services for asylum seekers and refugees are proposed.

The chapter by Sousa Nascimento, Dominguez Roberto e Correia dos Santos follows an ego network analysis approach to 1) evaluate how social capital changes from general to specific-health networks between Portuguese-speaking immigrants and non-migrants in Portugal while 2) evaluating network structural fluctuations among immigrants according to their length of time in the country. A convenience sample of 71 egos provided information on their general and health-specific networks, which was collected online through a network survey using a name generator (alters' names), name interpreter (alters' attributes), and position generator (social capital). Results revealed that migrants' networks were less efficient and had lower social capital than non-migrant networks. Among migrants, those living in Portugal for more than five years had more social capital, more efficient networks, and more bridging ties (non-migrants) than those living in the country for less than two years, which had more bonding ties. Insights on how social networks evolve to understand social determinants of migrant health are discussed and can inform stakeholders and enhance decision-making processes in migrations health.

Merone, De Falco, and Degani examine how Hispanic immigrant women in Philadelphia (Pennsylvania, the USA) with various immigration statuses and conditions, access and utilise sexual and reproductive services and describe the obstacles they face. The city of Philadelphia was chosen as the case study site due to the high foreign-born population, where an estimated number of 390,000 residents were immigrations or natives with immigrant parents. In addition, Philadelphia was estimated to have the largest undocumented immigrant population among the Northeast American cities. An exploratory qualitative study was designed with 18 in-depth ad hoc interviews with Hispanic women with the following immigration statuses: first- and second-generation immigrants, lawful permanent residents, naturalised citizens, and undocumented immigrants. The barriers were understood in terms of discrimination and inequitable access to healthcare under international human rights law. To detect the root causes of healthcare inequalities and lack of human rights fulfilment, the authors relied on an intersectionality perspective to analyse and understand the multiple sources of discrimination. The research yielded four key themes: historical cultural beliefs, practises, and languages; fear, stigma, and negative self-perception; the role of community and social services; and influence of socioeconomic status.

In the next chapter, Wong, Saravanakumar, and Shrestha-Ranjit illustrate the main features of migration-related health policy changes in New Zealand (NZ), a country with a long migration history. The paper compares NZ's policy about entitlement, access, and responsiveness to health services for legal migrants, refugees, asylum seekers, and undocumented migrants in 2014 and 2019. The results were organised into entitlement to services; access to services; responsiveness of services; and measures to achieve change, following the Migration International Policy Index model (MIPEX). The paper shows that there were minor differences between the 2014 and 2019 migrant health policies and no change in NZ's overall rating. Aggregation into overall migration categories masks a deficit in health policies for Asian and MELAA migrants particularly. Very high-level health policy was not congruent with lower-level policy for Asian and MELAA (Middle Eastern, Latin American, and African) migrants in 2014 and 2019. While NZ ranked top in the MIPEX health policy index in 2014, and among the top five countries in 2019, significant obstacles persist, in particular for undocumented migrants and asylum seekers. On the other hand, the study emphasises the importance of policies that ensure accessible, sufficient, appropriate, and responsive services that take into account the identity of ethnic, cultural, and religious sub-groups.

Fanny Christou and Nikky Christou analyse, in a comparative perspective, how the French and Swedish health systems acted during the pandemic in the provision of health services to migrants, with a focus on the articulation between the precarious situation of migrants and chronic digestive diseases. As the study shows, while France has used lockdown measures since the beginning of the pandemic, Sweden has favoured a culture of trust and relied on individual responsibility to deal with Covid-19. With two opposite perspectives in managing the pandemic crisis, these two countries face a common issue highlighting extensive inequalities in accessing health and an excess mortality rate concentrated in the most economic precarious areas, where migrant populations often settle. Overall, this paper aims to highlight the need for preventive measures linked to the Covid-19 pandemic for vulnerable migrant populations, as well as to question the various inequalities in accessing health.

Levy, Mensa-Kwao, Chuang, and Hernandez-Barco present an interesting case study from the USA. As gastroenterologists, they share first-hand experiences from the field and offer policy and practice suggestions that can help overcome the practical barriers migrants face in health centres. The authors recommend that medical systems provide free or low-cost transportation to help immigrant patients attend clinic appointments, obtain labs/imaging, and come in for procedures. Providing immigrants and refugees with a lanyard or paper form indicating their name and destination within a hospital can be a tremendous help due to language barriers. Whenever possible, matching patients with doctors of a similar cultural background who speak their native language can improve patient communication and medical adherence. Another recommendation is to provide patient navigators who can help steer patients through the insurance landscape, facilitate referrals, arrange transportation, and ensure all testing is performed. The paper also shows that it is important to allocate longer clinic visits for refugees and immigrants, as the interpretation and explanations require patience and more time. Finally, the authors argue that gastroenterologists and general practitioners should assess medical literacy and frequently check their understanding of medical recommendations at the end of each clinical, procedural, and hospital visit.

We would like to thank all the Authors for their valuable and unique contributions. As the editors of this volume, certain of the interest and usefulness of its contents, we wish you an enjoyable read.

Michela C. Pellicani & Gül Ince-Beqo

AN ANALYSIS OF MIGRATION AND HEALTH NEXUS

Gül Ince-Beqo[1] and Michela C. Pellicani[2]

Introduction

The reasons and conditions that induce human mobility are manifold. People are increasingly moving within and across national borders due to demographic dynamics, the economic and social structures of migration-receiving and sending countries, political and humanitarian crises, climate change, advanced transport and communication technologies, and so on. However, while neo-liberal economies promote the idea of the universal market and facilitate trade in goods, services and finance, the freedom of movement for people changes considerably based on origin and socioeconomic status. Those who manage to cross borders face other challenges in the country of arrival, depending not only on the rights granted but also on how those rights granted on paper are enforced in practice. Indeed, in its multilayered and complex nature, migration challenges the conceptualisation of sovereignty and citizenship in many countries, constantly redrawing the boundaries and meanings of the public spaces and services to which people with migration backgrounds have differentiated access. In accordance with the current political and policy-based conjuncture on migration-related issues, how migration-receiving countries conceptualise migration and efforts to regularise it through nation-state-based policies confirms that migration is considered a problem rather than a natural result of the economic development of global societies and an intrinsic component of social transformations (Castles, 2010). That said, assuming that "international migration is both a cause and a consequence of social transformations such as globalization" (Bilecen, 2019, p. 40), migration policies in general and health policies, in particular, are valuable tools for analysing the impact, consequences and understanding of such changes. Access to health services for migrants with different legal statuses is one of the most important aspects of the integration policies.

[1] Gül Ince-Beqo, University of Milan, Italy.
[2] Michela C. Pellicani, University of Bari, Italy.
Acknowledgement: This paper is the result of the collaboration between the two authors. In particular, the Introduction, Section 3, Section 4 and Conclusion have to be considered by the two authors: Section 1, Section 2 by Gül Ince-Beqo, and Section 5 by Michela C. Pellicani.

Current global estimations suggest a number of international migrants[3] of about 281 million by 2020, or 3.6 percent of the global population (IOM, 2022). With the growing numbers, globally and throughout the EU, access to health care has become a focal point in the debate on migration, and who has access to health care is determined by questions of citizenship, identity, belonging, and nationalism (Burns, 2017). As well as the conceptualisation and implementation of rights granted on the basis of legal status, many recent international dialogues have sought to provide promising tools, policies, and principles through new multilateral commitments to address the health needs of migrants, such as the UN 2030 Agenda for Sustainable Development, the debate on Advancing the Unfinished Agenda on Migrant Health at the 106th Council of the International Organization for Migration (IOM), the New York Declaration for Refugees and Migrants (NYD), and the decision of the 140th World Health Organization Executive Board (WHO EB) on Promoting the Health of Migrants (IOM, 2017).

In this chapter, our main aim is to illustrate some crucial aspects that link and shape migration and health spheres. First, we focus on the ways in which the relationship between health and migration is conceptualised and reproduced at different levels. We also analyse obstacles and barriers to accessing services according to migrants' legal status and categorisation. Finally, we examine the role of two key actors in health care provision and access: the general practitioner and the intercultural mediator.

1. How migration and health intersect at different levels

The relationship between migration and health may be analysed from

---

[3] In this paper, different terms are used for people with migration background. Below some brief definitions for each, according to the EMN Asylum and Migration Glossary.

Migrant: In the global context, a person who moves away from their place of usual residence, whether within a country or across an international border, temporarily or permanently, voluntarily or involuntarily, and for a variety of reasons.

Immigrant: In the global context, a non-resident (both national or alien) arriving in a State with the intention to remain for a period exceeding a year.

Irregular migrant: In the global context, a person who, owing to irregular entry, breach of a condition of entry or the expiry of their legal basis for entering and residing, lacks legal status in a transit or host country. In the ENM glossary, there is no specific definition of "undocumented migrant" which can be defined broadly as "all immigrants who reside in the country of settlement without legal status".

Refugee: In the global context, either a person who, owing to a well-founded fear of persecution for reasons of race, religion, nationality, political opinion or membership of a particular social group, is outside the country of nationality and is unable or, owing to such fear, is unwilling to avail themselves of the protection of that country, or a stateless person, who, being outside of the country of former habitual residence for the same reasons as mentioned before, is unable or, owing to such fear, unwilling to return to it.

Asylum seeker: In the global context, a person who seeks protection from persecution or serious harm in a country other than their own and awaits a decision on the application for refugee status under relevant international and national instruments.

different angles and perspectives regarding theoretical frameworks and context-based research. For instance, exploring migration and health nexus through a social transformation lens may capture how these two spheres constantly intersect at macro, meso, and micro levels (Bilecen, 2019).

The Macro Level

With the development of universal human rights within modern states, the distribution of rights and responsibilities between citizens of a nation-state and non-citizens aimed to be equitable, yet such a shift did not "inaugurate a new era of genuinely universal human rights" (Nash, 2009, p. 1070). In this sense, migration management is structured around categories that are based on intentions and arrival patterns in the destination, with each category determining who has access to which services and rights. At the macro level, migration and health intersect in conceptualising and defining legitimate beneficiaries of health services and the definition of public funds allocated to certain services targeting aliens (Bilecen, 2019).

Under this perspective, health moves from being a universal right to a citizenship-related right (Pace, 2011), subject to strict conditions and requirements to be met. Furthermore, immigrants are often depicted as potential welfare scroungers in exclusion discourses, particularly with regard to access to health services (Sollors et al., 2011). Morris (2013, p. 76) calls this "a clash of national interests with global culture" based on universalistic rights.

Such clashes also take place at the local level. Debates, approaches, and regulations implemented and practised at the national level are subject to deviations at the local level due to different interests and principles. Regarding our specific focus, in some cases, local environments opposing national regulations can improve unauthorised migrants' access to healthcare through local networks and the agency of street-level bureaucrats (Marrow, 2012).

The Micro Level

The analysis is micro when the unit of analysis is the migrant him/herself, who is embedded in the complex administrative-bureaucratic mechanisms in the host country based on the legal status they are entitled to. Migrants are often disadvantaged in social and political hierarchies in ways that expose them to health risks, limit their access to necessary care and restrict their ability to realise their skills and potential (Willen et al., 2021). Although there is an implicit consensus that the 'social' represents an area of great importance to a patient's ability to cope with treatment, addressing structural barriers to health is generally considered to be outside the scope of routine clinical practice (Bourgois et al., 2017). Empirical evidence at the micro level confirms this assumption. It shows how rapidly and dramatically changing socioeconomic and legal conditions affect the health of migrants, especially in the case of asylum seekers (Bilecen, 2019), those fleeing different forms of insecurity, undocumented and irregular migrants (Carruth et al., 2021).

Some cases with different obstacles and barriers to health access can be listed without claiming to be exhaustive. In the United States, Asian migrants are more hindered than other migrant groups in accessing insurance and health services (Clough et al., 2013). Some racial and ethnic minority groups excluded from employer-sponsored health insurance lacked equitable access to treatment and vaccines also during COVID-19 (Yearby et al., 2022). In Canada, known for its welcoming migration and refugee policies, the lack of cultural competence of those involved in providing services is one of the most significant barriers (Ahmed et al., 2016). Also, communication-related issues and the socioeconomic status of migrants affect health access.

The situation is not much different in Europe where, despite aspirations for equity, inequalities between migrants and autochthonous in health and access to health services persist (Lebano et al., 2020) and the main obstacles can be listed as follows:

- legal barriers to access to care for refugees and undocumented migrants;

- economic situation of migrants who may not have the means to pay for health services;

- lack of language and cultural competence to navigate health systems;

- exposure to discrimination.

In some cases, obstacles are even more numerous and policies designed to meet the health needs of migrants are not adequately utilised either by GPs or by migrants themselves. For example, research has shown that the government-sponsored reimbursement system for undocumented migrants' healthcare costs is rarely used in Brussels by GPs due to the complexity and length of paperwork and also by migrants due to fear of deportation, insufficient health knowledge and communication barriers (Goossens & Depoorter, 2011).

The Meso Level

The meso level, on the other hand, shifting attention to networks and kinship, conceptualises how family and social ties determine the well-being of migrants, highlighting why the public health of receiving countries needs to transcend nation-state borders to understand the different needs and expectations of ethnically and religiously diverse societies (Bilecen, 2019). Accordingly, researchers have analysed the link between social capital and mental health (Almedom, 2005; Tulin & Smith, 2020).

Research on climate refugees has shown how connecting and strengthening social ties in home and destination communities can increase resilience and mitigate some negative mental health outcomes (Torres & Casey, 2017). Research on Mexicans in the United States also highlights the importance of social ties, in general, and identity support and transnational social relationships, specifically, for more positive health outcomes (Viruell-Fuentes & Schulz, 2009). Indeed, the analysis of transnational social ties, as a driver of the "healthy immigrant effect," may be helpful in providing a source of medical information, treatment, and social support not measured in conventional surveys or health records (Bakhtiari, 2021).

2. How diseases are shaped by migration

If societies are becoming increasingly more diverse along a variety of dimensions, so do their needs and expectations. Indeed, another critical aspect needs to be investigated in the sphere where migration and health intersect: that related to female migrant care workers whose (often) undeclared employment substitutes public health services, creating the basis of informal welfare (Ambrosini, 2015). These women from underdeveloped or developing countries who move to Northern countries with a high need for elderly care are called "servants of globalization" (Parreñas, 2015). In their case, constant contact with illness in highly isolated contexts resulted in the so-called "Italy Syndrome"[4], an anxiety and depression status among Romanian in-household caregivers working intensively with Italian elders. In this case, the working contexts of migrant caregivers (mostly women) lead doctors in the home country to identify particular diseases by analysing the symptoms of women returning to their home country. In other cases, some specific symptoms which are believed to be an intrinsic characteristic of non-Western cultures, such as "Morbus mediterraneus" or "Morbus Bosphorus,"

---

[4] https://www.aljazeera.com/features/2019/2/12/why-romanian-migrant-women-suffer-from-italy-syndrome

referring to somatisation among Mediterranean and Turkey-related migrants in Germany, are coined by native doctors in the country of settlement. In this context, however, research (Viruell-Fuentes et al., 2012) shows how cultural explanations for immigrant health outcomes are limited in shedding light on how structural factors intersected along different lines produce and reproduce inequality in accessing health services.

3. The role of general practitioners in health access of migrants

There are some key actors involved in the different stages of migrants' access to health care who can facilitate or hinder the whole process. Among these, general practitioners (GPs) are a key link in the chain linking public health, social workers/volunteers/intermediaries, and migrants.

GPs work daily with multicultural, underserved, and vulnerable patient populations. Their broad scope, community focus, emphasis on prevention, and ability to manage chronic conditions make them well-placed to provide essential services to migrants and address their ongoing physical, psychological, behavioural, and social needs (Mishori et al., 2017). The knowledge of their patients' backgrounds is crucial to ensuring appropriate care, and they are the main initial points for access to various parts of the health system (Jensen et al., 2013).

As discussed above, legal status, migration backgrounds, and context-based conditions are key determinants of who will have access to a health service and to what extent. On the other hand, the specific types of health conditions are strongly influenced by premigration, migration, and postmigration resettlement, with different specific risks and exposures in each stage (Kirmayer et al., 2011). Under the perspective of these dynamics, refugees represent a specific category, being highly stigmatised at the public policy level.

As highlighted by Walden et al. (2017), across the continuum of care, GPs can interact with refugees in different roles and settings, and each brings its own unique challenges, including:

- increased incidence of emotional and physical trauma;
- undiagnosed and untreated chronic medical conditions;
- lack of preventive health screenings;
- potential family dysfunction due to social disruption;

13

- difficulty navigating the health system.

The primary care setting is crucial in assessing the health needs of refugees, as they may experience poorer health outcomes, both in terms of mental health and general well-being (Iqbal et al., 2022), and general practitioners(GPs) are gatekeepers to various parts of the mental health system, and knowledge of their patients' refugee background is crucial for appropriate care (Jensen et al., 2013).

Compared with the general population, refugees have higher rates of mood disorders and anxiety, and around half of refugees experience post-traumatic stress disorder (PTSD) (Hamrah et al., 2020). They may present with somatic symptoms, sleep disorders, fatigue, paranoia, or suicidal thoughts and PTSD may present years after arrival, even long after resettlement (Mishori et al., 2017).

Research showed that mental health problems may be exacerbated by a patient's history of trauma or torture. Comprehensibly, PTSD is more common in refugees who have been exposed to torture and violence which are more common among refugees; multiple studies show the prevalence to be more than 50% (Walden et al., 2017; Fazel et al., 2005; Kirmayer et al., 2011).

Another important aspect is the case of imported diseases. Due to the high prevalence in their countries of origin and the circumstances of their migration, some refugees arrive with a higher risk of certain diseases, and when refugee patients present with clinical signs and symptoms compatible with imported communicable diseases, a high index of suspicion is required, even if they occur months or years after arrival, as 50% of cases occur in the first five years after resettlement (Mishori et al., 2017).

Refugees from countries with inefficient health systems may not be able to undertake the recommended routine immunisations and screenings for cancer and chronic diseases also because they may not be accustomed to preventive care. Completing all routine health maintenance tasks during the first visit is unnecessary, but they should be addressed in subsequent meetings. Focusing on women's health, family planning, cancer screening (breast, colon, and cervix), oral health, vision, and chronic disease screening (hyperlipidemia, diabetes mellitus, hypertension, and hepatitis C) will help identify and address previously unmet health care needs (Terasaki G. et al., 2015).

There are organisational aspects to be taken into consideration. Due to language and other cultural barriers, newly resettled refugees may find it difficult to understand the first patient examination process; thus, in healthcare settings, a willingness to explore one's own prejudices and respect other cultures (cultural humility) is essential, as is flexibility in schedules, also due to transport-related issues which may contribute to non-attendance and late arrivals (Walden et al., 2017). On the other hand, scheduling frequent and regular follow-up visits can increase the therapeutic alliance and ensure comprehensive care, particularly in case of unfamiliar infectious diseases (Walden et al., 2017). This is also because promoting continuity of care and ensuring adequate resources are key aspects of integration processes (Robertshaw et al., 2017).

Caring for refugee patients can be rewarding for GPs and their staff and create deeper community bonds (Walden et al., 2017). Indeed, the research (Davison et al., 2023) outlined the GP's perceptions of refugee health provision and their commitment to it. GPs' perceptions of refugee care were very positive, reflecting on the benefits to themselves and the community at large while recognising the challenges of providing this specific type of health care. Another research (Harris et al., 2020) showed that the main challenges from the perspective of GPs in consultations with refugees in the field of mental health are language barriers, different perceptions of disease, different expectations of healthcare, and a feeling of lack of preparedness on the part of GPs. Regarding the meaning attributed to the commitment to vulnerable people, it was confirmed that a trusting patient-physician relationship facilitates consultations, and working with refugees with mental health problems was found meaningful and interesting. However, a holistic approach is essential in the consideration and evaluation of primary care for refugees. Indeed, the research highlighted the importance of analysing as well the perception and practice of administrative staff, such as health centre receptionists and managers, in facilitating or hindering access to primary health for refugees (Lindenmeyer et al., 2016).

4. Intercultural mediation in migration management

Migration makes social and interpersonal relationships more stratified and complex, and in this context, cultural mediation seems increasingly necessary and inevitable, offering endless opportunities to negotiate meanings and positions, promote symbolic reconciliation, and prevent and/or mitigate conflicts. In a very generic sense, cultural mediation is a therapeutic, discursive, conciliatory, and assertive process based on the management of complexity and conflict, shifting the interaction of conflict from the logic of *winners and losers* to *I win, you win* and seeking a just balance (Castelli, 1996, p.5). For Sybille de Pury Toumi (as cited in Pignataro, 2012), instead, mediation is not for creating consensus among parties and does not presuppose the imposition of a meeting. Indeed, mediation "is at the heart of the entire process, acting as its motor, fully responsible for what happens, because the translations s/he chooses will have an impact on the outcome of the exchange" (Pignataro, 2012, p. 73).

With this premise in mind, intercultural mediation plays a crucial role in migration management, especially if resources and capacities are used effectively. Mediation is particularly important in public spaces, where cultural, linguistic, and ethnical dynamics intertwine, creating communication problems that hinder service delivery. In this context, mediation can help to create the basis for peaceful coexistence and mutual respect, fostering positive relations between communities of origin and destination. Finally, by providing information on local regulations and migrants' rights and promoting an understanding of cultural differences and working practices, intercultural mediators can help prevent discrimination and social exclusion. It also helps to build a more inclusive and welcoming society by improving mutual understanding and overcoming cultural prejudices.

A crucial aspect of ensuring the quality of mediation services in the field of migration is the training of intercultural mediators. Many training programmes exist at both academic and non-academic levels across the globe. The training programmes are structured to endow the participants with an in-depth knowledge of the culture and the situation of migrants, as well as with the intercultural competences and intercultural communication necessary for the management of cultural diversity in migration contexts. In addition, these programmes may include participation in training events and networking between intercultural mediators and other professionals working in the field of migration.

To match, both globally operating organisations, such as UNESCO[5] and the Council of Europe[6], have developed frameworks that set common standards for the training of intercultural mediators. Yet, the European countries are autonomous in the provision of the legislative framework for mediation, resulting in a lack of harmonisation and uniform standards for intercultural mediation, despite European Union (EU) directives to regulate and

---

[5] https://unesdoc.unesco.org/ark:/48223/pf0000219768
[6] https://www.coe.int/en/web/reference-framework-of-competences-for-democratic-culture

systematise the role and competences of mediators[7].

5. Intercultural mediation in healthcare

The concept of health is very relative, partly because of the influence of culture and partly because it is inextricably linked to the concept of illness, and both being a social construction, belong to the human world of meaning (Mangone, 2012). Under this perspective, the healthcare provision and therapeutic relationship are complex processes since the concepts of health, disease, and care are heavily influenced by the culture and its associated symbolic values and meanings. Plus, there are several communication and relational barriers to accessing and continuing healthcare, particularly for migrants in more vulnerable socio-economic circumstances (Goldade, 2009). Furthermore, accessibility and quality of care for migrants and ethnic minorities are hampered mainly by language, socio-cultural barriers, and consequences of interethnic tensions, racism, and discrimination (Verrept & Coune, 2016).

In order to ensure effective communication, appropriate transfer of information, respect for cultural diversity, confidence building, and equitable access to care, intercultural language mediation in healthcare is essential since it promotes an inclusive and culturally sensitive healthcare environment and contributes to improving the quality of care for migrant patients (Christen & Balthasar, 2017). The empirical evidence highlighted the importance of effective communication in primary care. According to GPs' clinical experience, access to face-to-face interpreters improved their ability to meet the needs of refugees, in line with their consideration of the lack of language competencies as the main challenge in providing care. Furthermore, difficulties related to a lack of understanding of the health system were also alleviated by the employment of refugee community members as receptionists within the practice (Davison et al., 2023).

Verrept and Coune (2016) proposed a "ladder" model with the main tasks of intercultural mediators working in healthcare settings. The ladder represents advantages and disadvantages that are connected to the execution of several tasks, also in relation to mediators' visibility.

---

[7] https://includeu.eu/intercultural-mediation-how-to-guarantee-rights-and-access-to-services-for-third-country-nationals/

Figure 1. The "ladder" model of intercultural mediation

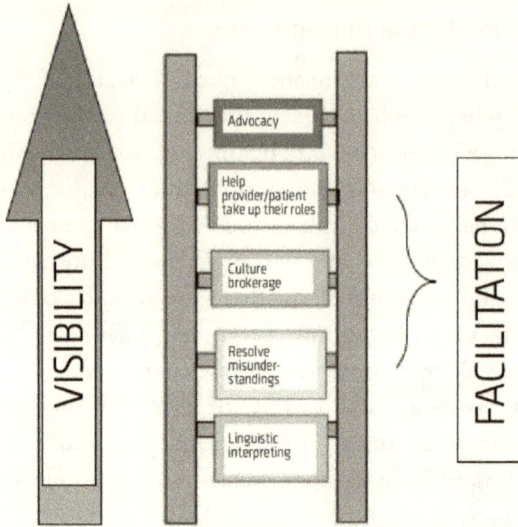

Source: Verrept & Coune, 2016

This model foresees these tasks (from bottom to top):

- linguistic interpreting;

- resolve misunderstandings;

- culture brokerage;

- help provider/patients take up their roles;

- advocacy.

Executing tasks higher on the ladder increases the mediator's visibility, and, at this level, it is much harder to formulate precise norms or standards. For that reason, the higher-placed tasks will only be executed when strictly necessary (Verrept & Coune, 2016, p. 8)

Finally, while intercultural mediation is an essential condition for shared understanding in the healthcare setting (Angelelli, 2012), the efficiency and effectiveness of intercultural mediation in healthcare are hindered by several factors, including a lack of skills, knowledge, and attitudes on the part of healthcare professionals and intercultural mediators (Verrept, 2008).

Conclusions

The experience of migration has a significant impact on health. In their countries of origin, migrants, particularly those from disadvantaged and vulnerable backgrounds, often face severe poverty, inequality and social exclusion, which can have a negative impact on their physical and mental health and well-being. The situation does not often change in the country of arrival, where they also face obstacles in accessing adequate and affordable health and social services. To address these challenges, research is needed to better understand the complex and multilayered relationship between migration and health. This should involve capturing diverse migrant voices and experiences, as well as developing nuanced migrant typologies to account for factors like immigration status, migration trajectory, and access to services (Wickramage et al., 2018). Ultimately, encouraging migrant-sensitive health policies enforced with an effective intervention of intercultural mediators is crucial to ensuring the right to health for all, regardless of legal status.

References

Ahmed, S., Shommu, N. S., Rumana, N., Barron, G. R., Wicklum, S., & Turin, T. C. (2016). Barriers to Access of Primary Healthcare by Immigrant Populations in Canada: A Literature Review. *Journal of immigrant and minority health*, 18(6), 1522–1540. https://doi.org/10.1007/s10903-015-0276-z

Almedom A. M. (2005). Social capital and mental health: an interdisciplinary review of primary evidence. *Social science & medicine (1982)*, 61(5), 943–964. https://doi.org/10.1016/j.socscimed.2004.12.025

Ambrosini, M. (2013). Immigration in Italy: between Economic Acceptance and Political Rejection. *International Migration & Integration* (14), 175–194. https://doi.org/10.1007/s12134-011-0231-3

Ambrosini, M. (2015). Irregular but Tolerated: Unauthorized Immigration, Elderly Care Recipients, and Invisible Welfare, *Migration Studies*, (3)2, 199-216.

Angelelli, C. (2004). Medical interpreting and cross-cultural communication. Cambridge: Cambridge University Press.

Angelelli, C. (2012). Challenges in interpreters' coordination of the construction of pain. In C. Baraldi & L. Gavioli (Ed.), Coordinating participation in dialogue interpreting. (pp. 251–268). Amsterdam & Philadelphia: John Benjamins.

Bakhtiari, E. (2021). Migration and health. In W. Cockerham (Ed.). The Wiley Blackwell Companion to Medical Sociology. (pp. 389-409). John Wiley & Sons Inc.

Bilecen, B. (2019). Social Transformation(s): International Mobility and Health. In A. Krämer & F. Fischer (Ed.), Refugee Migration and Health: Challenges for Germany and Europe (1 ed., pp. 39-48). (Migration, Minorities and Modernity; Vol. 4). Springer. https://doi.org/10.1007/978-3-030-03155-8_3

Bonizzoni, P. (2017). The shifting boundaries of (un)documentedness: a gendered understanding of migrants' employment-based legalization pathways in Italy, *Ethnic and Racial Studies*, 40(10), 1643-1662. https://doi.org/10.1080/01419870.2016.1229488

Bourgois, P., Holmes, S. M., Sue, K., & Quesada, J. (2017). Structural Vulnerability: Operationalizing the Concept to Address Health Disparities in Clinical Care. *Academic medicine : Journal of the Association of American Medical Colleges*, 92(3), 299–307.

https://doi.org/10.1097/ACM.0000000000001294

Burns, N. (2017). The human right to health: exploring disability, migration and health. *Disability & Society*, 32(10), 1463–1484. https://doi-org.ezproxy.unicatt.it/10.1080/09687599.2017.1358604

Carruth, L., Martinez, C., Smith, L., Donato, K., Piñones-Rivera, C., Quesada, J. & Migration and Health in Social Context Working Group (2021). Structural vulnerability: migration and health in social context. *BMJ global health*, 6(Suppl 1). https://doi.org/10.1136/bmjgh-2021-005109

Castelli, S. (1996). *La mediazione. Teorie e tecniche*. Milano, Raffaello Cortina Editore.

Castles, S. (2010). Understanding Global Migration: a Social Transformation Perspective, *Journal of Ethnic and Migration Studies*, 36(10), 1565–1586. https://doi:10.1080/1369183X.2010.489381

Christen, D., Balthasar, A. (2017). Approaches to improve the interaction between general practitioners and migrants - a systematic review of international literature. *International Journal of Migration, Health and Social Care*, 13(3), 321-333. https://doi.org/10.1108/ijmhsc-10-2015-0037

Clough, J., Lee, S., & Chae, D. H. (2013). Barriers to health care among Asian immigrants in the United States: a traditional review. *Journal of health care for the poor and underserved*, 24(1), 384–403. https://doi.org/10.1353/hpu.2013.0019

Davison, R., Hobbs, M., Quirk, F., & Guppy, M. (2023). General practitioners' perspectives on the management of refugee health: a qualitative study. *BMJ open*, 13(3). https://doi.org/10.1136/bmjopen-2022-068986

De Luca, G., Ponzo, M. & Andrés, A.R. (2013). Health care utilization by immigrants in Italy. *Int J Health Care Finance Econ*.13(1), 1–31.

Fazel, M., Wheeler, J., & Danesh, J. (2005). Prevalence of serious mental disorder in 7000 refugees resettled in western countries: a systematic review. *Lancet* (London, England), 365(9467), 1309–1314. https://doi.org/10.1016/S0140-6736(05)61027-6

Goldade, K. (2009). "Health is Hard Here" or "Health for All". Medical Anthropology Quarterly 23(4): 483–503. https://doi.org/10.1111/j.1548-1387.2009.01074.x

Goossens, M. C., Depoorter, A. M. (2011). Contacts between general practitioners and migrants without a residence permit and the use of "urgent" medical care. *Scandinavian journal of public health*, 39(6), 649–655. https://doi.org/10.1177/1403494811414249

Hamrah, M. S., Hoang, H., Mond, J., Pahlavanzade, B., Charkazi, A., & Auckland, S. (2020). The prevalence and correlates of symptoms of post-traumatic stress disorder (PTSD) among resettled Afghan refugees in a regional area of Australia. Journal of Mental Health, 1–7. https://doi:10.1080/09638237.2020.1739247

Harris, S. M., Binder, P. E., & Sandal, G. M. (2020). General Practitioners' Experiences of Clinical Consultations With Refugees Suffering From Mental Health Problems. *Frontiers in psychology*, (11)412. https://doi.org/10.3389/fpsyg.2020.00412

IOM (2017). *Health of migrants: resetting the agenda. Report of the 2nd global consultation.* https://www.iom.int/sites/default/files/our_work/DMM/Migration-Health/GC2_SriLanka_Report_2017_FINAL_22.09.2017_Internet.pdf

IOM (2022). *World Migration Report*. Retrieved from: https://worldmigrationreport.iom.int/wmr-2022-interactive/

Iqbal, M., Walpola, R., Harris-Roxas, B., Li, J., Mears, S., Hall, J., & Harrison, R. (2022). Improving primary health care quality for refugees and asylum seekers: a systematic review of interventional approaches. *Health expectations: an international journal of public participation in health care and health policy*, 25(5), 2065–2094. https://doi.org/10.1111/hex.13365

Jensen, N. K., Norredam, M., Priebe, S., & Krasnik, A. (2013). How do general practitioners experience providing care to refugees with mental health problems? A qualitative study from Denmark. *BMC family practice*, 14(17). https://doi.org/10.1186/1471-2296-14-17

Kirmayer, L. J., Narasiah, L., Munoz, M., Rashid, M., Ryder, A. G., Guzder, J., Hassan, G., Rousseau, C., Pottie, K., & Canadian Collaboration for Immigrant and Refugee Health (CCIRH) (2011). Common mental health problems in immigrants and refugees: general approach in primary care. *Canadian Medical Association Journal = Journal de l'Association medicale canadienne*, 183(12), 959–967. https://doi.org/10.1503/cmaj.090292

Lebano, A., Hamed, S., Bradby, H., Gil-Salmeron, A., Dura-Ferrandis, E., Garces-Ferrer, J., Azzedine F., Riza, E., Karnaki, P., Zota, D. & Linos, A. (2020). Migrants' and refugees' health status and healthcare in Europe: a scoping literature review. *BMC Public Health*, 20, 1039. https://doi.org/10.1186/s12889-020-08749-8

Lindenmeyer, A., Redwood, S., Griffith, L., Teladia, Z., & Phillimore, J. (2016). Experiences of primary care professionals providing healthcare to recently arrived migrants: a qualitative study. *BMJ open*, 6(9). https://doi.org/10.1136/bmjopen-2016-012561

Mangone, E. (2012). Le dimensioni culturali della salute e della malattia nella società globale. In R. Biancheri, M. Niero & M. Tognetti Bordogna (Ed.) *Ricerca e sociologia della salute fra presente e futuro. Saggi di giovani studiosi italiani.* (pp.131-145). Milano: FrancoAngeli.

Marrow, H.B. (2012). The power of local autonomy: expanding health care to unauthorized immigrants in San Francisco, Ethnic and Racial Studies, 35(1), 72-87. https://doi.org/10.1080701419870.2011.594168

Mishori R., Aleinikoff S. & Davis D., (2017). Primary Care for Refugees: Challenges and Opportunities, *American Family Physician*, Retrieved from: http://www.aafp.org/afp/2017/0715/p112.html

Morris, L. (2013). *Human Rights and Social Theory*, Bloomsbury Academic.

Nash, K. (2009). Between Citizenship and Human Rights, *Sociology*, 43(6), 1067-1083.

Pace, P. (2011). The Right to Health of Migrants in Europe. In B. Rechel, P. Mladovsky, W. Deville, B. Rijks, R., Petrova-Benedict, M. McKee (Ed.) *Migration and Health in the European Union.* (pp. 55–66) Maidenhead: McGrawHill OUP.

Parreñas, R. (2015). Servants of Globalization: Migration and Domestic Work. Stanford CA: Stanford University Press.

Pignataro, C. (2012). Interlinguistic and intercultural mediation in healthcare setting, *The Interpreters' Newsletter*, 17, 71-82.

Robertshaw L., Dhesi S. & Jones L.L. (2017). Challenges and facilitators for health professionals providing primary healthcare for refugees and asylum seekers in high-income countries: a systematic review and thematic synthesis of qualitative research. BMJ Open, 7(8).

Sollors, W., Jacobson, M., & Hee Park, L. S. (Ed.) (2011). Entitled to Nothing: The Struggle for Immigrant Health Care in the Age of Welfare Reform. (Nation of Newcomers: Immigrant History as American History). New York: New York University Press.

Terasaki, G., Ahrenholz, N. C., & Haider, M. Z. (2015). Care of Adult Refugees with Chronic Conditions. *The Medical clinics of North America*, 99(5), 1039–1058. https://doi.org/10.1016/j.mcna.2015.05.006

Torres, J.M., Casey, J.A. (2017). The centrality of social ties to climate migration and mental health. *BMC Public Health,* 17(600). https://doi.org/10.1186/s12889-017-4508-0

Tulin, M., Smith, S. (2020). Poverty and mental health among migrants: when is ingroup exposure more protective than social ties? *SSM - population health*, 11. https://doi.org/10.

1016/j.ssmph.2020.100599

Valero-Garces, C., Martin, A. (Ed.). (2008). Crossing Borders in Community Interpreting. Definitions and dilemmas. Amsterdam & Philadelphia: John Benjamins.

Verrept, H. (2008). Intercultural mediation: An answer to healthcare disparities? In C. Valero Garces, A. Martin (Ed.). Crossing Borders in Community Interpreting: Definitions and Dilemmas (pp. 187–201). John Benjamins Publishing Company.

Verrept, H. (2019). What are the roles of intercultural mediators in health care and what is the evidence on their contributions and effectiveness in improving accessibility and quality of care for refugees and migrants in the WHO European Region? Copenhagen: WHO Regional Office for Europe.

Verrept., H., Coune, I. (2016). Guide for Intercultural Mediation in Health Care. Brussels: FPS Health, Safety of the Food Chain and Environment.

Viruell-Fuentes, E. A., Schulz, A. J. (2009). Toward a dynamic conceptualization of social ties and context: implications for understanding immigrant and Latino health. *American journal of public health*, 99(12), 2167–2175. https://doi.org/10.2105/AJPH.2008.158956

Walden J., Valdman O., Mishori R. & Carlough M. (2017). Building Capacity to Care for Refugees, *Family Practise Management*, Retrieved from: www.aafp.org/fpm

Wickramage, K., Vearey, J., Zwi, A.B. Robinson, C. & Knipper, M. (2018). Migration and health: a global public health research priority, *BMC Public Health* 18(987). https://doi.org/10.1186/s12889-018-5932-5

Willen, S.S., Selim, N., Mendenhall, E., Lopez, M.M., Chowdhury, S.A. & Dilger, H. (2021). Flourishing: migration and health in social context. *BMJ global health*, 6(Suppl 1), https://doi.org/10.1136/bmjgh-2021-005108

Yearby, R., Clark, B., & Figueroa, J. F. (2022). Structural Racism In Historical And Modern US Health Care Policy. *Health affairs (Project Hope)*, 41(2), 187–194. https://doi.org/10.1377/hlthaff.2021.01466

REFUGEES' MENTAL HEALTH IN RELATION TO NEGATIVE ATTITUDES IN RECEIVING SOCIETIES: THEORETICAL PREMISES

Saskia Schubert[1] and Tobias Ringeisen[2]

Introduction

The number of displaced people worldwide has doubled in the last ten years. Due to wars, violent conflicts, and persecution, roughly 82,4 million people were forced to leave their homes and search for a safe place in another country, giving them the status of refugees as defined by the 1951 Refugee Convention (UN General Assembly, 1951). Its geographical location, political and economic stability, security, and standard of living made Europe one of the major destinations for refugees (IOM, 2020), of whom 1.23 million found shelter in Germany (UNHCR, Global Trend Report, 2021). With that, the country hosted the fifth-largest number of refugees across borders worldwide (UNHCR, 2021).

The receiving societies – and Germany in particular – face the challenge of better understanding the needs of refugees to help them receive healthcare support and a chance for healthy societal integration. However, this challenge is often overlooked or even seen as a communal burden (Reinke et al., 2022). Aside from traumatic experiences during the flight, refugees face multiple stressors throughout the process of arriving and resettling. Examples refer to negative attitudes, fear of contact among receiving society members, a lack of support in daily life, and discrimination (Kluge et al., 2020; Ringeisen et al., 2020). In different European countries, significant proportions of the population have been displaying negative attitudes towards refugees, whom they perceive as a threat to national security, cultural heritage, and social cohesion (for an overview, see Ceobanu & Escandell, 2010), which is associated with more significant risks of assaulting refugees verbally and/or physically (Çelebi et al., 2017; Karpenstein & von Nordheim, 2019). In light of these findings, studies started to examine the antecedents of attitudes and emotional responses towards refugees in different receiving societies and the implications these responses may have for the mental health of refugees.

The associations between attitudes, related emotions, and social behavior

[1] Saskia Schubert, Berlin School of Economics and Law, Germany.
[2] Tobias Ringeisen, Berlin School of Economics and Law, Germany.

toward groups, as well as mental health implications for the targeted groups, may be studied concerning the Integrated Threat Theory (ITT) (Stephan & Stephan, 2000). ITT specifies perceived threats as mediators between antecedents and attitude-related outcomes. Multiple studies provided evidence that these threats predict negative attitudes, negative affectivity, and antisocial behavior, such as rejection towards the respective outgroups (e.g., Stephan & Stephan 2000; Stephan et al., 2009), which in turn can cause psychological and physical harm for the targeted group, in this case, refugees (Çelebi et al., 2017; Karpenstein & von Nordheim, 2019).

The experience of pre-arrival stressors such as prosecution or violence, as well as stressors that many refugees encounter during the flight (e.g., violence, abuse, physical and/or psychological hardmanship), may already call for adequate treatment in the receiving societies (for an overview see e.g., Ringeisen et al., 2020). Experiences of rejection after arrival can aggravate these stress-related health impairments and may lead to multiple psychological anomalies that make it necessary for refugees to receive adequate healthcare treatment (Ringeisen et al., 2020; Kluge et al., 2020; Thöle et al., 2017). Regarding a downward spiral, refugees' mental health may deteriorate further if these needs are met insufficiently (Nesterko, 2020). In that sense, negative attitudes towards refugees can cause and aggravate mental health issues and obstruct refugees' access to mental health care services (Penka et al., 2015; Karpenstein & von Nordheim, 2019).

In light of these patterns, this chapter presents theoretical approaches and associated research results on psycho-social determinants of mental health in refugees about negative attitudes among members of receiving societies. Where available, the chapter focuses on European research results, emphasizing Germany. The country deserves special attention in attitude research because Germany hosted the third-largest number of refugees across country borders worldwide (UNHCR, 2021) while the political and social conditions towards refugees have worsened over the past few years (Liebe et al., 2018). As a result of the open border policy adopted by the federal government in 2015, Germany has taken in more refugees than any other country in the EU, with a majority of the population initially taking a positive view of this course (Konle-Seidl, 2018; Trines, 2017). Consistent with this welcoming attitude, Gehrsitz and Ungerer (2017), examining the short-term impact of the refugee influx in 2015, showed that refugees did not take local people's jobs and that crime only increased slightly. Despite some variance in the results, surveys in Germany in the following years revealed increasingly negative attitudes towards refugees and skepticism about their immigration (for an overview, see Liebe et al. 2018).

Refugees' mental health in the light of resources and stressors

The negative attitudes among the population in the receiving countries promote adverse reactions towards refugees, which can stress the psychological and physical health of the refugees. From a resource-oriented perspective, stress arises either if refugees have too few resources that enable adequate coping efforts and/or if the stress-triggering conditions exceed their resources (for an overview, see e.g., the Conservation of Resources Theory, COR theory in short) (Buchwald & Hobfoll, 2020). According to COR theory, the loss of resources is a central reason for stress reactions. Buchwald and Hobfoll (2020) systematize resources by categorizing them into (1) objects (e.g., spaces, means of communication and transportation, clothing), (2) conditions related to living conditions (e.g., status, security, social networks, credit-worthiness), (3) personal characteristics (e.g., self-esteem, available coping strategies, social skills) and (4) energy resources (money, time, knowledge, language skills). Although resources may be valued with significant interindividual variability, some resources, such as close support networks or a portfolio of effective coping strategies, can be named, with cross-cultural importance confirmed (e.g., Schubert & Ringeisen, 2020). Aside from scarce resources, the confrontation with strains forms the starting point of the stress process, whereby four categories can be distinguished, which comprise (1) contextual, (2) situational, (3) social, and (4) personal stressors (Samarasinghe & Arvidsson, 2002). The effect of these stressors on refugees accumulates from the beginning of their flight through settling in the destination country. It deals with adaptation to all aspects of everyday life (for an overview, see Eggerth & Flynn, 2020).

Prior to fleeing, *contextual stressors* often occur as trauma from wars, violence, and/or persecution (Sinnerbrink et al., 1997; Steel et al., 2002). With the decision to flee, those affected lose their living environment and job, leading to a deterioration in their financial status and promoting the development of clinical and psychological symptoms (e.g., Löbel & Jacobsen, 2021; Lie, 2002). Costs often arise from paying smugglers to cross the border illegally. The families who stay behind often support the flight financially and expect to share in the anticipated economic benefits of the emigrants (Eggerth & Flynn, 2020). Once admitted to an EU country, refugees are not allowed to pursue paid employment, training, or university studies until their asylum application has been approved (Samarasinghe & Arvidsson, 2002).

Finding work is further hindered by a lack of recognition of skills or educational achievements. As a result, refugees are often willing to accept jobs, wages, and working conditions that workers with choices would refuse (Orrenius & Zavodny, 2009). In addition, refugees face difficulties accessing medical care and social assistance, especially if their status has not been legalized (Silove et al., 1999). Regarding energy resources, it is therefore crucial to provide refugees with language courses, vocational training, and qualification options (for an overview, see Reinke et al., 2022).

Situational stressors overlay the effect of contextual stressors during the flight and after arrival in the receiving country. In addition to a cramped living situation in the reception and interim camps, which is characterized by a lack of essential privacy and a lack of control over aspects of daily life, there are often physical (e.g., noise, extreme temperatures), requirement-related (e.g., dealing with authorities) and temporal stressors (e.g., quick action during the flight; long waiting times, dealing with authorities in the target country) (Mehran et al., 2021; Porter & Haslam, 2005). The experience of traumatization before or during the flight can impede handling situational stressors (Steel et al., 2002).

Regarding social stressors, many refugees experience changes in relationships with family or friends associated with isolation and a lack of social and emotional support (Segal & Mayadas, 2005). Many refugees are separated from their families indefinitely and fear never seeing them again (Sinnerbrink et al., 1997; Steel et al., 2002). They may suffer from a complete loss of family ties or a sense of helplessness when they keep in touch with the abandoned family, knowing about the threats and difficult living conditions their family faces in their home country, yet being unable to help (Löbel & Jacobsen, 2021). Refugees usually need several years to have their relatives join them after a recognized asylum procedure (Grzywacz et al., 2006). Although refugees mainly depend on social support due to the loss of family networks, many experience a lack of receptiveness in the host country (Samarasinghe & Arvidsson, 2002). Negative attitudes towards refugees, such as xenophobia and related behaviors like rejection, discrimination, or attacks, form a subset of refugees' social stressors (Çelebi et al., 2017; Segal & Mayadas, 2005). The effect of negative behavior maximizes the refugees' experience of stress when they have lost their social networks and feel lonely (Samarasinghe & Arvidsson, 2002; Löbel & Jacobsen, 2021). Against this background, digital communication media, whenever possible, enable the exchange with loved ones at home and thus the maintenance of social networks.

In addition, ***personal stressors*** and low personal resources cause an increased experience of stress. Personal stressors include uncertainty about one's fate and that of relatives left behind (Samarasinghe & Arvidsson, 2002) and fear of being deported to the home country (De Genova, 2002). Upon arrival, learning a foreign language is the most significant and most apparent barrier immigrant people face (Segal & Mayadas, 2005). Poor language skills and/or a low level of education may lead to insecurities and misunderstandings in everyday life, which can cause acculturative stress and impaired well-being (Zick, 2010). Acculturation marks an unplanned, mostly unconscious process by which groups or individuals from different cultural backgrounds influence each other as they adapt to life in a new country (for an overview, see Zick, 2010). Refugees confronted with multiple stressors and experience xenophobic aggression while resources such as social support are declining show an increased risk of acculturative stress (Çelebi et al., 2017; Karpenstein & von Nordheim, 2019). Resources such as participation in intercultural training or coaching can support refugees to (re)appraise and better understand cultural gaps between the receiving societies and their home country, which enhances their capacities to deal with acculturative stress (Hettich et al., 2020). In terms of secondary advantages, such interventions help refugees to integrate the different cultural socialization influences and form beneficial bi- or multicultural identities, which in turn may take on the form of personal resources that enable them to actively pursue integration as an acculturation strategy (cf. Berry et al., 2006; Schmitz & Berry, 2011). Other personal resources such as higher education, good language skills, self-efficacy, or culturally sensitive coping strategies may also be beneficial to reduce acculturative stress (Chen, 2008).

Stress-related clinical symptomology and its prevalence among refugees

As a result of traumata and accumulating exposure to severe stressors before and during the flight, after arrival, and while settling in the receiving societies, the risk increases that those affected will develop mental health issues (Eggerth & Flynn, 2020; Hollifield et al., 2002; Ringeisen et al., 2020). The most common clinical diagnoses comprise affective and/or anxiety disorders, post-traumatic stress disorders, internalizing behavioral disorders, or conduct disorders (Fazel et al., 2005; Möhrle et al., 2016). As indicated by a meta-analysis, refugees' prevalence of developing generalized anxiety disorder is 11% (95% CI 6.75-15.43); for depression, the prevalence is 31.5% (95%, CI 22.64-40.38), and for post-traumatic stress disorder (PTSD) 31.46%, respectively (95%, CI 24.43-38.5) (Blackmore et al., 2020). Other research suggests that these rates may be even higher, as up to 86% of refugees met the criteria for PTSD (Hollifield et al., 2002; Knipscheer & Kleber, 2006). The prevalence rates were exceptionally high when refugees came from war zones or experienced violence in armed conflicts. The risk of comorbid diagnoses also increases. For example, 45% of a sample of Bosnian refugees in Croatia met diagnostic criteria for depression, PTSD, or both (Mollica et al., 2001).

Aside from determining prevalence rates, several longitudinal studies have examined the development of well-being among refugees. Most studies found evidence that refugees' mental health was impaired even years after their flight (e.g., Mollica et al., 2001; Silove et al., 1999) or even deteriorated over time (Lie, 2002). Few studies have identified improvements (Steel et al., 2002). Marshall et al. (2005) found high rates of PTSD (62%) and depression (42%) in Cambodian refugees two decades after immigrating to the United States. The risk of long-term impairment of mental health is severe when refugees have experienced trauma such as war or violence. These groups are at higher risk for mental disorders and physical health problems (Hollifield et al., 2002; Robertson et al., 2006). Reduced social support in the destination country is also associated with increased rates of PTSD, anxiety disorders, and depression among refugees (Gerritsen et al., 2006). The absence of support can be caused by the interaction anxieties of members of the receiving society, a lack of awareness of refugees' emotional and informational needs (Schubert et al., 2021b), or because of discrimination resulting from negative attitudes against refugees (Karpenstein & von Nordheim, 2019; Kluge et al., 2020; Thöle et al., 2017).

Antecedents and effects of attitudes towards refugees

Research on the determinants of attitudes towards refugees intensified in recent years, based on extensive panel studies on attitudes towards migration and immigration.[3] The Integrated Threat Theory (ITT) is suitable for analyzing the determinants. Stephan and colleagues (2009) specify assumptions on the emergence and effect of negative attitudes toward selected groups – here, towards refugees. According to ITT, prejudice, negative attitudes, and accompanying negative emotions towards members of a perceived outgroup occur as a defensive response when individuals feel

---

[3] e.g., the ALLBUS study by the Leibniz Institute for Social Sciences: Diekmann et al., 2015; the MITTE studies by the University of Leipzig: Decker et al., 2014; the European Social Survey: Siegert & Kogan, 2010

threatened by their values and beliefs and those of their social group. Determining group membership is subjective and varies depending on the context and/or the salience of group-constituting characteristics. The number and size of identifiable groups thus result from the considered diversity criteria (Dick & Stegmann, 2016).

The ITT proposes four central threat dynamics that can influence attitudes of members of a (perceived) ingroup towards the outgroup: (1) *intergroup anxiety* (anxious responses ingroup members experience when interacting with outgroup members, for example, uncertainty about how to address someone) (2) *realistic threat* (perceptions of competition and conflicting goals as well as threats to the physical and economic well-being of the ingroup, for example, perceiving competition regarding jobs), (3) *symbolic threat* (perceived differences in values, beliefs, and norms, for instance, perceiving a threat to one's cultural heritage), and (4) *negative stereotypes* (negative expectations of ingroup members about the behavior of outgroup members, for instance, perceiving members of an outgroup as criminals) (Stephan et al., 2009). Negative experiences with refugees can intensify the threatened sense of security and be associated with increased intergroup anxiety. Those affected may have had these experiences through direct contact with refugees or observation (Murašovs et al., 2015). Regarding a realistic threat, half of the respondents in eight out of ten European countries expressed concern about the security implications of receiving refugees associated with an increased risk of terrorism (Wike et al., 2016)[4].

The perception of symbolic threat from refugees by members of a receiving community is especially relevant when people with heterogeneous values or different religious backgrounds meet. It increases further when respondents lean towards a party whose politicians reject cultural diversity (Harteveld et al., 2017). Right-wing forums on the internet and social media are of great importance, especially in the German context, for fueling refugee threat scenarios (Simpson, 2016). Person-centered antecedents to threat perception, especially to symbolic threat, such as cultural solid *group identification* with one's nationality or few to no intercultural contact experiences, have been linked to negative attitudes towards cultural outgroup members such as refugees (Stephan & Stephan, 2000; Bernak & Chung, 2018; Schubert et al., 2021a). In turn, negative attitudes towards cultural diversity go hand in hand with hostile behavior, coercion, and aggression towards foreign cultural

---

[4] The survey on Global attitudes towards refugees from 2016 included data from the United Kingdom, Germany, France, Sweden, Netherlands, Spain, Greece, Poland, Italy and Hungary (Wike et al., 2016).

groups, as studies in Poland and New Zealand have shown (Golec De Zavala et al., 2010; Ward & Masgoret, 2006). A salient social identity can reinforce attitudinal adverse reactions toward refugees (van Dick & Stegmann, 2016). Suppose social identity emerges in an intercultural interaction between natives and refugees. In that case, the perceived threat is more likely to lead to aggressive reactions (Fischer et al., 2010), which can negatively affect the mental health of refugees (Çelebi et al., 2017). This means that behavioral tendencies towards refugees are more influenced by beliefs and values derived from group membership and less by the quality of the interaction per se.

Looking on the bright side of research about threat perceptions and their antecedents, van Assche's (2019) review reports multiple evidence that **positive intergroup contact** reduces prejudice and anti-immigration attitudes in intercultural settings significantly (Pettigrew & Tropp, 2006; Donth et al., 2014). Positive social contact between members of the host community and migrants may buffer threat perceptions and related negative emotions, such as intergroup anxiety in intercultural settings, indirectly reducing prejudice (Trines, 2017). For instance, a German study (Schubert et al., 2021b) showed that positive intercultural contact experiences may be directly and indirectly linked to better perspective-taking towards refugees, helping Germans as the receiving community to improve their attitudes towards refugees and to become more aware of the refugees' support needs.

Verkuyten (2006) argues that advocating cultural diversity in pluralistic societies promotes positive attitudes towards immigration and can thus promote subjective security in terms of reduced perceived symbolic threat. Confirming these assumptions, surveys in the Netherlands showed that advocates of a multicultural ideology expressed fewer prejudices against Muslims and evaluated the Muslim-Turkish proportion of the population more positively (Gonzalez et al., 2008; Verkuyten, 2006). According to Crawley and McMahon (2016), locals also judged refugees more positively when top politicians actively supported immigration. In addition, there are initial indications that media coverage of salient events and discussion forums in social media can influence the appreciation of cultural diversity or attitudes toward refugees. For example, reporting on drowning during a sea crossing or the arrival of refugees in Germany contributed to an appreciation of diversity and lower xenophobia (cf. Simpson, 2016). In an attempt to conceptualize these buffering effects, Ward and Masgoret (2006) suggested including positive attitudes towards multiculturalism and the extent of positive contact with migrants as additional antecedents within the framework of ITT because both contribute to reduced threat perceptions towards outgroups in intercultural settings.

Refugees' access to mental health care services

Upon their arrival in the receiving society, refugees may have differentiated needs regarding health care and social support (Reinke et al., 2022; Asfaw et al., 2020). In order to be effective, interventions should correspond to respective needs, covering all domains such as safety and security (e.g., approved legal status or housing), relatedness (e.g., having close relationships), societal participation (e.g., a sense of acceptance), self-determination (e.g., accomplishing personal and professional goals) as well as the need for physical and mental integrity (e.g., psychotherapeutic care) (for an overview see Reinke et al., 2022). Anders and Christiansen (2016) conducted a systematic literature review on the effectiveness of psychotherapeutic interventions for unaccompanied refugees. The authors found satisfactory effects for narrative exposure therapy and cognitive-behavioral therapy. Other studies suggest that multi-faceted methods in counseling and family counseling of refugees also help refugees cope with physical and mental problems (Björn et al., 2013). In order to be effective, however, psychotherapeutic care needs to take culturally varying expressions of clinical symptoms and an understanding of the refugees' cultural background into account (Marshall et al., 2005). In a similar vein, the involvement of bicultural counselors can have a positive impact on the treatment's success (Karageorge et al., 2018).

Despite these promising findings on how to shape and implement adequate therapeutic services, there are certain obstacles to their accessibility for refugees. Aside from administrative hurdles, one general problem is the massive gap between available psychotherapeutic services and the extent of the demand, especially in less urbanized areas (BAFF e.V., 2018; Asfaw et al., 2020). Another obstacle is that many refugees are unaware of the different health services they can access (Kortas, 2017). Hence, they need advocacy to find out which services they may use efficiently and to which extent (Reinke et al., 2022).

Besides, negative experiences with people working in health care services and with members of the host society, in general, can lead to a lack of perceived emotional support and further obstruct the reception of inadequate information on how to get help (Penka et al., 2015; Sandhu et al., 2013). The everyday experiences of refugees with members of the receiving society shape the level of trust perceived by refugees. In that sense, laypeople are necessary information providers for refugees to support them in seeking help when they need it (Hebbani et al., 2017). It is up to the members of the host community to develop awareness of the health-related needs of refugees and further act on it to foster the well-being of arriving refugees and to allow them to become part of the receiving society (Bohn, 2016; Reinke et al., 2022; Schubert et al., 2021b).

So far, research has found empathy to be a basis for solidarity towards another person or group and, therefore, to be of great importance for the readiness to help a group in need (Batson et al., 2002; Johnston & Glasford, 2018). In a study with children in Northern Ireland, defining Syrian refugee children as the target group, Glen and colleagues (2019) induced empathy and found changing outgroup attitudes to predict the willingness of Northern Irish children to help arriving refugee children in a meaningful way. Also, positive contact experiences with others who are perceived as an outgroup, such as other ethnical groups or refugees, have been shown to increase the intention to provide help by reducing negative attitudes against the outgroup (Glen et al., 2019; Johnston & Glasford, 2018; Schubert et al., 2021b; for an overview see van Assche, 2019). For instance, Schubert et al. (2021b) found intercultural contact experience to be an essential direct antecedent of empathy and attitudes towards refugees and an indirect antecedent of Germans' awareness of the informational needs of refugees regarding mental health services.

Conclusion and future directions

Refugees are confronted with many situational, personal, and social stressors before and during their flight. Additionally, contextual stressors, such as lack of privacy and inadequate housing, and social stressors, such as experiences of rejection and discrimination, may add to the stress experienced after they arrive in the host country. A lack of resources, for instance, inadequate socio-emotional and informational support, can further worsen the mental health of refugees. Accumulating stressors, in combination with lowered resources, contribute to the onset of clinical symptomatology, such as PTSD, anxiety disorders, or depression among refugees.

Threat perceptions and negative attitudes towards refugees can trigger negative behavioral interactions between receiving society members and refugees. With this, intergroup anxiety, symbolic and realistic threat perceptions, and harmful stereotypes have shown to be of most significant importance (Stephan et al., 2000). Threat perception and resulting negative attitudes towards refugees may be fueled by a salient social identity as well as by negative attitudes towards a culturally diverse society. Moreover, negative attitudes among receiving society members pose a multi-faceted obstacle because they deprive refugees of getting adequate information on how to access mental health services. They also hinder refugees from developing trust in the receiving society and feeling emotionally supported. On the other hand, positive intercultural interactions and empathy can serve as protective factors, improve attitudes toward refugees, and foster the readiness to support them.

Besides medical professionals, lay people and their attitudes play a crucial role in refugees' access to mental health care services because it is them refugees interact with daily. As such, members of the general population could offer the needed emotional and informational support. So far, however, most studies have concentrated on the attitudes of medical professionals. At the same time, research on the gate-keeping role of general members of the receiving society for refugees' access to mental health care is scarce. A good starting point could be previous positive intercultural contact experiences with migrants, as these may lower the host communities' threat perceptions and improve their awareness of the support needs of refugees via more positive attitudes (Schubert et al., 2021a; 2021b). Future research should continue exploring the role that members of the receiving societies play in refugees' access to mental health care services. Also, it appears worth searching for answers to how to foster an understanding of the needs of refugees, which helps to integrate refugees ultimately into the society they arrived in.

References

Anders, M., & Christiansen, H. (2016). Unbegleitete minderjährige Flüchtlinge. Eine systematische Übersicht über psychologische Interventionen. *Kindheit und Entwicklung*, *25*(4), 216–230. https://doi.org/10.1026/0942-5403/a000201

Asfaw, B.B., Beiersmann, C., Keck, V. et al. (2020). Experiences of psychotherapists working with refugees in Germany: a qualitative study. *BMC Psychiatry* 20, 588. https://doi.org/10.1186/s12888-020-02996-0

BAFF e.V. - Bundesweite Arbeitsgemeinschaft der psychosozialen Zentren für Flüchtlinge und Folteropfer e.V. (2018). *Musterverwaltungsvorschrift für Psychotherapien im AsylbLG*. Retrieved on February 16, 2022 from: http://www.baff-zentren.org/wpcontent/uploads/2008/05/Musterverwaltungsvorschrift-f%C3%BCr-Psychotherapien-im-AsylbLG.pdf

Batson, C., Chang, J., Orr, R., & Rowland, J. (2002). Empathy, Attitudes, and Action: Can

Feeling for a Member of a Stigmatized Group Motivate One to Help the Group? *Personality and Social Psychology Bulletin, p.* 28, 1656–1666. https://doi/10.1177/014616702237647

Bemak, F., & Chung, R. (2018). Race Dialogues in Group Psychotherapy: Key Issues in Training and Practice. International Journal of Group Psychotherapy, *69*(2), 1–20. https://d oi. Org/ 10. 1080/ 00207284. 2018. 14987 43

Berry, J. W., Phinney, J. S., Sam, D. L., & Vedder, P. (2006). Immigrant youth: Acculturation, identity, and adaptation. *Applied Psychology, 55*(3), 303–332. https://doi.org/10.1111/ j.1464-0597.2006.00256.x

Björn, G. J., Gustafsson, P. A., Sydsjö, G., & Berterö, C. (2013). Family therapy sessions with refugee families; a qualitative study. *Conflict and health, 7*(1), 7. https://doi.org/10.1186/ 1752-1505-7-7

Blackmore, R., Boyle, J. A., Fazel, M., Ranasinha, S., Gray, K. M., Fitzgerald, G., Misso, M., & Gibson-Helm, M. (2020). The prevalence of mental illness in refugees and asylum seekers: A systematic review and meta-analysis. PLoS medicine, *17*(9), e1003337. https://doi.org/10.1371/journal.pmed.1003337

Bohn, I., Landes, B., Seddig, N., & Warkentin, S. (2016). Ich brauche hier nur einen Weg, den ich finden kann. Ankommen und Einleben in NRW aus der Sicht geflüchteter Kinder und Jugendlicher. Frankfurt a. M.: Institut für Sozialarbeit und Sozialpädagogik e.V. Retrieved October 11, 2020 from: https://www.iss-ffm.de/fileadmin/assets/ veroeffentlichungen/ downloads/641_yr-zwischenbericht_web_neuesimpressum_einzeln.pdf

Buchwald, P., & Hobfoll, S. (2020). Die Theorie der Ressourcenerhaltung: Implikationen für den Zusammenhang von Stress und Kultur. In P. Genkova, T. Ringeisen & F. T. L. Leong (Eds.), Handbuch Stress und Kultur (pp. 127–138). Springer VS. http://dx.doi.org/10. 1007/978-3-658-27825-0_9-1

Celebi E., Verkuyten M., & Bagci S.C. (2017). Ethnic identification, discrimination, and mental and physical health among Syrian refugees: The moderating role of identity needs. *European Journal of Social Psychology*, 47, 832–843. https://doi.org/10.1002/ejsp.2299

Ceobanu, A., & Escandell, X. (2010). Comparative Analyses of Public Attitudes Toward Immigrants and Immigration Using Multinational Survey Data: A Review of Theories and Research. *Annual Review of Sociology. 36*(1), 309-328. https://doi: 10.1146/annurev.soc. 012809.102651

Chen, C.P. (2008). Career Guidance with Immigrants. In J. A. Athanasou, & R. Van Esbroeck (Eds.), *International Handbook of Career Guidance* (pp. 419–442). Springer. https://doi.org/10.1007/978-1-4020-6230-8_21

Crawley, H., & McMahon, S. (2016). Beyond fear and hate: Mobilising people power to create a new narrative on migration and diversity. Ben and Jerry's. http://www.benjerry.co.uk/ files/live/sites/uk/files/our-values/Beyond-Fear-and-Hate-v1.5-FINAL.pdf

De Genova, N. P. (2002). Migrant "Illegality" and deportability in Everyday Life. Annual Review of Anthropology, *31*, 419–447. http://www.jstor.org/stable/4132887

Decker, O., Kiess, J., & Brähler, E. (2014). Die stabilisierte Mitte- Rechtsextreme Einstellung in Deutschland 2014. Universität Leipzig.

Dhont, K., Van Hiel, A., & Hewstone, M. (2014). Changing the ideological roots of prejudice: Longitudinal effects of ethnic intergroup contact on social dominance orientation. Group Processes & Intergroup Relations, 17(1), 27–44. https:// doi. org/ 10. 1177/13684 30213 497064

Dick, R. van, & Stegmann, S. (2016). Diversity, Social Identity und Diversitätsüberzeugungen. In P. Genkova & T. Ringeisen (Eds.), *Handbuch Diversity Kompetenz. Band 1: Perspektiven und Anwendungsfelder* (pp. 3–15). Springer Fachmedien.

Diekmann, A., Fetchenhauer, D., Kreuter, F., Kurz, K., Liebig, S., Wagner, M., Westle, B., GESIS - Leibniz-Institut für Sozialwissenschaften (2015). Allgemeine Bevölkerungsumfrage der Sozialwissenschaften ALLBUS 2014. GESIS Datenarchiv, Köln. ZA5240 Datenfile Version 2.1.0.

Eggerth, D. M., & Flynn, M. A. (2020). Immigration: Implikationen für Stress und Gesundheit. In P. Genkova, T. Ringeisen & F. T. L. Leong (Eds.), *Handbuch Stress und Kultur: Interkulturelle und kulturvergleichende Perspektiven* (S. 343–359). SpringerVS. http://dx.doi.org/10.1007/978-3-531-93449-5_20

Fazel, M., Wheeler, J., & Danesh, J. (2005). Prevalence of serious mental disorder in 7000 refugees resettled in western countries: A systematic review. *Lancet, 365*(9467), 1309–1314. https://doi.org/10.1016/s0140-6736(05)61027-6

Fischer, P., Haslam, S. A., & Smith, L. (2010). „If you wrong us, shall we not revenge?" Social identity salience moderates support for retaliation in response to collective threat. *Group Dynamics: Theory, Research, and Practice, 14*(2), 143–150. http://dx.doi.org/10.1037/a0017970

Gehrsitz, M., & Ungerer, M. (2017). Jobs, crime, and votes: A short-run evaluation of the refugee crisis in Germany. Institute of Labor Economics. No. 10494. Retrieved on June 21, 2018 from: http://ftp.iza.org/dp10494.pdf

Gerritsen, A. A., Bramsen, I., Deville, W., van Willigen, L. H., Hovens, J. E., & Van der Ploeg, H. M. (2006). Physical and mental health of Afghan, Iranian, and Somali asylum seekers and refugees in the Netherlands. *Social Psychiatry and Psychiatric Epidemiology, 41*(1), 18-26. https://doi.org/10.1007/s00127-005-0003-5

Glen, C., Taylor, L., & Dautel, J. (2019). Promoting prosocial behavior towards refugees: Exploring the empathy attitude-action model in middle childhood. In Children and Peace: From Research to Action (pp. 71-87). Springer. https://www.springer.com/ gp/ book/9783030221751

Grzywacz, J. C., Quandt, S. A., Early, J., Tapia, J., Graham, C. N., & Arcury, T. A. (2006). Leaving family for work: Ambivalence and mental health among Mexican migrant farmworker men. *Journal of Immigrant and Minority Health, 8*(1), 85–97. https://doi.org/10.1007/s10903-006-6344-7

Golec De Zavala, A., Cislak, A., & Wesolowska, E. (2010). Political conservatism, need for cognitive closure, and intergroup hostility. *Political Psychology, 31*(4), 521–541. http://www.jstor.org/stable/20779582

Gonzalez, K. V., Verkuyten, M., Weesie, J., & Poppe, E. (2008). Prejudice towards Muslims in the Netherlands: Testing integrated threat theory. *British Journal of Social Psychology, (4)*47, 667–685. https://doi.org/10.1348/014466608x284443

Harteveld, E., Kokkonen, A., & Dahlberg, S. (2017). Adapting to party lines: The effect of party affiliation on attitudes to immigration. *West European Politics, 40*(6), 1177–1197. https://doi.org/10.1080/01402382.2017.1328889

Hebbani, A., Colic-Peisker, V., & MacKinnon, M. (2017). Know thy Neighbour: Residential Integration and Social Bridging among Refugee Settlers in Greater Brisbane. *Journal of Refugee Studies, 31*, 82-103. https://doi.org/10.1093/jrs/fex016

Hettich, N., Seidel, F. A., & Stuhrmann, L. Y. (2020). Psychosocial Interventions for Newly Arrived Adolescent Refugees: A Systematic Review. *Adolescent Research Review, 5*, 99–114. https://doi.org/10.1007/s40894-020-00134-1.

Hollifield, M., Warner, T. D., Lian, N., Krakow, B., Jenkins, J. H., & Kesler, J. (2002). Measuring trauma and health status in refugees: A critical review. *Journal of the American Medical Association, 288*(5), 611–621. https://doi.org/10.1001/jama.288.5.611

IOM (International Organization for Migration) (2020). *World Migration Report*. Retrieved February 16, 2022 from: https://publications.iom.int/system/files/pdf/wmr_2020.pdf

Johnston, B. M., & Glasford, D. E. (2018). Intergroup contact and helping: How quality contact and empathy shape outgroup helping. *Group Processes & Intergroup Relations, 21*(8), 1185–1201. https://doi.org/10.1177/1368430217711770

Karpenstein, J., & Nordheim, F. (2019). Die Situation (unbegleiteter) minderjähriger und junger volljähriger Geflüchteter in Deutschland. Auswertung der Online-Umfrage 2019. Berlin: Bundesfachverband unbegleitete minderjährige Flüchtlinge e.V. Retrieved April 13, 2021 from:

https://b-umf.de/src/wp-content/uploads/2019/12/bumfumfrage2019_web_v03.pdf

Karageorge, A., Rhodes, P., & Gray, R. (2018). Relationship and Family Therapy for Newly Resettled Refugees: An Interpretive Description of Staff Experiences. *Australian and New Zealand Journal of Family Therapy, 39*, 303–319. https://doi.org/10.1002/anzf.1325

Kluge, U., Aichberger, M.C., Heinz, E., Udeogu-Gözalan, U., & D. Abdel-Fatah (2020). Rassismus und psychische Gesundheit. *Nervenarzt, 91*, 1017–1024. https://doi.org/10.1007/s00115-020-00990-1

Knipscheer, J. W., & Kleber, R. J. (2006). The relative contribution of posttraumatic and acculturative stress to subjective mental health among Bosnian refugees. *Journal of Clinical Psychology, 62*(3), 339–353. https://doi.org/10.1002/jclp.20233

Konle-Seidl, R. (2018). Integration of refugees in Austria, Germany, and Sweden: Comparative analysis. Retrieved June 21, 2018 from http://www.europarl.europa.eu/ RegData/ etudes/STUD/2018/614200/IPOL_STU(2018)614200_EN.pdf

Kortas, A. M. (2017). *Bedürfnisorientierung und passende Angebote für Geflüchtete*. Retrieved October 11, 2020, from https://www.ghst.de/fileadmin/jahresbericht2016/_d/ ynRqYj/u/ abschlussbericht_kortas2017.pdf

Lie, B. (2002). A 3-year follow-up study of psychosocial functioning and general symptoms in settled refugees. *Acta Psychiatrica Scandinavica, 106*(6), 415–425. https://doi.org/10.1034/j.1600-0447.2002.01436.x

Liebe U., Meyerhoff J., Kroesen M., Chorus C., & Glenk K. (2018). From welcome culture to welcome limits? Uncovering preference changes over time for sheltering refugees in Germany. *PLoS ONE 13*(8): e0199923. https://doi.org/10.1371/journal.pone.0199923

Löbel, J.-M. & Jacobsen, J. (2021). Waiting for kin: a longitudinal study of family reunification and refugee mental health in Germany. *Journal of Ethnic and Migration Studies.* https://doi.org/10.1080/1369183X.2021.1884538.

Marshall, G. N., Schell, T. L., Elliot, M. N., Berthold, S. M., & Chun, C. (2005). Mental health of Cambodian refuges 2 decades after resettlement in the United States. *Journal of the American Medical Association, 294*(5), 571–579. https://doi.org/10.1001/jama.294.5.571

Mehran, N., Jumaa, J., Lazaridou, F., Foroutan, N., Heinz, A., & Kluge, U. (2021). Spatiality of Social Stress Experienced by Refugee Women in Initial Reception Centers. Journal of International Migration and Integration / Revue de l'intégration et de la migration internationale. http://doi.org/10.1007/s12134-021-00890-6.

Mollica, R. F., Sarajlic, N., Chernoff, M., Lavelle, J., Vukovic, I. S., & Massagli, M. P. (2001). Longitudinal study of psychiatric symptoms, disability, mortality, and emigration among Bosnian refugees. *Journal of the American Medical Association, 286*(5), 546–554. https://doi.org/10.1001/jama.286.5.546

Möhrle, B., Dölitzsch, C., J. M. Fegert, & Keller, F. (2016). Verhaltensauffälligkeiten und Lebensqualität bei männlichen unbegleiteten minderjährigen Flüchtlingen in Jugendhilfeeinrichtungen in Deutschland. *Kindheit und Entwicklung, 25*(4), 204–215.

https://doi.org/10.1026/0942-5403/a000206.

Murašovs, V., Ruža, A., Raščevskis, V., & Dombrovskis, V. (2015). Expecting refugees in Latvia: Intergroup anxiety. Social Sciences Bulletin, 2, 60–74.

Nesterko, Y., Jäckle, D., Friedrich, M., Holzapfel, L., & Glaesmer, H. (2020) Factors predicting symptoms of somatization, depression, anxiety, post-traumatic stress disorder, self-rated mental and physical health among recently arrived refugees in Germany. *Conflict and Health, 14.* https://doi.org/10.1186/s13031-020-00291-z

Orrenius, P. M., & Zavodny, M. (2009). Do immigrants work in riskier jobs? Demography, 46(3), 535–551.

Penka, S., Faißt, H., Vardar, A., Borde, T., Mösko, M.O., Dingoyan, D., Schulz, H., Koch, U., Kluge, U., & Heinz, A. (2015). Der Stand der interkulturellen Öffnung in der psychosozialen Versorgung- Ergebnisse einer Studie in einem innerstädtischen Berliner Bezirk. *Psychotherapie, Psychosomatik, Medizinische Psychologie, 65,* 353-362. https://doi.org/10. 1055/s-0035-1549961.

Pettigrew, T., & Tropp, L. (2006). A Meta-analytic test of intergroup contact theory. Journal of personality and social psychology., *90*(5), 751–783. https:// doi. org/ 10. 1146/ annur ev. psych. 49.1. 65

Porter, M., & Haslam, N. (2005). Predisplacement and postdisplacement factors associated with mental health of refugees and internally displaced persons: A meta-analysis. *Journal of the American Medical Association, 294*(5), 602–612. https://doi.org/10.1001/jama.294.5.602

Reinke, H., Kärner, T., & Ringeisen, T. (2022) Need-centered support for young refugees in Germany. In: S. Mozes, & M. Israelashvili (Eds.), Youth without family to lean on. Routledge. https://doi.org/ 10.4324/9781003124849-15

Ringeisen, T., Mahat-Shamir, M., Ben-Ezra, M., Hamama-Raz, Y., & Schubert, S. (2020). Krank durch beidseitige Fremdheitserfahrung? Zur Rolle von Stressoren und Einstellungen für die Gesundheit von Einheimischen und Geflüchteten [. In: P. Genkova & A. Riecken (Eds.) *Handbuch Migration und Erfolg* (pp. 1-13), Springer Reference Psychologie. Springer. https://doi.org/10.1007/978-3-658-18403-2_5-1

Robertson, C. L., Halcon, L., Savik, K., Johnson, D., Spring, M., & Butcher, J. (2006). Somali and Oromo refugee women: Trauma and associated factors. *Journal of Advanced Nursing, 56*(6), 577–587. https://doi.org/10.1111/j.1365-2648.2006.04057.x

Sandhu, S., Bjerre, N. V., Dauvrin, M., Dias, S., Gaddini, A., Greacen, T., Ioannidis, E., Kluge, U., Jensen, N. K., Lamkaddem, M., Puigpinós i Riera, R., Kósa, Z., Wihlman, U., Stankunas, M., Straßmayr, C., Wahlbeck, K., Welbel, M., & Priebe, S. (2013). Experiences with treating immigrants: a qualitative study in mental health services across 16 European countries. Social psychiatry and psychiatric epidemiology, 48(1), 105–116. https://doi.org/10.1007/s00127-012-0528-3

Samarasinghe, K., & Arvidsson, B. (2002). It is a different war to fight here in Sweden'- the impact of involuntary migration on the health of refugee families in transition. *Scandinavian Journal of Caring Sciences, 16*(3), 292–301. https://doi.org/10.1046/j.1471-6712.2002.00089.x

Schmitz, P. G., & Berry, J. W. (2011). Structure of Acculturation Attitudes and their relationships with personality and psychological adaptation: A study with immigrant and national samples in Germany. In F. Deutsch, M. Boehnke, U. Kühnen, & K. Boehnke (Eds.), *Rendering borders obsolete: Cross-cultural and cultural psychology as an interdisciplinary, multi-method endeavor: Proceedings from the 19thInternational Congress of the International Association for Cross-Cultural Psychology.* Retrieved from: https://scholarworks.gvsu.edu/iaccp_papers/80. Accessed: October 10, 2020.

Schubert, S. J., Hamama-Raz, Y., Ben-Ezra, M., Mahat-Shamir, M., & Ringeisen, T. (2021a, Juli 6-10). *How perceiving refugees as threat may backfire on German's health: An integrated threat theory approach* [Paper presentation]. The Migration Conference, online.

Schubert, S. J., Kluge, U., Klapprott, F., & Ringeisen, T. (2021b, July 7-8). *"All you need is.." - what? How Germans perceive the support needs of accommodated refugees* [Paper presentation]. 42nd International Conference of the Stress Trauma Anxiety and Resilience Society, online.

Schubert, S. J., & Ringeisen, T. (2020). Stressbewältigung im Kulturvergleich [coping from a cross-cultural perspective]. In T. Ringeisen, P. Genkova & F.T.L. Leong (Eds.), Handbuch Stress und Kultur: interkulturelle und kulturvergleichende Perspektiven. Wiesbaden: Springer.

Segal, U. A., & Mayadas, N. S. (2005). Assessment of issues facing immigrant and refugee families. *Child Welfare, 84*(5), 563–583. PMID: 16435651.

Siegert, M., & Kogan, I. (2010). *Einstellungen gegenüber ethnischen Minderheiten in Europa: Analysen mit dem European Social Survey.* Bamberg: University Press. https://fis.uni-bamberg.de/handle/uniba/242

Silove, D., Steel, Z., McGorry, P., & Drobny, J. (1999). Problems Tamil asylum seekers encounter in accessing health and welfare services in Australia. *Social Science & Medicine, 49*(7), 951–956. https://doi.org/10.1016/s0277-9536(99)00188-4

Sinnerbrink, I., Silove, D., Field, A., Steel, Z., & Manicavasagar, V. (1997). Compounding of premigration trauma and postmigration stress in aslym seekers. *The Journal of Psychology, 131*(5), 463–470. https://doi.org/10.1080/00223989709603533

Simpson, P. A. (2016). Mobilizing meanings: Translocal identities of the far right web. *German Politics & Society, 34*(4), 34–53. http://dx.doi.org/10.3167/gps.2016.340403

Steel, Z., Silove, D., Phan, T., & Bauman, A. (2002). Long-term effect of psychological trauma on the mental health of Vietnamese refugees resettled in Australia: A population-based study. *Lancet*, 360, 1056–1062. https://doi.org/10.1016/s0140-6736(02)11142-1

Stephan, C.W., & Stephan, W.G. (2000). An Integrated Threat Theory of Prejudice In S. Oskamp (Ed.), *"The Claremont Symposium on Applied Social Psychology" Reducing prejudice and discrimination* (p. 23–45). Lawrence Erlbaum Associates Publishers. https://psycnet.apa.org/record/2000-03917-001

Stephan, W.G., Ybarra, O., & Rios, K. (2009). *Intergroup threat theory.* In T. D. Nelson (Ed.), Handbook of prejudice, stereotyping, and discrimination, S. 43–59. Psychology Press. https://psycnet.apa.org/record/2008-09974-003

Thöle, A.-M., Penka, S., Brähler, E., Heinz, A., & Kluge, U. (2017). Psychotherapeutische Versorgung von Geflüchteten aus der Sicht niedergelassener Psychotherapeuten in Deutschland. *Zeitschrift für Psychiatrie, Psychologie und Psychotherapie. 65.* 145-154. http://doi.org/10.1024/1661-4747/a000315

Trines, S. (2017). Lessons from Germany's refugee crisis: Integration, costs, and benefits. Online article. World education news & reviews. Retrieved on June 2, 2017 from: http://wenr.wes.org/2017/05/lessons-germanys-refugee-crisis-integration-costs-benefits

United Nations General Assembly, Convention Relating to the Status of Refugees, 28 July 1951, *United Nations, Treaty Series*, vol. 189, p. 137. Retrieved February 19, 2022 from: https://www.refworld.org/docid/3be01b964.html

United Nations High Commissioner for Refugees (UNHCR) 2021. Global Trends – Forced Displacement in 2021. In: UNHCR. 2021. Retrieved on February 14, 2023 from https://www.unhcr.org/publications/brochures/62a9d1494/global-trends-report-2021.html.

Van Assche, J. (2019). Ethnic diversity, ideological climates, and intergroup relations: A person x context approach. Psychologica Belgica, 59(1), Article 33-49. https://doi.org/10.5334/pb.465

Verkuyten, M. (2006). Multicultural recognition and ethnic minority rights: A social identity perspective. *European Review of Social Psychology, 17*(1), 148–184. https://doi.org/10.1080/10463280600937418

Ward, C., & Masgoret, A. M. (2006). An integrative model of attitudes toward immigrants. *International Journal of Intercultural Relations,* 30, 671–682. https://doi.org/10. 1016/j.ijintrel.2006.06.002

Wike, R., Stokes, B., & Simmons, K. (2016). Europeans fear wave of refugees will mean more terrorism, fewer jobs. Online article. Pew Research Centre. Retrieved on June 10, 2018 from: http://www.pewglobal.org/2016/07/11/europeans-fear-wave-of-refugees-will-mean-more-terrorism-fewer-jobs/

Zick, A. (2010). *Psychologie der Akkulturation- Neufassung eines Forschungsbereiches*. Springer. https://doi.org/10.1007/978-3-531-92183-9

SAFE, BUT WORRIED ABOUT FOOD:

THE CASE OF SYRIAN REFUGEES IN CANADA

Ginny Lane[1] and Hassan Vatanparast[2]

Introduction

Food insecurity is a persistent problem in Canada, especially among vulnerable population groups, such as ethnic minorities, immigrants, and refugees. In Canada, 12.7% of households were food insecure in 2017-2018; however, newcomers (immigrants and refugees) within their first five years in Canada more commonly experienced food insecurity (17.1%), as compared to longer-term newcomers (13.8%), and the Canadian-born (12.2%) (Tarasuk & Mitchell, 2020). Arab or West Asian households (immigrants and Canadian-born) were at particularly high risk of food insecurity (20.4%) (Tarasuk & Mitchell, 2020). The Canadian Community Health Survey (CCHS) does not present information on distinct immigration categories so refugee food security status distinct from that of economic immigrants cannot be determined. Other Canadian studies using the CCHS food security module have documented high rates of food insecurity among refugees, varying from 55% in Saskatchewan to 57% in Ontario (Lane et al., 2019; Tarraf et al., 2018). These two studies may have reached more vulnerable refugees that were excluded from the CCHS due to not speaking one of Canada's two official languages (Tarasuk & Mitchell, 2020).

Tarasuk and Mitchell (2020) state, "Food insecurity is a serious public health problem in Canada because individuals' health and wellbeing is tightly linked to their household food security status," indicating the prominent role of food security related to public health. Food insecure adults have been noted to be at higher risk of inadequate nutrient intake (Davison et al., 2017; Gucciardi et al., 2009; Kirkpatrick & Tarasuk, 2008); chronic diseases such as heart disease, diabetes and hypertension (Gucciardi et al., 2009; Vozoris & Tarasuk, 2003); poor physical health, low level of physical activity, major depression and psychological distress (Davison et al., 2017; Gucciardi et al., 2009; Vozoris & Tarasuk, 2003). Food insecure children have been noted to

[1] Ginny Lane, Margaret Ritchie School of Family and Consumer Sciences, University of Idaho. School of Public Health, University of Saskatchewan, Canada.
[2] Hassan Vatanparast, School of Public Health, University of Saskatchewan. College of Pharmacy and Nutrition, University of Saskatchewan, Canada.

consume less fruits, vegetables, and dairy products, as well as a more energy dense diet (Kirkpatrick & Tarasuk, 2008). Food insecure children have been found to be at higher risk of poor health, asthma, and depression (Kirkpatrick et al., 2010; McIntyre et al., 2017). In summary, food insecure individuals are at risk of consuming suboptimal diets, developing diet-related chronic diseases, and mental health conditions.

Income is one of the most important determinants of food security. In 2018, food insecurity was highest among Canadian households with lower incomes and those receiving social assistance (Tarasuk & Mitchell, 2020). Food insecurity was also high among single-parent families headed by women and households with children under the age of 18 years. Although the impact of educational attainment on food security status was not mentioned in the most recent report, Tarasuk et al. (2016) found that individuals with post-secondary education were less likely to be food insecure than those with less education.

Food Insecurity among Newcomers (immigrant and refugees)

Among newcomers, food insecurity has been linked to several poor health outcomes. Food insecure adults have been noted to be at increased risk for physical and emotional health problems, including anxiety, depression, and respiratory and gastrointestinal problems (Marin-Leon et al., 2005; McIntyre et al., 2000; Lee & Frongillo, 2001). Analysis of the US National Health Interview Survey (2011 to 2015) indicate that food insecurity among adult immigrants is associated with higher odds of being diagnosed with coronary heart disease (CHD) (57%), angina pectoris (81%) and heart attack (220%), reporting poor health (280%), and being obese (126%) compared to food secure immigrants (Smith & Coleman-Jensen, 2020). It is possible that the stress associated with food insecurity and/or the high cost of healthy food items such as whole grains, lean proteins, and fresh products, which are vital to the prevention and management of chronic conditions, contribute to these poor health outcomes (Berkowitz et al., 2017; Gundersen & Ziliak, 2014; Berkowitz et al., 2014).

Among immigrant children aged 4-8 years, food insecurity has been linked with consuming fewer servings of dairy products, less protein, as well as inadequate amounts of vitamin B12 and calcium (Lane et al., 2019). They have also been observed to be at higher risk for learning disabilities (Weigel et al., 2007). A recent analysis of a nationally representative sample of preschool aged children from the US Early Childhood Longitudinal Study–

Birth Cohort reported that children of immigrants from food insecure households experience worse parent-reported health than their native peers from food insecure households (Huang et al., 2018). It is possible that food insecurity could impact children's development and health by altering family processes. Food insecurity can induce stress, which may negatively impact parents' emotional well-being and quality of interactions with their children, resulting in adverse child outcomes (Gershoff et al., 2005). A suboptimal diet could put food-insecure immigrant children at risk of not growing and developing during an important developmental period.

Premigration experiences may impact current newcomer food security. Refugees may have experienced food deprivation prior to migration and are then confronted with a sudden expansion of food choices in their host country, which can lead to under and over-nutrition (Rondinelli et al., 2011). In addition, resettled refugees have reported feeling guilty about eating well when family members left behind in their country of origin are food insecure. (Gallegos et al., 2008). Families may feel pressure to send money to their family members left behind.

Economic factors have often been linked to higher risk of food insecurity among newcomers, such as low income (Anderson et al., 2014; Gichunge et al., 2015; Lane et al., 2019; Peterman et al., 2013; Tarraf et al., 2018); use of food aid programs (Doad, 2016; Patil et al., 2009; Peterman et al., 2013); receiving social assistance benefits and borrowing money or goods (Anderson et al., 2014; Tarraf et al., 2018); budgeting difficulties due to other pressing needs beyond food (Lane et al., 2019); financially supporting family members abroad (Gallegos et al., 2008); and the high cost of healthy or ethnic foods (Gallegos et al., 2008; Hadley et al., 2007; Patil et al., 2009). Family composition, such as being a single or widowed mother and having more than one child have been linked with increased risk of food insecurity (Nisbet, 2011; Peterman et al., 2013; Tarraf et al., 2018).

Figure 1 describes many social factors common to the immigrant experience have been linked with higher risk of food insecurity. For example, fewer years in the host country (Tarraf et al., 2018), low social support (Gichunge et al., 2015), low host language skills and difficulties with shopping in a new food environment (Dharod et al., 2013; Peterman et al., 2013) have been associated with higher risk of food insecurity. Due to not owning cars, refugees have reported challenges with transportation to ethnic grocery stores (Lane et al., 2019). Sometimes newcomers are not able to find traditional ingredients and report having to substitute less nutritious ingredients (Renzaho & Burns,

2006). They have also noted that available foods lack taste or are not fresh (Piwowarczyk et al., 2008; Dharod et al., 2013), or perceive chemicals in food (Hadley & Sellen, 2006). The extensive time requirements to prepare traditional meals (Piwowarczyk et al., 2008), and children's demands for Western foods (sugar sweetened beverages, fast food, etc.) (Dharod et al., 2013; Piwowarczyk et al., 2013) may also increase risk of food security.

Low educational achievement has often been linked with food insecurity (Gichunge et al., 2015); however, more recent evidence has reported that families with parents or mothers that are high school graduates were at three to four times higher risk of household food insecurity compared to households with less-educated parents (Lane et al., 2019, Al-Kharabsheh et al., 2020). It is possible that immigrant families with higher education come to Canada with high expectations of maintaining a good lifestyle when then arrive and become disillusioned when their dream does not materialise. These families likely had middle to higher class lifestyles in their country of origin, but after they arrive and find that their foreign qualifications are not immediately recognised or that their language skills are not sufficient to secure the type of employment they were expecting, they are faced with the stark reality of living on a low income for an extended period. These families may not have the coping or food preparation skills that may help them to cope with low resources, in contrast to other immigrants with agricultural or rural backgrounds that may have stronger skills in these areas. As such, families accustomed to living on a low income may have coping strategies, such as accessing community supports and services and working cooperatively with their neighbours, as well as advanced food preparation skills that allow them to prepare foods from scratch and preserve foods for future consumption, which position them to thrive better in low resource environments.

Figure 1. Socioecological framework explaining factors associated with food security status of refugees

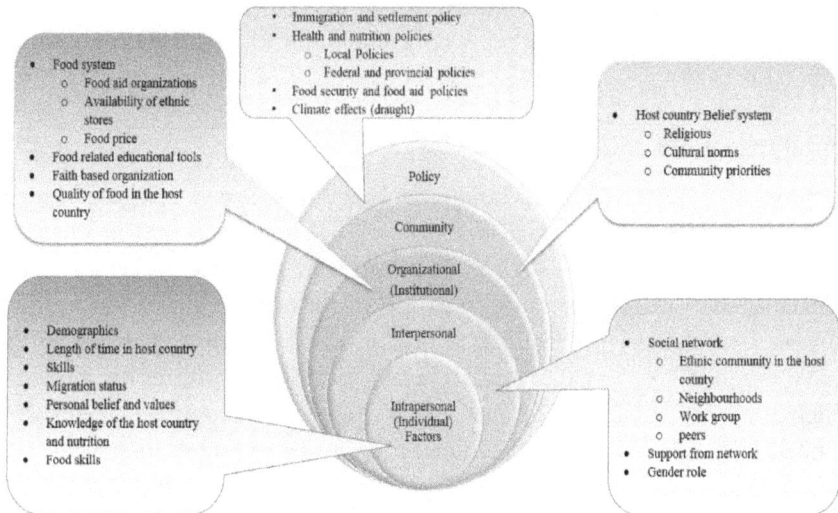

Source: Khakpour, 2019

Syrian Refugees

Between November 4, 2015, and October 31, 2021, almost 45,000 Syrian refugees arrived in Canada (IRCC, 2021). This large influx within a short period likely placed substantial demands on Canada's refugee resettlement services and raises the question of whether available supports were sufficient to assure refugees' food security.

The Syrian refugee population includes government-assisted refugees (GAR), privately sponsored refugees (PSR) and blended sponsorship refugees (BSR). These groups differed on several sociodemographic characteristics. A higher proportion of GARs and BSRs were under the age of 17 (59%, 57% respectively), than PSRs (35%); only 4% of GARs and 3% of BSRs had more than thirteen years of schooling, compared to 34% of PSRs; 29% of GARs and 26% of BSRs had no education, compared to 15% of PSRs; and GAR households included an average of 4.6 people, while BSR households averaged 4.2 people, and PSRs 2.3 people. (IRCC, 2021).

A recent evaluation of the reception of Syrian refugees resettled between 2010 and 2014 indicates that Syrian refugees received orientation regarding where to purchase food, including halal food, etc. Due to the small number of BSRs, the report focuses on GARs and PSRs. Almost 94% of GARs and

97% of PSRs agreed that they "understood how to shop for groceries and get other essentials" (IRCC, 2016). About 74% of GARs and 50% of PSRs used a food bank at least once. Of families that accessed a food bank, almost 25% of GARs and 23% of PSRs received a minimum of seven food hampers (IRCC, 2016).

Food Insecurity among Syrian Refugees

A series of recent Canadian studies indicate that Syrian refugees across Canada are experiencing high levels of food insecurity - 52% in Quebec (Chevrier et al., 2023)[1], 80% in Toronto and 92% in Saskatoon (Al-Kharabsheh et al., 2020). These rates are comparable with those observed among other refugee populations in Saskatchewan (55%) (Lane et al., 2019) and Ontario (57%) (Tarraf et al., 2018) using the CCHS food security module. High levels of food insecurity have also been observed among refugees in the United States and Australia, varying from 40 to 85% (Anderson et al., 2014; Dharod et al., 2013; Gallegos et al., 2008; Hadley et al., 2010; Hadley & Sellen, 2006; Hadley et al., 2007; Piwowarczyk et al., 2008).

The recent Canadian studies suggest some areas of concern related to food security among Syrian refugees. Among the Syrian refugees located in Toronto and Saskatoon, low-income households were at four times higher risk of food insecurity (Al-Kharabsheh et al., 2020); while those living in Quebec also indicated they had insufficient income to assure their food security (Chevrier et al., 2023). Food insecurity among refugees due to lack of financial resources has been commonly mentioned in the literature (Anderson et al., 2014; Dharod et al., 2013; Gichunge et al., 2015; Hadley et al., 2010; Lane et al., 2019; Nisbet, 2011; Peterman et al., 2013; Piwowarczyk et al., 2008; Tarraf et al., 2018; Masri & Srour, 2014; Vahabi et al., 2011). Poor official language proficiency and lack of recognition of educational qualifications and past work experience have been cited as significant barriers to well-paying employment among refugees (Vahabi & Damba, 2013; Vahabi et al., 2011; IRCC, 2016).

Al-Kharabsheh et al. (2020) reported that Syrian families that included a woman who was a high school graduate or had higher education were four times more likely to be food insecure compared to households that included

---

[1] This study is a collaboration between the University of Saskatchewan and the Université de Montréal that aimed to quantify the extent of food insecurity among Syrian refugees, as well as describe the experience from the perspective of refugees and service providers. Data was collected in 2017 from 50 Syrian refugees and nine service providers living in the greater Montreal area and other mid-sized cities in Quebec.

a woman with less education. While this has not been a common finding in food security research, Lane et al. (2019) also found that newcomer households with parents that were high school graduates or had some postsecondary training were at three times higher risk of food insecurity than families with parents that did not complete high school or those with university degrees. It is possible that less-educated families may be more resilient at dealing with financial hardship by drawing on strong social support networks and coping strategies to secure adequate food (Dean & Sharkey, 2011). In addition, the perception of food security among better educated families that likely did not have to worry about food security in their home countries, may be distinct from less educated families that may have adapted to dealing with food scarcity over the longer term. Overall, the food security of new Syrian refugees suddenly thrust into a foreign environment is a complex phenomenon, beyond the typical socioeconomic factors of educational level and income.

In the Quebec study, the higher food insecurity levels observed among Syrian refugees living in the greater Montreal area compared to other areas suggest concerns with greater financial costs of living in an urban area (Chevrier et al., 2023). Refugees living in greater Montreal may experience higher accommodation or living costs, challenges with accessing food aid, lack access to bulk buying from farms, and/or lack gardens to grow food. Few studies have reported on how place of resettlement may impact food security. However, refugees living in densely populated immigrant enclaves have been noted to have good access to ethnic foods (Pereira et al., 2010).

Syrian foods were widely available in the greater Montreal area, and although available outside this area, it was not always consistently available in the required quantities (Chevrier et al., 2023). However, many families noted they overcame transportation challenges to access traditional foods by receiving rides to food stores from theirs sponsors or more established Syrians. Wide availability of ethnic foods has been linked to enhanced food security among Cambodian refugees in the United States (Peterman et al., 2013). Syrian refugee families settled in Quebec reported difficulties with navigating the food environment, including locating reliable merchants of halal meat and traditional bread. Similar challenges to sourcing religiously acceptable foods among immigrants and refugees in Ontario, Canada has been reported (Moffat et al., 2017).

The Quebec study highlighted some concerns with accessing food banks. Chevrier et al., (2023) reported that not all Syrian refugee families knew they could receive food from food banks, while others were unsatisfied with the quality of foods from food banks or encountered challenges with eligibility requirements. Refugees' low use of food bank amidst high rates of food insecurity has been previously documented (Piwowarczyk et al., 2008).

Some Syrian refugee families in Quebec described that they were now cooking foods from scratch that they would normally have purchased ready-made in their home country, and they were substituting cheaper ingredients in place of more expensive ingredients to cope with high food costs (Chevrier et al., 2023). In the same study, some Syrian refugee families reported increased reliance on restaurant food to cope with demanding schedules when they were in French language training, which negatively impacted their budget available to purchase ingredients for home cooking. This finding seems contradictory to efforts to maintain food security through judicious use of available resources; however, families described being under pressure to be in language training for extended periods and not having the time or cooking facilities to prepare food at their educational setting. This is similar to an American study that found schedule demands impacted time available for home cooking (Patil et al., 2009). Thus, although families were attempting to cope with their limited income to purchase food, the added task of learning the host country language to improve employment prospects can temporarily increase food insecurity.

The higher level of food insecurity observed among PSRs compared to GARs in Quebec may be related to financial difficulties (Chevrier et al., 2023). In this study, GARs reported receiving a stable income during their first year, while PSRs did not always reliably receive their anticipated monthly support. GARs also received orientation and support from settlement organizations, including a grocery store orientation, while PSRs received variable levels of support. In addition, since GAR families were on average larger families, they would benefit from a larger monthly child tax credit amount than PSRs. There is a lack of research regarding the impact of refugee immigration category on food security status, likely because the private sponsorship program is not common in all parts of the world.

Conclusion

The experience of food insecurity among Syrian refugees in Canada is distinct from the typical Canadian experience. Syrian refugees may arrive with highly specialised skills that provided them with a good salary and comfortable life in Syria, but their lack of language skills makes it difficult to integrate into suitable employment during the first few years. Accordingly, Syrian refugees with higher levels of education suddenly need to cope with living on a limited income and the associated risk of food insecurity. This situation may contribute to adults being at higher risk of developing chronic diseases and children being at risk of poor health and development.

In order to improve food security, we need to adopt a more comprehensive strength-based approach that builds on Syrian refugees' skills and abilities. In the Quebec study, many families came from agricultural backgrounds, grew their own foods, canned products, and cooked meals from scratch (Chevrier et al., 2023). In light of these skills, improving access to garden plots, community kitchens, and/or organising collective purchasing groups to source food from farmers could enhance community food security. Broad policy level efforts to improve food security among Syrian refugees should involve a review of minimum income requirements to meet basic needs.

References

Al-Kharabsheh, L., Al-Bazz, S., Koc, M., Garcia, J., Lane, G., Engler-Stringer, R., White, J., & Vatanparast, H. (2020). Household food insecurity and associated socio-economic factors among recent Syrian refugees in two Canadian cities. *Border Crossing, 10*(2), 203-214. https://doi.org/10.33182/bc.v10i2.1161

Anderson, L., Hadzibegovic, D. S., Moseley, & J. M., Sellen, D. W. (2014). Household food insecurity shows associations with food intake, social support utilization and dietary change among refugee adult caregivers resettled in the United States. *Ecology of food and nutrition, 53*(3), 312-332. https://doi.org/10.1080/03670244.2013.831762

Berkowitz, S. A., Gao, X., & Tucker, K. L. (2014). Food-insecure dietary patterns are associated with poor longitudinal glycemic control in diabetes: results from the Boston Puerto Rican Health study. *Diabetes care, 37*(9), 2587-2592. https://doi.org/10.2337/dc14-0753

Berkowitz, S. A., Berkowitz, T. S., Meigs, J. B., & Wexler, D. J. (2017). Trends in food insecurity for adults with cardiometabolic disease in the United States: 2005-2012. *PloS one, 12*(6), e0179172. https://doi.org/10.1371/journal.pone.0179172

Chevrier, J., Lane, G., Khakpour, M., Vatanparast, H., & Batal, M. (2023). Food security among Syrian refugee families in Quebec, Canada. Ecology of Food and Nutrition (Revision submitted February 20, 2023, Submission ID: 227693582 currently out for review).

Dean, W. R., & Sharkey, J. R. (2011). Food insecurity, social capital and perceived personal disparity in a predominantly rural region of Texas: an individual-level analysis. *Social Science & Medicine, 72*(9), 1454-1462. https://doi.org/10.1016/j.socscimed.2011.03.015

Davison, K. M., Gondara, L., & Kaplan, B. J. (2017). Food Insecurity, Poor Diet Quality, and Suboptimal Intakes of Folate and Iron Are Independently Associated with Perceived Mental Health in Canadian Adults. *Nutrients, 9*(3), 274. https://doi.org/10. 3390/nu9030274

Dharod, J. M., Croom, J. E., & Sady, C. G. (2013). Food insecurity: its relationship to dietary intake and body weight among Somali refugee women in the United States. *Journal of *nutrition education and behavior, 45*(1), 47-53. https://doi.org/10.1016/j.jneb.2012.03.006

Doad, S. (2016). *Food receipts analyses: Examining food choices and shopping practices of newly arrived refugee families in the U.S.* [mémoire de maîtrise, University of North Carolina]. NC Digital Online Collection of Knowledge and Scholarship. https://libres.uncg.edu/ir/ uncg/ f/ Doad_uncg_0154M_12139.pdf

Gallegos, D., Ellies, P., & Wright, J. (2008). Still there's no food! Food insecurity in a refugee population in Perth, Western Australia. *Nutrition & Dietetics, 65*(1), 78-83. https://doi.org/10.1111/j.1747-0080.2007.00175.x

Gershoff E. T., Aber J. L., & Raver C. C. (2005). Child poverty in the United States: An evidence-based conceptual framework for programs and policies. In Learner R. M., Jacobs F., Wertlieb D. (Eds.), *Applied developmental science* (pp. 269-324). Thousand Oaks, CA: Sage.

Gichunge, C., Harris, N., Tubei, S., Somerset, S., & Lee, P. (2015). Relationship between food insecurity, social support, and vegetable intake among resettled African refugees in Queensland, Australia. *Journal of Hunger & Environmental Nutrition, 10*(3), 379-389. https://doi.org/10.1080/19320248.2014.929544

Gucciardi, E., Vogt, J. A., DeMelo, M., & Stewart, D. E. (2009). An exploration of the relationship between household food insecurity and diabetes mellitus in Canada. *Diabetes care, 32*(12), 2218-2224. https://doi.org/10.2337/dc09-0823

Gundersen, C., & Ziliak, J. (2014). Food insecurity and health outcomes among multigenerational households (805.11). *The FASEB Journal, 28*, 805-11. https://doi.org/10.1096/fasebj.28.1_supplement.805.11

Hadley, C., & Sellen, D. (2006). Food security and child hunger among recently resettled Liberian refugees and asylum seekers: a pilot study. *Journal of Immigrant and Minority Health, 8*(4), 369-375. https://doi.org/10.1007/s10903-006-9007-9

Hadley, C., Zodhiates, A., & Sellen, D. W. (2007). Acculturation, economics and food insecurity among refugees resettled in the USA: a case study of West African refugees. *Public health nutrition, 10*(4), 405-412. https:// doi,org/10.1017/S1368980007222943

Hadley, C., Patil, C. L., & Nahayo, D. (2010). Difficulty in the food environment and the experience of food insecurity among refugees resettled in the United States. *Ecology of food and nutrition, 49*(5), 390-407. https://doi.org/10.1080/03670244.2010.507440

Huang, Y., Potochnick, S., & Heflin, C. M. (2018). Household Food Insecurity and Early Childhood Health and Cognitive Development Among Children of Immigrants. *Journal of Family Issues, 39*(6), 1465–1497. https://doi-org.cyber.usask.ca/10.1177/ 0192513X17 710 772

Khakpour, M. (2019). *Food (In) Security of Protracted Refugees: A Global Crisis.* PhD Thesis, Under H. Vatanparast supervision. University of Saskatchewan, College of Graduate Studies and Research. https://harvest.usask.ca/handle/10388/12435

Kirkpatrick, S. I., & Tarasuk, V. (2008). Food insecurity is associated with nutrient inadequacies among Canadian adults and adolescents. *The Journal of nutrition, 138*(3), 604-612. https://doi.org/10.1093/jn/138.3.604

Kirkpatrick, S. I., McIntyre, L., & Potestio M. (2010). Child hunger and long-term adverse consequences for health. *Archives of Pediatrics and Adolescent Medicine, 164*(8),754-62. https://doi.org/10.1001/archpediatrics.2010.117

Lane, G., Nisbet, C., & Vatanparast, H. (2019). Food insecurity and nutritional risk among Canadian newcomer children in Saskatchewan, *Nutrients, 11*, 1744; https://doi.org/10. 3390/nu11081744.

IRCC, Immigration, Refugees and Citizenship Canada. (2016). *Rapid Evaluation of the Syrian Refugee Initiative.* https://www.canada.ca/content/dam/ircc/ migration/ircc/ english/

resources/evaluation/pdf/evaluation-syrian-refugee-initiative.pdf

IRCC, Immigration, Refugees and Citizenship Canada. (2021). Syrian Refugees – Monthly IRCC Updates. https://open.canada.ca/data/en/dataset/01c85d28-2a81-4295-9c06-4af792a7c209

Lee, J. & Frongillo, E. (2001). Nutritional and health consequences are associated with food insecurity among US elderly persons. *J. Nutr., 131*, 1503–1509. https://doi.org/10.1093/jn/131.5.1503

Marin-Leon, L., Segal-Correa, A., Panigassi, G., Maranha, L., Sampaio, M., & Perez-Escamilla, R. (2005). Food insecurity perception in families with elderly in Campinas, Sao Paulo, Brazil. *Cad. Saúde Pública, 21*, 1433–1440. https://doi.org/10.1590/S0102-311X200 5000 500016

Masri, S., & Srour, I. (2014). Assessment of the impact of Syrian refugees in Lebanon and their employment profile. Regional Office for the Arab States. Beirut: International Labour Organization. Retrieved from http://www.ilo.org/ beirut/publications/WCMS_240134/lang--en/index.htm

McIntyre, L., Connor, S., & Warren, J. (2000). Child hunger in Canada: Results of the 1994 National Longitudinal Survey of Children and Youth. *CMAJ, 163*, 961–965.

McIntyre, L., Wu, X., Kwok, C., & Patten, S. (2017). The pervasive effect of youth self-report of hunger on depression over 6 years of follow up. *Soc Psychiatry Psychiatr Epidemiol, 52*, 537-547. https://doi.org/10.1007/s00127-017-1361-5

Moffat, T., Mohammed, C., & Newbold, K. B. (2017). Cultural dimensions of food insecurity among immigrants and refugees. *Human Organization, 76*(1), 15-27. https://doi.org/10.17730/0018-7259.76.1.15

Nisbet, C. N. (2011). *Have we forgotten the children? Health and nutrition issues in refugee and immigrant newcomer children* [Thesis, University of Saskatchewan]. https://harvest.usask.ca/bitstream/handle/10388/etd-08302011-005857/Nisbet_Christine_MScNutrition_thesis_August_2011.pdf?sequence=1&isAllowed=y

Patil, C. L., Hadley, C., & Nahayo, P. D. (2009). Unpacking dietary acculturation among new Americans: results from formative research with African refugees. *Journal of Immigrant and Minority Health, 11*(5), 342-358. https://doi.org/10.1007/s10903-008-9120-z

Pereira, C. A., Larder, N., & Somerset, S. (2010). Food acquisition habits in a group of African refugees recently settled in Australia. *Health & Place, 16*(5), 934-941. https://doi.org/10.1016/j.healthplace.2010.05.007

Peterman, J. N., Wilde, P. E., Silka, L., Bermudez, O. I., & Rogers, B. L. (2013). Food insecurity among Cambodian refugee women two decades post resettlement. *Journal of Immigrant and Minority Health, 15*(2), 372-380. https://doi.org/10.1007/s10903-012-9704-5

Piwowarczyk, L., Keane, T. M., & Lincoln, A. (2008). Hunger: the silent epidemic among asylum seekers and resettled refugees. *International Migration, 46*(1), 59-77. https://doi.org/10.1111/j.1468-2435.2008.00436.x

Renzaho, A. M., & Burns, C. (2006). Post-migration food habits of sub-Saharan African migrants in Victoria: A cross-sectional study. *Nutrition & Dietetics, 63*(2), 91-102. https://doi.org/10.1111/j.1747-0080.2006.00055.x

Rondinelli, A. J., Morris, M. D., Rodwell, T. C., Moser, K. S., Paida, P., Popper, S. T., & Brouwer, K. C. (2011). Under-and over-nutrition among refugees in San Diego County, California. *Journal of Immigrant and Minority Health, 13*(1), 161-168. https://doi.org/10.1007/s10903-010-9353-5

Smith, M., & Coleman-Jensen, A. (2020). Food insecurity, acculturation and diagnosis of CHD and related health outcomes among immigrant adults in the USA. *Public Health Nutrition, 23*(3), 416-431. doi:10.1017/S1368980019001952

Tarasuk, V., Dachner, N., & Mitchell, A. (2016). *Household food security in Canada, 2014.* Toronto: Research to identify policy options to reduce food insecurity (PROOF). https://proof.utoronto.ca/resources/proof-annual-reports/annual-report-2014/

Tarasuk, V., & Mitchell, A. (2020). Household food insecurity in Canada, 2017-18. Toronto: Research to identify policy options to reduce food insecurity (PROOF). https://proof.utoronto.ca/wp-content/uploads/2020/03/Household-Food-Insecurity-in-Canada-2017-2018-Full-Reportpdf.pdf

Tarraf, D., Sanou, D., Blanchet, R., Nana, C. P., Batal, M., & Giroux, I. (2018). Prevalence and determinants of food insecurity in migrant Sub-Saharan African and Caribbean households in Ottawa, Canada. *International Journal of Migration, Health and Social Care, 14*(2), 160-173. https://doi.org/10.1108/IJMHSC-07-2016-0027

US Early Childhood Longitudinal Study–Birth Cohort, https://nces.ed.gov/ecls/Birth.asp

US National Health Interview Survey, https://www.cdc.gov/nchs/nhis/index.htm

Vahabi, M., Damba, C., Rocha, C., & Montoya, E. (2011). Food insecurity among Latin American recent immigrants in Toronto. *Journal of Immigrant and Minority Health, 13*, 929–939. https://doi.org/10.1007/s10903-010-9384-y

Vahabi, M., & Damba, C. (2013). Perceived barriers in accessing food among recent Latin American immigrants in Toronto. *International Journal for Equity in Health*, 12(1), 1. https://doi.org/10.1186/1475-9276-12-1

Vozoris, N. T., & Tarasuk, V. S. (2003). Household food insufficiency is associated with poorer health. *The Journal of nutrition, 133*(1), 120-126. https://doi.org/10. 1093/ jn/ 133.1.120

Weigel, M., Armijos, R., Hall, Y., Ramirez, Y., & Orozco, R. (2007). The household food insecurity and health outcomes of U.S.-Mexico border migrant and seasonal farmworkers. *J. Immigr. Minor. Health, 9*, 157–169. https://doi.org/10.1007/s10903-006-9026-6

ITALIAN ASYLUM RECEPTION SYSTEM AND HEALTH CHALLENGES: THE APULIAN CASE

Michela C. Pellicani[1] and Gül Ince-Beqo[2]

Introduction

During 2019, in a pre-Pandemic situation, an estimated 11.0 million people were newly displaced[3] and by the end of 2019, the number of people forcibly displaced due to war, conflict, persecution, human rights violations and events seriously disturbing public order had grown to 79.5 million, the highest number on record according to available data. The number of displaced people was nearly double the 2010 number of 41 million and increased from the 2018 number of 70.8 million. The Democratic Republic of the Congo (DRC), Burkina Faso, the Syrian Arab Republic (Syria), the Bolivarian Republic of Venezuela (Venezuela) and Yemen represent just a few of the many hotspots in 2019 driving people to seek refuge and safety within their country or flee abroad to seek protection. The proportion of the world's population who were displaced continued to rise. One per cent of the world's population in 2019 – or 1 in 97 people – was forcibly displaced.

[1] Michela C. Pellicani, University of Bari, Italy.
[2] Gül Ince-Beqo, University of Milan, Italy.

Acknowledgements: This paper is the result of the collaboration between the two Authors in the frame of both the Research Project of Relevant National Interest (PRIN) project 2018, "International Migrations, State, Sovereignty and Human Rights: Open Legal Issues" and the AMIF project "Prevenzione 4.0". In particular, the Introduction and Conclusion have to be considered by the two authors: Section 2, Section 3 and Section 4 by Michela C. Pellicani, and Section 1 by Gül Ince-Beqo.

[3] In this paper, different terms are used for people with migration background. Below are some brief definitions for each, according to the EMN Asylum and Migration Glossary.

Migrant: In the global context, a person who moves away from their place of usual residence, whether within a country or across an international border, temporarily or permanently, voluntarily or involuntarily, and for a variety of reasons.

Immigrant: In the global context, a non-resident (both national or alien) arriving in a State with the intention to remain for a period exceeding a year.

Irregular migrant: In the global context, a person who, owing to irregular entry, breach of a condition of entry or the expiry of their legal basis for entering and residing, lacks legal status in a transit or host country. In the ENM glossary, there is no specific definition of "undocumented migrant" which can be defined broadly as "all immigrants who reside in the country of settlement without legal status".

Refugee: In the global context, either a person who, owing to a well-founded fear of persecution for reasons of race, religion, nationality, political opinion or membership of a particular social group, is outside the country of nationality and is unable or, owing to such fear, is unwilling to avail themselves of the protection of that country, or a stateless person, who, being outside of the country of former habitual residence for the same reasons as mentioned before, is unable or, owing to such fear, unwilling to return to it.

Asylum seeker: In the global context, a person who seeks protection from persecution or serious harm in a country other than their own and awaits a decision on the application for refugee status under relevant international and national instruments.

This compares with 1:159 in 2010 and 1:174 in 2005 as the increase in the world's forcibly displaced population continued to outpace global population growth.

At the end of 2019, Syrians continued to be by far the largest forcibly displaced population worldwide (13.2 million, including 6.6 million refugees and more than 6 million internally displaced people). When considering only international displacement situations, Syrians also topped the list with 6.7 million persons, followed by Venezuelans with 4.5 million. Afghanistan and South Sudan had 3.0 and 2.2 million, respectively.

Turkey hosted the highest number of people displaced across borders, 3.9 million, most of whom were Syrian refugees (92%). Colombia followed, hosting nearly 1.8 million displaced Venezuelans. Germany hosted the third largest number, almost 1.5 million, with Syrian refugees and asylum-seekers constituting the largest groups (42%). Pakistan and Uganda hosted the fourth and fifth largest number, with about 1.4 million each (UNHCR, 2020).

Europe saw a spike in the number of new asylum seekers in 2014, largely because of the outbreak of conflict in eastern Ukraine. It experienced another spike in new asylum requests in 2015. As the war in Syria intensified and conflicts in Iraq and Afghanistan worsened, an increasing number of people risked their lives to cross the Mediterranean Sea in search of safety and protection. More than one million people arrived in Europe by boat – the vast majority from these three refugee-producing countries. More than 1.5 million new asylum claims were lodged in the major European destination countries, including Germany and Sweden. Arrivals in Cyprus, Greece, Malta, Italy, and Spain continued in subsequent years but remained below 200,000 between 2017 and 2019 (UNHCR, 2020). In the EU member states 612,700 first-time asylum seekers have been registered in 2019, up by 12% compared with 2018 (EUROSTAT, 2020).

In 2019, Italy registered 43,783 first-time asylum seekers, mainly men (73.3%). The principal origin countries were Pakistan (19.9%), Nigeria (8.0%), Bangladesh (6.7%), El Salvador (5.8%) and Peru (5.6%). 15.1% were minors and 1.5% unaccompanied minors. Refugees and asylum seekers present in 2019 in the Italian reception centres were: 91.424 (CPAs: 66.958; SAIs: 24.388; Hot Spots: 78) (Ministero dell'Interno, 2020).

The demographic structure of the people displaced across borders differs from the population of the 272 million international migrants and the 7.7 billion world population. Children represent a larger proportion of the displaced population than they do in the international migrant population. In fact, at the end of 2019, around half of refugees were children[4], compared to an estimated 31% of the world population and just 10% of the international migrant population. Young adults between the ages of 18 and 24 also represent a greater proportion of refugees (13%) when compared to 11% of the world population and 9% of international migrants. In contrast, older persons make up a smaller proportion of the refugee population (4%) compared to the world population (12%) and international migrants (17%) (UNHCR, 2020).

Migrants face multiple barriers to accessing healthcare basically due to a lack of cultural and structural competency (Hiam et al., 2019). For asylum and international protection seekers, the issues are even more complex because they have limited knowledge of the territory, lifestyle, health system, and current legislation on health protection. For this category of migrants, medical care is generally provided within the reception system. However, linguistic, information, legal-bureaucratic, and cultural barriers create serious difficulties both in the fruition of the right to health and in the establishment of a relationship of trust between doctor and patient.

Of course, the COVID-19 pandemic aggravated the existing problems because it disrupted social support systems, devastated incomes and livelihood opportunities, and heightened anxieties about falling ill. For those already dealing with the stress of being uprooted, this created an added psychological burden. Many who previously coped well became less able to cope with the multiple stressors generated by the Pandemic, which abruptly raised new threats to freedom of movement, social support systems, education, and social contact.

For what concerns Italy's migration policy, since its first formulation, it has been considered emergency-based, and later-comer (Ambrosini, 2013), ranging between security concerns, humanitarian claims, and functionalist perspectives (carried on by social and political pro-business actors) and producing confused and unplanned policy emerged with a deficient legal framework (Marchetti, 2014; Andriopoulou et al., 2022).

At first glance, this is confirmed by the following preliminary data. Regarding access to primary care through the right to be assigned a General Practitioner (GP), according to data from Medici senza Frontiere (2018), one-third of

---

[4] Refugee children face specific challenges, such as access to education. An estimated 3.7 million refugee children were out of school in 2018. Enrolment rates of refugee children at primary and secondary level have improved in recent years, but only 3% were able to access higher education in 2018 (UNHCR, 2020).

refugees who have been in Italy for several years are not yet registered with the National Health Service (NHS), and two-thirds of those eligible do not have a GP or a freely chosen paediatrician (Barbati et al., 2023).

Another critical issue is the lack of comprehensive person-centred care (as envisaged by the primary care model), which constitutes an additional barrier to accessing healthcare services. This gap is often filled by voluntary associations and NGOs with limited forms of agreement with the NHS.

Without a comprehensive and coherent national framework regulating migration-related issues, the local level assumes an essential role in implementing policies (Campomori & Caponio, 2013). In the Italian context, we decided to focus, in particular, on Apulia, the South-Eastern region of Italy, for several reasons. First of all, Apulia represents one of the main Mediterranean routes for asylum seekers heading to Europe. Even more peculiar is that the Apulian region represents an exception in the Italian national territory thanks to regional autonomy in offering health services under a universalistic principle. Medical treatments and services provided for Italians are, in fact, extended to regular, irregular, and illegal migrants as well.

It is worth mentioning, however, that regional autonomy created some disruptions in the governance of health access in particular for vulnerable groups, such as asylum seekers and irregular migrants. Furthermore, the Covid-19 Pandemic, which destabilised the NHS, has strengthened the existing inequalities in terms of access to public health care for these disadvantaged groups.

The research is structured as follows: First, we briefly analyse European, Italian, and Apulian normative frameworks regarding health access. Then, we illustrate our case study and research methodology. The following section is on data analysis. In the last section, some conclusions are presented.

1. Social and health care in Italy of vulnerable populations: an overview

The health issues fall within the list of matters for which the EU member states have always been reluctant to surrender their sovereignty and in turn the EU has also maintained a role of support and coordination of their actions (as provided for in Article 168 TFEU[5]). This is primarily due to the

---

[5] Article 168 of the Treaty on the Functioning of the European Union (TFEU) provides that "a high level of health protection shall be ensured in the definition and implementation of the Union policies and activities". Nevertheless, according to Article 6, letter a of the same treaty, the Union can only support, coordinate or complement the action of EU countries in the health sector, since Union acts cannot entail the harmonisation of laws or regulations of member states (Arbia & Biz, 2020).

significant differences that exist between the various national healthcare systems and, undoubtedly, also to the economic impact that healthcare policies have on the financial system of each member state. For these reasons, the EU has always been very cautious about providing rules that could alter the financial burden of the member states[6].

In the Pandemic context, for instance, EU role has been instrumental in adopting common policies regarding asset mobility (masks, respirators, and other personal protection equipment), human mobility, and border zone management. Plus, on the mandate received from the health ministers of the member states[7], the European Commission has also presented a European strategy to accelerate the development, production, and dissemination of vaccines against Covid-19, as a key tool to achieve a permanent solution to the Pandemic.

Among the EU member states, Italy is a laudable exception in terms of codifying the right to health protection, as it expressly includes it in its own Constitutional Charter (Zagrebelsky, 2016). Art. 32 of the Constitution mentions: "The Republic protects health as a fundamental right of the individual and in the interest of the community and guarantees free care to the indigent". It is evident that the protection of health is part of the set of fundamental rights. The careful choice of the word "individual" also indicates that this right applies to all human beings, regardless of their citizenship or legal status (Baglio & Affronti, 2019). In this direction, the national law n. 40 of 1998, which regulates immigration issues, guarantees the right to medical care for all foreign citizens.

Consequently, even in the Consolidated Act on Immigration of 1999[8], it is stipulated that even foreign citizens who are in the national territory in a condition of irregularity (that is not in compliance with the rules on entry and residence), are nevertheless assured in public and accredited health accommodations, any urgent or essential medical care[9].

---

[6] On the relationship between the economy and social rights see, among others, Gambino, 2015.

[7] For more information see: European Commission, (17.6.2020). https://commission.europa.eu/strategy-and-policy/coronavirus-response/public-health_en

[8] Art. 35 of the Consolidated Act of the provisions concerning the discipline of immigration and norms on the condition of the foreigner, Presidential Decree 31.8.1999, No. 394.

[9] Urgent care refers to those that cannot be postponed without danger to the life or health of the individual. Essential care, on the other hand, relates to healthcare, diagnostic, and therapeutic services concerning non-immediate or short-term dangerous conditions, but which over time could lead to greater harm to health or life risks (complications, chronic conditions, or aggravations). This category also includes ongoing care for illness and injury and preventive medicine programs for the safeguarding of individual and collective health.

Particular attention is paid to foreign women during the period of pregnancy and maternity by guaranteeing them equal rights to Italian women. Among the most protected categories we can find minors as well. In addition to the Consolidation Act on Immigration of 1999, minors' rights are also enshrined in the Convention on the Rights of the Child of November 20, 1989, ratified, and made enforceable in Italy in May 1991.

However, despite these highly inclusive principles, for the Italian universalist-inspired NHS the enjoyment of the full right is significantly differentiated according to the legal status of the foreign citizen (regular or irregular), so it follows "parallel tracks" based on the "regularity" of his or her stay.

All foreign citizens regularly present in the national territory (including asylum seekers waiting for a response) have equal rights with Italian citizens in the health care field; foreigners who are in the national territory in a condition of irregularity, i.e., not in compliance with the rules on entry and stay, as we saw, are guaranteed only urgent and essential medical care.

Another critical issue is that the NHS regionally based administrative set-up can determine a framework of fragmented access to services that has created significant inequalities in the management of health emergencies and institutional frictions in the State-Region relationship regarding health issues governance. This local autonomy has produced, therefore, a series of dissimilarities among the regions with respect to the measures adopted and the modalities of implementation of health policies towards foreigners (Pasini, 2011). The one who has suffered most is the vulnerable part of the population which has found itself faced with inequalities in terms of supply and access to health services according to the region in which it lives.

More than this, the absence of a national framework produces the politicisation of the migration issue at the regional level, in some cases leading to exclude migrants from various types of benefits and rights (Ambrosini, 2013). In fact, at a formal level, while the right to medical assistance is obtained at the time the asylum application is filed, delays in the allocation of the tax code in some regions hinder the practice of that right[10].

In accordance with the principle of continuity of urgent and essential care, the complete therapeutic and rehabilitative cycle concerning the possible resolution of the disease event must also be ensured. The requirement of urgency or essentiality must be documented in the clinical records and in all requests for services (Circular No. 5, 24.03.2000, Application Guidelines of Legislative Decree 25.07.1998, No. 286 Consolidated Text of provisions concerning immigration discipline and rules on the condition of foreigners - Provisions on healthcare. Official Gazette 1.6.2000, No. 126).

[10] For the practical obstacles, see: https://asylumineurope.org/reports/country/italy/reception-conditions/health-care/

Beyond these considerations, if we observe the national scenario, we can resume the differences in the access to basic health services through a brief comparative analysis between the migrant and Italian populations.

Medical examinations: lower likelihood of seeking a medical examination; greater difficulty in communicating one's health status to the doctor and understanding what the doctor says and greater difficulty in carrying out bureaucratic-administrative procedures (Petrelli, 2017).

Emergency and urgent care (ER accesses): higher rates of inappropriate access for the migrant population compared to the Italian population (Di Napoli et al., 2022).

Chronic diseases (diabetes mellitus): higher risk of inadequate management for the foreign population in terms of therapy and follow-up visits; increased risk of avoidable hospitalisation in the male migrant population for diabetes-related conditions (Seghieri et al., 2019; Dalla Zuanna et al., 2020).

Maternal and child health: higher frequency of incomplete prenatal care (fewer than 5 ultrasounds performed per pregnancy and missed first visit after the 12th week of pregnancy); higher risk of adverse perinatal outcomes (macrosomia, gestational diabetes, very low birth weight, very preterm delivery); higher neonatal and post-neonatal mortality (Caruso et al., 2021).

Infectious diseases (HIV): more frequent late presentation (late arrival at diagnosis of HIV seropositivity, with all its consequences), more defections to follow-up (Sullis et al., 2014).

Prevention (cancer screenings and vaccinations): lower access to cervical screening, mammographic and colorectal cancer screenings; low vaccination coverage and higher risk of contracting vaccine-preventable diseases (WHO, 2022).

Mental health: limited access and low use of community mental health centres with a further average reduction in the number of first visits and in the percentage of patients returning for follow-up visits during the Covid-19 pandemic period from, namely since March 2020 (Tarricone et al. 2012).

We can consider avoidable hospitalisation (AH) as an indicator of poor access to primary care (PC). Both documented and undocumented migrants face considerably higher risk of AH compared to Italians. More precisely, compared with Italians, undocumented and documented migrants adjusted odd ratios (OR) for the risk of AH were 1.422 (95% CI 1.322-1.528) and 1.243 (95% CI 1.201-1.287), respectively. Documented migrants showed

ORs not significantly greater than 1 for AH due to chronic diseases compared with the Italians, while undocumented immigrants registered higher adjusted OR for all AH categories − chronic (OR 1.187; 95% CI 1.064-1.325), acute (OR 1.645; 95% CI 1.500-1.803) and vaccine-preventable (OR 2.170; 95% CI 1.285-3.664) (Allegri et al., 2022).

2. Specificity of Apulia Region

The Apulia Region, due to its geographical position overlooking the Mediterranean Sea and its traditional openness to reception, has been, since the 1990s, an important destination for people who have embarked on the path of migration. The analysis of Italian Institute of Statistics (ISTAT) data, which witnesses a considerable increase in the foreign presence in Apulia[11], determines that this Region is not only a land of passage towards the rest of Italy and Europe, but it represents a land of permanent settlement as well. The growth of the migrant population in Apulia and the consolidation of this phenomenon has made it necessary to adopt structural and lasting interventions which led to nominate in 2011 this region the most "migrant friendly" region in Italy on the sanitary field[12]. In fact, the regional administration promotes the implementation of an integrated system of interventions and services for the inclusion of the migrant population and for the full protection of rights.

The second reason of our interest is, therefore, related to the governance of the health issues of the immigrant population which is one of the areas of intervention in which Apulia has differed the most from the policy line followed both by other Italian regions and by the central government.

It is important to underline that, according to Title V of the Constitution, as anticipated in paragraph 1, the Italian regions are endowed with legislative autonomy in the healthcare field as they are the public authority closest to the citizens.

We can say that Apulia Region is an exception in the exception in fact in the Apulia Region the constitutional principle of health protection for all is fully implemented, both as an individual right for every human being and as a collective interest for the community commonwealth. Regional Law n. 32 of

---

[11] On January 1, 2010, foreigners residing in Apulia were 84,320. On January 1, 2015, the number rises to 117,732. As of January 1, 2020, the growth continues, recording 133,690 foreign citizens with a slight male predominance (ISTAT, Data Warehouse).
[12] See Conferenza delle Regioni e delle Province Autonome, 2011.

2009[13] extends the right to basic medical care to all persons present in the regional territory regardless of their citizenship or legal status. The regional law defines that even irregular immigrants have the possibility to have a GP and a paediatrician for their children. Starting in 2009, in Apulia, even irregular immigrants can receive treatment for any illnesses without waiting for their spread to reach an emergency stage, as required by national law (Pellicani et al., 2022).

For the implementation of the regional law, guidelines have been drawn up for the integrated care of immigrants by a multidisciplinary team, including psychologists, intercultural mediators, paediatricians, anthropologists, social workers (Mastrorocco & Calò, 2019).

To reduce the barriers and the heterogeneity in the access to the health services, as well as to improve the services themselves by making them more incisive and targeted to the needs of refugees and asylum seekers on the regional territory, a recent intervention has been the "Prevention 4.0" AMIF[14] project. Unique in all of Italy, it was launched in 2018 and implemented in the region thanks to the collaboration between competent partners such as the University of Bari, the Regional Strategic Agency for Health and Social Care (AReSS), the National Consortium for Social Innovation (NOVA Onlus) and the Regional Administration itself, as coordinator of the activities. Its main aim was to create an integrated system of prevention, diagnosis, treatment and rehabilitation of asylum seekers and refugees.

An in-depth field survey was carried out with reference to the context of intervention as well as an analysis of the needs and supply of health services in order to target the planned activities better and maximise the results. The development of an integrated model of psycho-social health care and the formalisation of agreement protocols by AReSS to test the model were also planned.

Thanks to an e-health system capable of responding to the health needs in a more efficient way, the project also included the design and installation of a computerised Totem, located in the reception centres, and connected to medical devices (pulse oximeter, blood pressure monitor, scale, thermometer, glucometer, electrocardiogram) for the direct use of guests. The data

---

[13] Regional Law n. 32 of 2009 on "Norms for the reception, civil coexistence and integration of immigrants in Apulia".
[14] Asylum, Migration and Integration Fund of the European Commission. The project was co-funded by the Italian Ministry of the Interior.

collected by the devices were transmitted in real time to a Control Room that collected all the data and created the health profile of each user. The system has been completed by an app for smartphones through which it was possible to perform autonomously the medical check-up and to monitor health status. Considering that all asylum seekers and refugees have a smartphone, the app has been created to improve the diffusion of different kinds of information as well.

A series of training and information meetings plus the development of a multilingual glossary, allows the beneficiaries to acquire a good level of health literacy, useful not only for the proper use of the devices, but also to have a greater awareness of their health status and treatments to be followed. The project also provided the strengthening of the skills of the operators of health facilities and reception centres through specific training courses. Finally intercultural mediators were trained to become ethno-clinical mediators.

3. Methods and data

We started our quantitative analysis basing on two types of sources: European and Italian databases for data related to the relevant context (Eurostat, IOM, UNHCR, ISTAT, Ministry of Labor and Social Policy, Ministry of the Interior, etc.) and reports published by international, national, and regional organisations and research institutes.

We have unfortunately observed that in the migration related health sphere, a preliminary critical aspect is the scarcity of data on the health access of asylum seekers and refugees. In fact, if, on one hand, we assist to a deluge of data on refugees and asylum seekers, on the other hand, when we try to find data on refugees and asylum seekers' access to health services, we realise that the information is very fragmented mainly because of the absence of an institutional monitoring process. Consequently, often the data are scant and based mainly on non-representative samples presenting serious methodological issues.

In this paper we tried to overcome some of these obstacles and explore the specificities of the refugees and asylum seekers' population using the data and information on needs and supply of health services provided by our survey within the AMIF project "Prevention 4.0". These data have been very valuable first of all because they are not available in any other national or local database. We continued our study developing the aspect related to the migrants' rights to health in the framework of another research project on "International Migrations, State, Sovereignty and Human Rights" funded by the Italian Ministry of Education, Universities and Research (MIUR).

Southern Italian regions located on the Mediterranean coast are the first reception sites being the main areas of arrival for asylum seekers. Among the top 30 provinces by the average capacity of their reception centres, only one was in the North (Bolzano), confirming the strong imbalance between North and South of Italy (Openpolis - Action Aid, 2021).

Not by chance, in Italy, in 2018, the first-level reception centre (CPA[15]) with the highest number of places was the CARA in Mineo, in the province of Catania in Sicily (2,400 places), followed by four others: Isola di Capo Rizzuto, in the province of Crotone[16] in Calabria (1,216 places), Bari-Palese in Apulia[17] (774 places), Castelnuovo di Porto, near Rome (650 places), and Borgo Mezzanone, in the province of Foggia still in Apulia (636 places)[18]. The following year, two mega centres were closed: first the CARA in Castelnuovo di Porto and then that of Mineo. In addition to the CARAs in Bari-Palese and Borgo Mezzanone, in Puglia there was a third CARA in Brindisi (Brindisi-Restinco) with a capacity of 128 places.

In terms of CASs, in 2018 Sassari was the province with the largest average centres: 105.2 places per centre, for a total of 25 centres, with the smallest having a capacity of 30 places and the largest of 248. The Sardinian province was followed by eight others in the South (Catanzaro, Brindisi, Bari, Siracusa, Trapani, Foggia, Campobasso, and Salerno). Refugees and asylum seekers present in 2019 in the Apulian reception centres were: 4,523 (CPA-CARA: 2,181; SAI: 2,342). (Ministero dell'Interno, 2020)

---

[15] In Italy, the reception system operates on two levels: first-level reception, which includes the Hotspots and first-level reception centres (CPA) that include, in turn, the Reception Centre for Asylum Seekers (CARA), and second-level reception centres, which include the SIPROIMI (Protection System for Holders of International Protection and Unaccompanied Foreign Minors), which, with the Security Decree 3.12.2018, No. 281, replaced the SPRAR (Protection System for Asylum Seekers and Refugees). The name has further changed and is currently SAI (Reception and Integration System). Finally, there are the CAS (Extraordinary Reception Centres), which represent a hybrid between first and second-level reception.

Migrants, upon arrival in Italy, are collected in Hotspots where they receive initial medical care, undergo health screening, are identified and photographed, and can apply for international protection. After an initial assessment, migrants who apply for asylum are transferred to first-level reception centres. Those who do not apply for asylum, although few, are taken to CPRs (Centres for Detention pending Repatriation), formerly known as CIEs (Centres for Identification and Expulsion).

[16] Crotone is being recalled with a very tragic event: the Cutro Shipwreck. On February 26, 2023, a boat carrying migrants from Turkey sank off in Cutro in the province of Crotone; of the 180 on board, 94 died at sea, including 34 children.

[17] The six main cities in Apulia are: Foggia, Barletta-Andria-Trani, Bari, Taranto, Brindisi and Lecce. Bari is the regional capital.

[18] It is not uncommon for the stated capacity of both CARAs and CASs to be exceeded during periods of increased arrivals especially in summertime.

As anticipated in paragraph 2, in 2019 we drafted and organised a field survey in every reception centre (CPA-CARA, CAS, and SAI) of the region hosting refugees and asylum seekers with the main aim of analysing the socio-demographic characteristics of the migrants present in these centres, obtaining useful information on the health services guaranteed all along the reception procedures and detecting further medical and health needs[19].

To avoid problems of representativeness of the sample, we involved the entire population of asylum seekers and refugees present in the first and second-level reception centres of the region.

The questionnaire was realised *ad hoc* and composed by 50 closed-ended questions and collected data were both quantitative and qualitative. The questions included in the questionnaire were clustered into four sections, each responding to precise purposes such as:

- capturing the main socio-demographic characteristics of reception centres' guests (amount, gender, age, nationality, legal status, length of stay, language skills, vulnerability status, etc.);

- describing the health services demand and supply of the reception system (symptoms/pathologies, type of intervention, type of staff, etc.);

- detecting strengths, weaknesses, and needs in the health and social fields;

- collecting the opinion of centres' operators (both employees and volunteers) with in-depth interviews regarding the usefulness of some project actions (specialised training, multilingual glossary, app, totem, Operational Services Centre, etc.).

Furthermore, to better understand the nature of organisational discomforts caused by the Covid-19 Pandemic and how to cope with them, semi-structured interviews were added in 2020 both with representatives of local authorities of the Regional Administration and the AReSS (Regional Agency for Health and Social Care), and with representatives of the reception centres present in the region.

In this study, we present quantitative data only on first-level reception centres (CPA-CARAs) because of limited space and because they are the centres

---

[19] Because the field survey took place during 2019, we asked data and information referring to the concluded previous solar year (2018).

where the vulnerability of asylum seekers is most experienced. We assimilated the CASs to the centres of first-level reception due to their characteristics.

4. Results

4.1 Pre-Pandemic context

Main socio-demographic characteristics

The analysis of the socio-demographic profile of the migrant in the reception centres helps us to better understand their needs in terms of health support.

The interviewed asylum seekers and refugees present at the moment of our survey in the CPA-CARAs plus CASs were 2,555: 2,225 men (87.1%), 330 women (12.9%) strongly concentrated, for both sexes, in the age class 18-40 years (93.8% for the men and 78.6% for the women). Minors were only 106 (4.1%) with an equal distribution by sex. The difficulties and dangers of the journey constitute a strong deterrent for women and other age groups. The presence of children, aged 0-5 years, indicates that migration involves families as well.

Among the guests of the first-level reception centres, the most common nationality is Nigerian[20] (21.4% of the total in CPA-CARA/CAS). Besides Nigeria, other countries from West Africa such as Gambia (7.8%), Senegal (6.7%), Ivory Coast (6.7%), Guinea (5.8%), and Mali (5.2%) represent 53.6% of the total.

The most represented country after Nigeria is Eritrea (13.4%). Just under one-fifth of the presence comes from Asia (Middle East and the Indian subcontinent) with countries such as Iraq (7.4%), Pakistan (7.1%), and Bangladesh (4.7%). The remaining countries are poorly represented.

---

[20] Nigerians are predominantly young people from rural areas with little education and few employment opportunities. Socially and economically disadvantaged, rural areas are often overlooked by economic policies and rarely involved in agricultural or educational development projects, which increases social exclusion and poverty high levels. Far from industrialised centres or large cities, these young men and women have few chances of integrating into a saturated job market that offers very little. Their best prospect is to survive with small, informal, and poorly paid daily jobs in large cities, far from their families. For this reason, families themselves decide to invest in one of their children, sending him to Europe in the hope that he will find work and, through remittances, contribute to the family's upkeep. There are inhabitants of the Niger Delta regions as well. These are regions rich in oil, the extraction of which has devastating consequences for the ecosystem and for the populations that mainly rely on agriculture and fishing. Environmental migrants (a status rarely recognised in host countries) leave these regions, forced into exile due to the devastation of the territory in which they reside, compromising their own survival. From Nigeria also come a large number of girls who are victims of trafficking. These are young girls, sometimes minors, who, eager to reach Europe for a better life, often rely on smugglers with the promise of work as maids or domestic helpers. After their arrival, they are often forced into prostitution.

Female presence is significant for Nigeria, Ivory Coast, Eritrea, and Iraq; absent for Pakistan, Bangladesh, Gambia, Mali, and Senegal. 70% of minors are evenly divided between Iraq, Nigeria, and Eritrea, countries marked by strong political, economic, and social disruptions.

Regarding their legal status, as these are first-level reception centres, we find almost exclusively asylum seekers (94.4%) accompanied by a few refugees (2.1%), few holders of other forms of international protection (2.6%), and Unaccompanied Foreign Minors (MSNA) (0.9%).

Duration of Stay

The length of stay analysis is useful to highlight a long-standing issue in the rotation between first and second level reception that complicates and delays the general integration process, including social and health integration. The first-level reception was created for the purpose of providing migrants with first aid. In these centres, asylum seekers receive initial medical care, undergo health screening, and are identified and photographed to start the international protection *iter*.

Although it is expected that the timeframes for these procedures are quick and respectful of the rights, it often happens that, due to the considerable number of migrants received and the heterogeneity of cases, the timeframes are lengthened and delay the inclusion of guests in the second reception programs SAI. The latter, while widely recognised as a good practice in many respects and has grown steadily over the years, it has never taken off quantitatively. Few local authorities choose to join in such a system even though the Ministry of the Interior with the National Fund for Asylum Policies and Services finances the entire project. The immediate consequence is that the number of applications often exceeds the availability of places in the second-level reception centres extending the duration of stay in the first-level reception centres (Pellicani & Tafuri, 2020).

Confirming what has been highlighted, we have found that 15.1% of guests remain in the CPA-CARAs and CASs for a duration of 12 months, and a significant 29.0% for a period exceeding 18 months, while only 26.0% stay for a duration of less than 6 months.

Professional Figures

Among the main professional figures operating in the centres emerge, in addition to the more purely healthcare personnel (doctors, healthcare operators, psychologists/psychotherapists), social assistants, intercultural mediators, legal operators, and Italian language teachers.

These figures play a fundamental role in the reception and integration process of asylum seekers and/or beneficiaries of international protection, acting as a bridge to the knowledge of the territory and social context (Graph 1).

Graph 1. Operators in the first-level reception centres by typology, Apulia, 2018

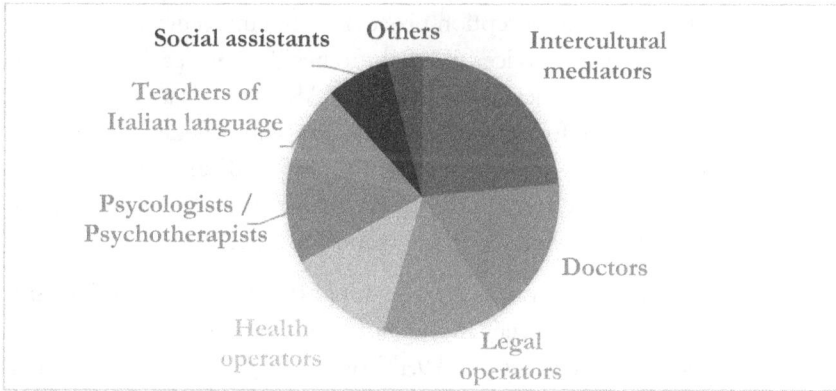

Source: field survey - AMIF project "Prevention 4.0"

The **intercultural mediator** is an important figure, especially upon arrival when migrants are introduced to a new world and lifestyle. The intercultural mediator accompanies the guests throughout their integration process. Through the mediators, guests are informed about the procedure to enter the reception project, as well as their rights and duties within this process (centre regulations, offered services, reception times and modalities). The contribution of the intercultural mediators remains valuable throughout the asylum seekers' integration process, as they also assist them in their relationships with local institutions (police, schools, health services, etc.), making communication easy for both parties.

It has emerged from the survey carried out in CPA-CARA that, during medical visits, migrants are always accompanied by an intercultural mediator, which is essential to facilitate the relationship and communication, both linguistic and cultural, between individual beneficiaries and healthcare sector operators, helping both parties in the process of "translating" cultural and language codes. The mediator also helps to "decode" the beneficiary's needs and "recode" the response in a language that is accessible and understandable to them, as well as managing relational complexities and overcoming communication barriers. Their presence is particularly useful, especially in the process of certification of violence, torture, and other serious forms of physical, psychological, or sexual violence. From our interviews it emerges clearly that the centre' operators emphasise the usefulness of having in their staff an ethno-clinical intercultural mediator with specialised professional training in the healthcare field.

What differentiates the CPA-CARA from second-level reception centres is the inclusion of **doctors and nurses/health assistants** in the internal staff. Indeed, in all phases of the reception process, from emergency assistance to the ordinary use of health services, the right to health is protected. However, each phase has its peculiarities: while in CPA-CARA there is an internal first aid service, always active for emergency situations, and a medical clinic open at certain times, in SAI guests must go to external structures for any eventuality (hospitals, ER, etc.). In the medical clinics present in CPA-CARA, there are also specialist doctors who intervene when necessary.

Doctors and healthcare operators are also supported by **psychologists and psychotherapists** who intervene in 54.5% of cases with scheduled meetings, 36.4% of cases with open access, and 9.1% of cases upon operators' warning (Graph 2). It should be noted that, for many years, due to an underestimation of the specific issues of asylum seekers and refugees, psychological support has been severely neglected and only in recent years has it been introduced more regularly and systematically.

So currently, there is a significant presence of these professional figures because many guests come from traumatic situations resulting from different circumstances depending on the country of origin, travel difficulties, and obstacles in the integration process. The presence of psychologists helps guests to open up, address their vulnerabilities, and accept new living conditions less abruptly.

In fact, many of the experiences lived, both in the countries of origin and during the migration journey, as well as upon arrival in a new context (war with its devastating effects, loss of friends and family, difficulties in adapting to a completely new and different environment, language barriers, etc.), are potentially disturbing and/or traumatising for migrants. The psychological consequences range from stress to perpetual anxiety, passing through very deep states of depression, and even reaching depersonalisation, the rooting of violent behaviours, and tendencies towards self-harm.

Among the most present professional figures we find the **legal operator** as well, who is tasked with supporting guests during the procedure for the recognition of international protection through legal information and orientation. It is not necessary for this role to be filled by a lawyer; it is sufficient for one or more operators with legal expertise in asylum law, procedure for submitting applications, rights and duties related to different statuses and legal conditions, and current legislation in Italy and Europe to be present.

Graph 2. Access to psychological support in the first-level reception centres, Apulia, 2018

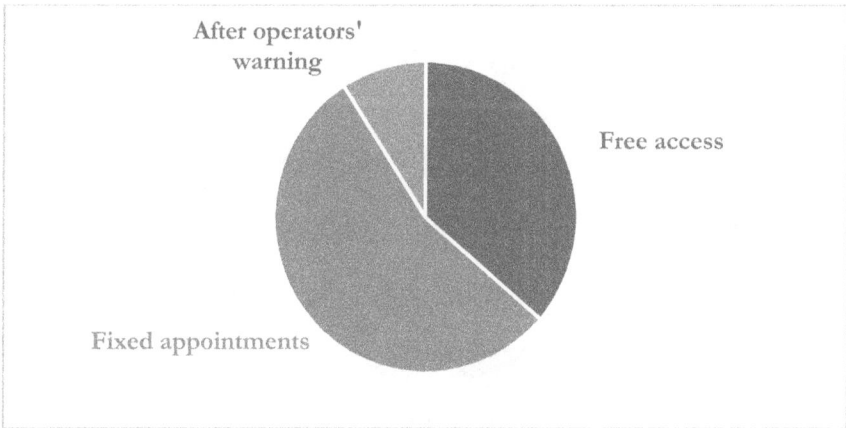

Source: field survey - AMIF project "Prevention 4.0"

Fundamental to the effective social integration in a broad sense are the **Italian language teachers** who are already present in the first-level reception centres to emphasise the importance for asylum seekers of learning the language of the host country even before knowing the outcome of the application submitted.

The category of "other professional figures" also includes **social assistants**. These help guests express their needs and facilitate relationships with local services, including health services, by providing information on current regulations and access modalities.

Screening and pathologies

All first-level reception centres open a personal medical record for each guest in which every information related to their health status, conditions, needs, and treatments is registered. First of all, the results of the medical screenings are recorded upon arrival.

This practice is also provided for in the Guidelines for health checks on arrival. This document, in fact, recommends offering a comprehensive health and psychological assessment to all new arrivals as soon as possible (and no later than one month), emphasising the importance of obtaining consent for the visit and verifying the patient's actual understanding of the information received.

Regarding the health assessment, the Guidelines recommend reconstructing the patient's clinical and family history, medications taken, any allergies, etc.. Specific attention is paid to detecting possible tuberculosis infections through chest X-rays, Mantoux and Quantiferon tests (Graph 3).

Graph 3. Medical screenings in the first-level reception centres, Apulia, 2018

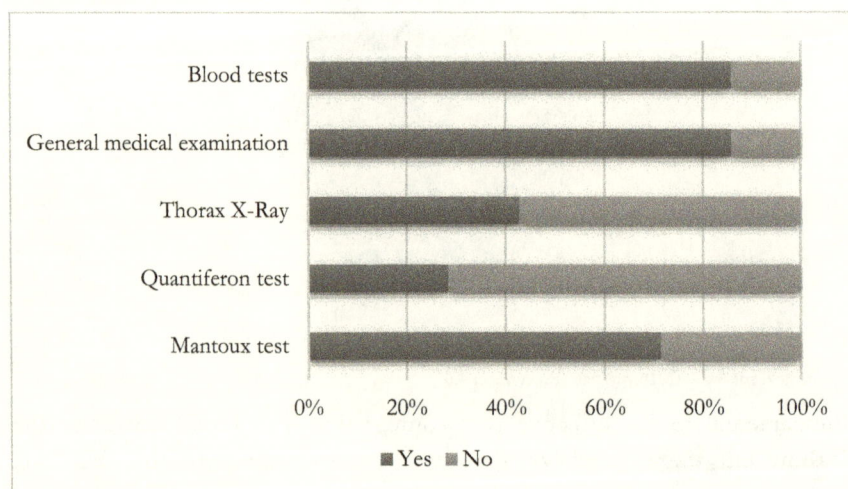

Source: field survey - AMIF project "Prevention 4.0"

It is known that mainly the younger and healthier individuals undertake the journey, confirming the so-called *healthy migrant effect* based on a self-selection process at departure (Fennely, 2007). However, once they arrive at their destination, it is often observed the *exhausted migrant effect* (Bollini & Siem, 1995). The precarious living conditions they find themselves in, mainly due to the uncertainty of their legal status, the persistence of disadvantaged living conditions, overcrowding in reception centres and its consequences, as well as the separation from their families, cause psycho-physical distress that requires medical care.

From Graph 4, it emerges that among the most common symptoms in first-level reception centres are those related to skin infections, joint pain, psychological/psychiatric discomfort, and respiratory problems.

Graph 4. Main symptoms and pathologies in the first-level reception centres, Apulia, 2018

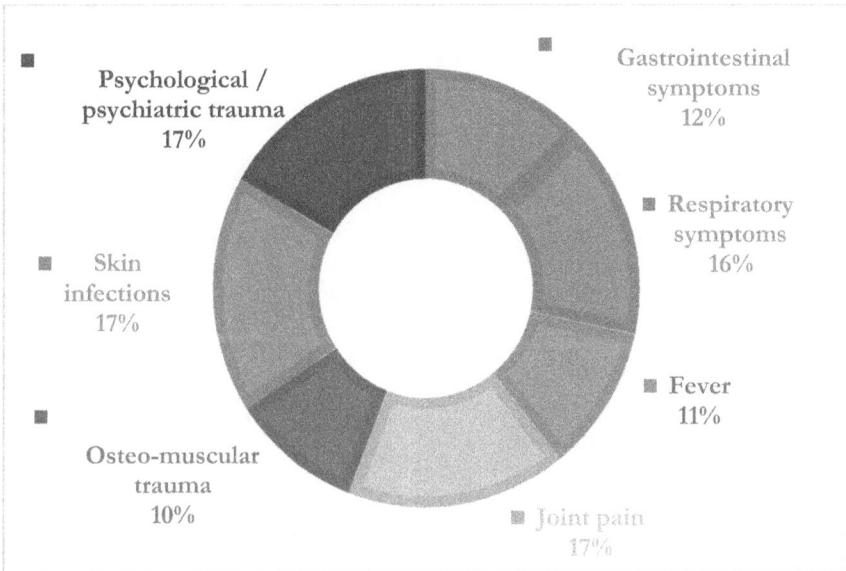

Source: field survey - AMIF project "Prevention 4.0"

In the reception process, the medical service proves to be crucial, and the absence of constant monitoring of their health can lead to the worsening of symptoms that are not visible and not treated promptly, resulting in psycho-physical imbalance.

Language Proficiency

Knowledge of the language of the host country (or at least its basics) is fundamental for any integration process. For this reason, we decided to dedicate a part of the survey questionnaire to this aspect. In order to better understand the language proficiency of the guests, we differentiated each language into written and spoken forms.

The most common languages are English, French, Italian, and Arabic. The knowledge of English and French stems from the colonial past of the countries of origin. Italian, on the other hand, is found as the language of the host country[21].

According to the linguistic needs of the guests, the foreign languages most commonly used by the operators (particularly by the intercultural mediators)

---

[21] The Italian language is more widespread among guests of the SAI due to their longer stay in the territory.

are, in order: French, English, and Arabic.

Graph 5. Languages used in the first-level reception centres, in written (W) and spoken (S) forms, Apulia, 2018

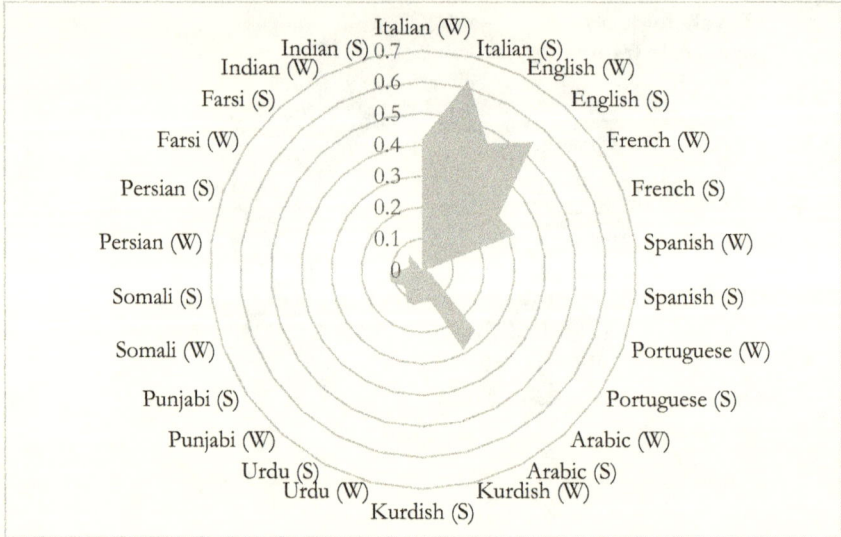

Source: field survey - AMIF project "Prevention 4.0"

For all the above-mentioned languages, it emerged from the survey that guests have greater oral expression skills than reading and writing. This information proved to be particularly useful as it highlighted the significant discrepancy between oral and written language skills. It is important to keep this information in mind when organising informative initiatives regarding the right to healthcare and the possibilities and modalities of accessing healthcare services. While this confirms the strategic role of intercultural mediators, it also leads us to further considerations about the effectiveness of communication and information channels and tools.

Communication and Information

Thanks to the survey results, the need expressed by the guests for "More complete and widespread dissemination of information" has emerged very clearly.

In the CPA-CARAs and CASs, among the information tools proposed in the survey, the "Multilingual Glossary" was considered the most useful. It is a multilingual glossary containing the main words and definitions used for the prevention, protection, and healthcare of asylum seekers/refugees, as well as the types of services available in the area. An oral version of the multilingual glossary has been planned to be added in the app.

Both for the guests and for the operators, the most useful proposed information channel indicated was the "Operational Services Centre" (OSC). This type of support has been designed to reduce the number of users who daily turn to the services of the NHS.

The OSC, once implemented, would be a physical place where operators (mediators, doctors, psychologists, dieticians, healthcare operators) are present to interact directly with the users and provide personalised solutions remotely. In this way, it would go beyond the dissemination of information, representing, at the same time, a valuable intervention tool.

Graph 6. Most useful project activities

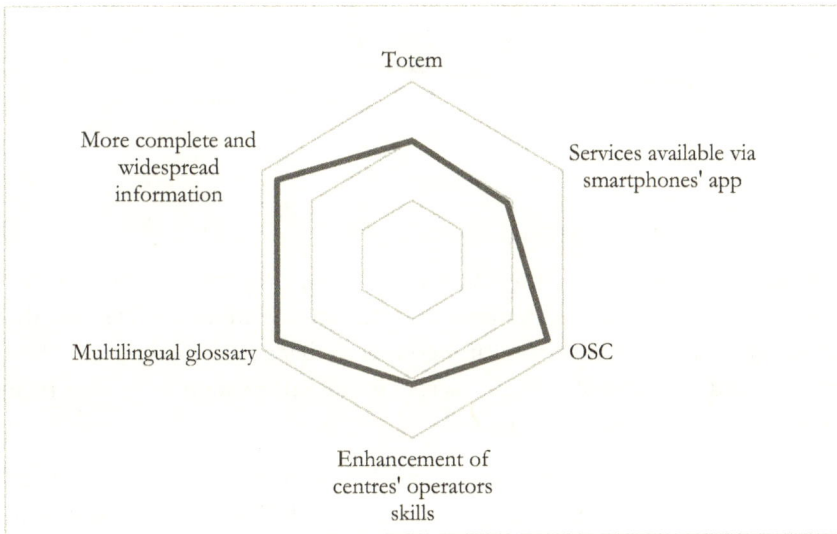

Source: field survey - AMIF project "Prevention 4.0"

Based on what emerged about language skills and with the help of modern technologies, the use of video and audio tools should be encouraged, able to reach a large number of recipients thanks to the widespread use of smartphones among migrants. In fact, from the survey data, it emerges that all guests own a smartphone because it is an essential means of communication and information, or even of survival.

The smartphone is fundamental for migrants before, during, and after the journey to a new country. Even before leaving their home, future migrants use them to organise their itinerary, informing themselves about available routes through both official websites and social media.

They read the information provided by their compatriots who have taken a certain route, the advice on the safety of one route compared to another, the warnings about traffickers' scams, the suggestions on how to behave with the authorities of the destination country, and so on.

Graph 7. Most useful app features

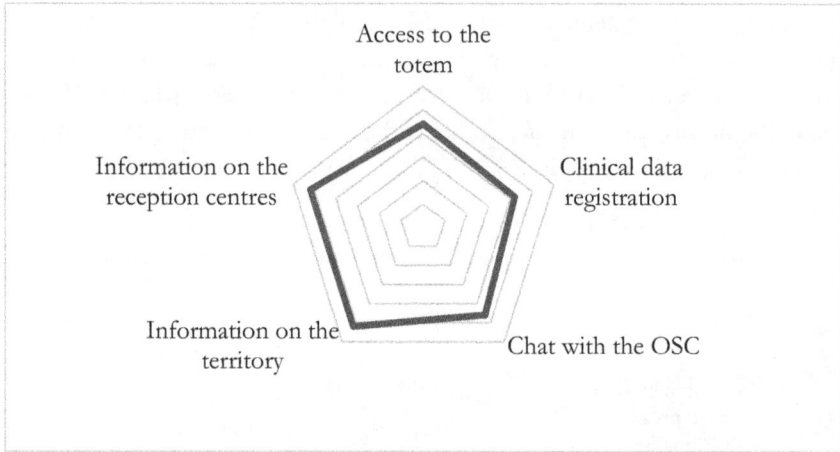

Source: field survey - AMIF project "Prevention 4.0"

Regarding the availability and access to services, even the operators of the centres have prioritised the need to illustrate, through educational videos, the procedures for accessing healthcare services so that guests can improve their physical and mental wellness and receive useful information to protect their health and prevent possible illnesses.

The most used apps are: Whatsapp and Viber to stay in touch with their families of origin, Google Maps for travel, Google Translate to translate in real-time and facilitate communication with reception staff and the local population. Even social media like Facebook and platforms like Youtube become important tools for integration and learning the language, customs, and habits of the host country.

Finally, regarding information about the location of places, guests have shown greater interest, on the one hand, in healthcare facilities (hospitals, clinics, and pharmacies) and, on the other hand, in the Prefecture, Police headquarters, and Municipality. For those who have just entered the reception network, knowing where institutions like the Police headquarters, Prefecture, and Municipality are located is mainly linked to their primary concern of defining their legal status.

Graph 8. Points of interest

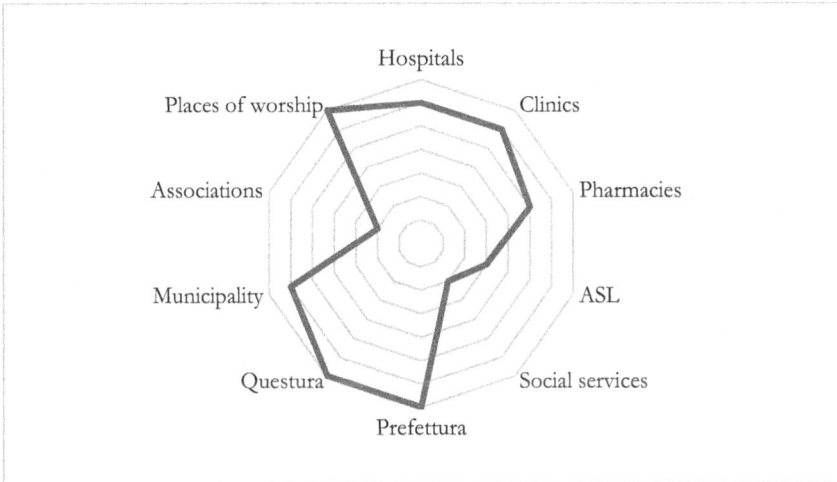

Source: field survey - AMIF project "Prevention 4.0"

Finally, it is worth noting the desire for information about places of worship. The distance from their families and friends leads them to turn to places of worship in search of a part of their identity within an unfamiliar context. A significantly lower interest is expressed for associations, social services, and Local Health Units (ASL) [22].

4.2 During the Pandemic

Europe received 40% fewer arrivals via Mediterranean routes in 2020 as compared to 2019, with sharp decreases in Greece, mainland Spain and Malta. However, arrivals tripled in Italy and increased almost eightfold in the Canary Islands (UNHCR, 2022).

The stop of mobility due to the Covid-19 Pandemic seemed to have been a short-term effect[23]: within a month and a half, arrivals began to grow again returning to the previous trend and reaching the usual seasonal peak during the summer (Villa, 2020). Flows were coming mainly from Tunisia and Libya which gather flows from sub-Saharan Africa and the Middle East countries[24].

The Covid-19 Pandemic stressed the entire national (and world) health

---

[22] ASL (Aziende Sanitarie Locali) are the administrative bodies of the NHS on the territory at the province level.
[23] In March 2020, irregular arrivals on Italian coasts decreased by 80% due to the complete stop of mobility worldwide (Villa, 2020).
[24] https://www.aspeninstitute.it/attivita/flussi-migratori-tempo-di-pandemia-esperienze-acquisite-e-nuovi-strumenti-una-migliore-gest

system due to the increased level of complexity in the organisation and in the delivery of health services. Like the health system, the reception system for asylum seekers and refugees had to deal with this increased complexity that strengthened the existing inequalities in terms of access to public health care of these disadvantaged groups of migrants.

In such a context, the Covid-19 Pandemic has highlighted how essential it is, on one hand, to adapt the policies in place to the circumstances of local reality and, on the other hand, echoing the principles of the Constitution, it reminded us that the health of all depends on the health of each person.

Following this principle, the Apulia Region has not set up differentiated rules for migrants to stop the spread of the virus. However, while the legislation adopted has covered the entire population living in the region, specific measures have been implemented for migrants to compensate the difficulties of both housing and linguistic and cultural diversity. In the Ordinance n. 190 adopted by the President of the Regional Council to cope with the Pandemic, a series of activities were provided in support of people in difficulty, including migrants. Reference was made, in this case, to migrants living in shelters, minors, women victims of violence, etc.. Below are the main interventions.

Mobile Units

The above-mentioned Regional Ordinance provided the organisation of mobile units for the protection of the homeless or in a state of psycho-physical fragility, such as migrants and victims of trafficking.

The Convention with the Regional Strategic Agency for Health and Social Care (AReSS) and the Local Health Units (ASL) of Foggia and Lecce allowed the activation of multidisciplinary mobile units in informal settlements[25] of migrants for prevention and treatment activities managed by three NGOs[26].

These mobile units dealt with infectious screening and social-health support distributing health kits, health and hygiene counselling, adequate information on all prevention measures to be taken with pictograms more understandable

---

[25] Informal settlements are places adapted to housing structures where migrants of different categories (those who have not been accepted in reception facilities, seasonal workers, those waiting to renew their residence documents, etc.) live in overcrowded conditions. They are pseudo-housing structures characterised by a lack of adequate supply of drinking water and sanitary services, with no protection from extreme weather conditions. These settlements are isolated, in fact they are completely detached from any urban or rural centre, and they can be defined as proper ghettos. On informal settlements see: Medici senza Frontiere (2018).
In Apulia these ghettos are located mostly around the cities of Foggia and Lecce where agricultural labour (too often undeclared jobs) is more needed.
[26] Cuamm, InterSos and Solidaunia.

to foreign users and to minors too. Among the group of volunteers there were intercultural mediators who served in the mobile units to help the medical staff to do their best work with vulnerable population and overcome the difficulties caused by socio-cultural differences.

The planned activities of the AMIF project "Prevention 4.0" have been reorganised to adapt to the needs derived from the health emergency and the implementation of some actions aimed at coping with the ongoing Pandemic has been incorporated.

Reorganisation of Spaces and Activities

Reorganising the spaces according to the measures adopted for the Covid-19 emergency has not been very complicated. Reception centres adopted prevention measures in accordance with national and regional regulations, including stopping the exits from the centre, the distribution of hygiene kits, installation of sanitising gel dispensers in all areas of the centre, reorganisation of common areas, provision of quarantine areas. However, from the interviews conducted with the managers of the reception centres it emerges that the reaction of the CARA of Bari-Palese to the health emergency was more anticipatory. In fact, it moved in full autonomy as soon as the risk of a health emergency was recognised by adopting measures that preceded the national or regional legislation on the containment of contagion.

This centre activated immediately the necessary measures to contain the infection through the posting of posters, translated into several languages and placed in the points of greatest concentration of guests. In presence of positive cases, the person was isolated in a detached room and all his/her contacts were isolated in another room to perform fiduciary isolation.

In addition to the ordinary work of the operators and intercultural mediators, the medical-nursing service was also increased, providing constant supervision of the guests by the medical staff of the centres. Both the psychological support for cases already reported as vulnerable and the monitoring of psychiatric patients was maintained. Obviously, the use of common areas was reorganised and as the contagion increased in the country, it became compulsory to suspend various activities up to the almost total blockade. Social distancing and prohibition to assemble took over as well.

Measures for New Arrivals

The asylum seekers received in the centres were obliged to be tested and the negative result was transmitted before their arrival. The result of the test was needed also to leave the centre. At their arrival at the centres, the guests were obliged to a preventive isolation. Throughout this period, doctors and nurses were always present for temperature measurement and other checks. Subsequently, in agreement with the Local Health Unit, guests were also given the opportunity to undergo spontaneous serological testing in order to early detection of risk situations to prevent their occurrence.

Vaccine Program

On January 2, 2021, the National Strategic Plan for Covid -19 vaccination[27] was adopted in Italy, due to the rapid spread of infections that exposed regional and national health systems to a constant overload.

Based on the principles of the Italian Constitution regarding equity and promotion of health and well-being, it was intended to guarantee the vaccine to the entire population to achieve herd immunity. However, due to the initial limited availability of vaccines, the Strategic Plan identified a gradual order of vaccination. The first phase of the program involved the vaccination of health and social care workers, staff and guests in residential facilities for the elderly, population over 60 years, and the population with at least one chronic comorbidity. In the following phases, as the number of available vaccine doses increased, it was the turn of teachers and school staff, police, military and prison staff.

No specification has been made in the National Strategic Plan regarding asylum seekers and holders of international protection because the Plan made no differentiation based on nationality or legal status, only certain specific professions of public utility and age groups have been considered.

Conclusions

In the Italian scenario, even though the Apulia regional legislation on social and health care is very extensive and guarantees full rights in terms of health protection for all kinds of migrants, there have been some critical issues in its implementation. We refer, in particular, to the complexity of the regulatory framework related to the legal status of foreigners, which posed relevant problems of interpretation and correct application of the rules especially in the case of missing services in informal settlements. For instance, obstacles

---

[27] Elements of preparation of the vaccination strategy, presented by the Italian Minister of Health to the Parliament on December 2, 2020 (Decree January 2, 2021) (https://www.trovanorme.salute.gov.it/norme/renderPdf.spring?seriegu=SG&datagu=24/03/2021&redaz=21A01802&artp=1&art=1&subart=1&subart1=10&vers=1&prog=002).
Ministry of Health, National Vaccine Prevention Plan-PNPV 2017-2019 (http://www.salute.gov.it/imgs/C_17_pubblicazioni_2571_allegato.pdf).

of a bureaucratic-administrative nature that, too often, delay entry into second-level reception centres and, consequently, integration times.

Furthermore, it is worth underlining that the positive effects of the autonomy of the Apulia region on health policies have been mitigated by some disruptions in the governance of health access particularly for vulnerable groups, such as asylum seekers and refugees due to some frictions occurred between the local and the national governance that complicated the respect of health rights emphasising the socio-sanitary discomfort that migrants experience.

That is a clear demonstration that enriching the enjoyment of rights is not always sufficient to achieve the aims for which the regulation itself has been created. We could say that it is a necessary but not sufficient condition. It is, therefore, fundamental to adopt effective implementation plans so that all beneficiaries can be aware of their rights and can take advantage of them.

Interventions in this field should aim to maximise the accessibility of services, focusing especially on combating barriers that may hinder such accessibility. For accessibility and the right to care to be effective, migrants should be enabled to access them, starting with adequate information about the existence of such rights. Otherwise, it risks remaining merely a "paper right" (Rinaldi et al., 2013).

In primis, it is important that health support be accompanied by legal advice on the right to health protection and on the organisation of healthcare services, both at the national and regional levels.

Our research has confirmed that information is a fundamental element in the concrete enjoyment of the right to health and that there is a need to review the tools for its dissemination. Increased use of visual and verbal information channels, also taking advantage of technological tools such as smartphones equipped with appropriate apps.

Another important aspect of improving access to healthcare services for asylum seekers and refugees is the need to overcome cultural and linguistic barriers through the support of intercultural mediators. Not by chance, reception centres considered very useful to be able to count on ethno-clinical mediators. At the same time, it is necessary to inform healthcare professionals about the specific needs of these patients and further incentivise the training of doctors and healthcare professionals by introducing both an intercultural perspective and explicit references to the duty of the professional to take into account the different cultural identities of patients (INMP, ISS e SIMM,

2017).

Considering the burden of avoidable hospitalisations, another proposal could be to ensure primary care (including preventive and ambulatory care) for all migrants who arrive in or are present on the national territory, regardless of their legal status (even undocumented ones), by providing them with a GP and a paediatrician for their children.

The improvement of technological tools can aid not only in the dissemination of information but also for this purpose, for example, with the use of telemedicine. Our research clearly shows the interest and usefulness of the Operational Services Centre (OSC), which has enabled the initiation of a new prevention model through the use of e-health technologies and the definition of personalised empowerment pathways tailored to the specific needs of users.

Our analysis showed another best practise like the vaccination campaign extended to all the people on the territory regardless to their legal status (nationals, regular, irregular, and illegal migrants).

Finally, we would like to mention an important best practice implemented for the first time in Italy that specifically concerns asylum seekers and refugees and that is based on the "holistic intake". In 2022, an extremely timely, inclusive, and widespread channel of reception was piloted: the temporary protection for refugees fleeing Ukraine. That has been possible thanks to the activation of the Directive established in 2001 by the European Commission to address the possible exodus of Balkan populations after the breakup of the former Yugoslavia (Campomori, 2022). This measure, unused for twenty-one years, enabled asylum seekers from Ukraine to quickly benefit from basic measures removing many of the obstacles other asylum seekers and refugees still face in entering and remaining in the EU and Italy (Barbati et al., 2023).

A much more generous policy, in fact, concerned Ukrainian refugees by granting them one year of protection (subsequently renewed due to the ongoing conflict), immediate access to healthcare and education systems, and the opportunity to seek regular employment. Furthermore, the management of reception was entrusted to the Civil Protection, establishing a new channel of assistance for refugees, which differed from the existing ones (CARA, CAS, and SAI). The Civil Protection immediately issued an ordinance that, in Article 1, speaks of "widespread reception". It recognised the need to integrate the public offer of reception services by addressing third sector entities, voluntary service centres, registered associations, and civilly recognised entities. These private entities were asked to ensure full involvement of municipalities through the signing of partnership agreements.

For the first time, Italian public institutions have recognised autonomy and responsibility among refugees, treating them as capable adults able to take care of themselves, encouraging them, for example, to seek independent housing and receiving a direct contribution of 300 euros per month for each adult and 150 euros for each minor, for a period of three months (Ambrosini, 2023).

The Ukrainian case has thus modified the cultural parameters with which asylum seekers and refugees were usually considered and Italian ability to receive them. It is noteworthy that the reception did not provoke political controversies, social resistance, or media speculation. It would be difficult to argue that Ukrainian refugees do not impact the welfare system, yet no one has objected.

For all these reasons, the extension of the model used for Ukrainian refugees would indeed be worthy of consideration because there are no understandable reasons why such a model cannot be applied to people fleeing from other armed conflicts and humanitarian, economic, or even climate crises.

As we saw, some measures have been adopted to address the existing inequalities, however, our research shows that there is still much to be done in terms of political intervention to eliminate barriers at correct and effective access to regular medical visits and exams; emergency treatments; follow-up of chronic diseases; assistance to mothers and newborns; detection of infectious diseases; prevention, mental disorders treatments, etc.

The main challenge is to adopt a multidisciplinary and multidimensional approach embedded within a framework of healthcare and psychological support, thereby overcoming fragmented and often purely emergency-based interventions. This kind of approach would help to make effective the motto of WHO: "No public health without refugee and migrant health".

References

Allegri, C., Banks, H. & Devillanova, C. (2022). Avoidable hospitalizations and access to primary care: comparisons among Italians, resident immigrants and undocumented immigrants in administrative hospital discharge records, *eClinicalMedicine*, 46, 101345, Retrieved from: https://www.thelancet.com/journals/eclinm/article/PIIS2589-5370 (22)00075-X/fulltext

Ambrosini, M. (2013). 'We are against a multi-ethnic society': policies of exclusion at the urban level in Italy, *Ethnic and Racial Studies*, 36(1), 136-155.

Ambrosini, M. (2023). Le politiche migratorie italiane: contraddizioni attuali e innovazioni possibili, *Dossier Statistico Immigrazione 2023*, (pp. 113-118). Roma: IDOS.

Andriopoulou, A., Angelucci, A., Barberis, E., De Blasis F., Ince-Beqo, G., Pitzalis, S. & Rossi, F. (2023). Local practices of integration and local networks. The case of Fermignano, Italy. Progetto PISTE – "Participation in small and medium–sized towns: Experiences, Exchanges, Experiments", In Schenkel K., Messerschmidt, S., Grossman, K. (Ed.) *Practices of integration and local networks in Small and Medium-Sized Towns: Insights from the project PISTE*, (pp. 79-143). Urbino: Urbino University Press.

Arbia, E., Biz, C. (2020). *L'Unione europea contro la pandemia di COVID-19: tra solidarietà per gestire l'emergenza sanitaria e adattamento degli strumenti esistenti, alla ricerca di un piano comune di rilancio*, in Diritto dell'emergenza Covid 19, n. 1012, Giustizia Insieme, Retrieved from: https://www.giustiziainsieme.it/en/news/74-main/123-diritto-ue/1012-l-unione-europea-contro-la-pandemia-di-covid-19-tra-solidarieta-per-gestire-l-emergenza-sanitaria-e-adattamento-degli-strumenti-esistenti-alla-ricerca-di-un-piano-comune-di-rilancio

Aspen Institute, Retrieved from: https://www.aspeninstitute.it/attivita/flussi-migratori-tempo-di-pandemia-esperienze-acquisite-e-nuovi-strumenti-una-migliore-gest

Baglio, G., Affronti, M. (2019). *Il dovere dell'accoglienza*, in Salute Internazionale, Retrieved from: https://www.saluteinternazionale.info/2019/05/il-dovere-dellaccoglienza/

Barbati, A., Cocco, N., Corsaro, A., Formenti, B., Mammana, L., Marchese, V., Nicoli, F., Russo, G. & Testa, J. (2023). Migranti e salute: opportunità mancate e proposte per migliorare accoglienza e inclusione, in *Dossier Statistico Immigrazione 2023*, (pp. 204-208). Roma: IDOS.

Bollini, P., Siem, H. (1995). No real progress towards equity: Health of migrants and ethnic minorities on the eve of the year 2000, *Social Science & Medicine*, 41(6), 819-828.

Campomori, F. (2022). La crisi ucraina e la (ri)organizzazione del sistema di accoglienza: tra lodevoli aperture e preoccupanti disparità di trattamento dei profughi, *Social Policies*, 2, 325-332.

Campomori, F., Caponio, T. (2013). Competing frames of immigrant integration in the EU: Geographies of social inclusion in Italian regions. *Policy Studies* 34(2), 162–179.

Caruso, G., Marcoccia, E., Brunelli, R., Candelieri, M., Schiavi, M.C., Zannini, I., Perrone, S., Capri, O., Muzii, L., Perrone, G. & Galoppi, P. (2021). Immigration and Adverse Pregnancy Outcomes in an Italian Free Care Hospital, *International Journal of Women's Health*, 13, 911-917, Retrieved from: https://www.tandfonline.com/doi/full/ 10.2147/ IJWH. S322828?scroll=top&needAccess=true

Cassarà, G. (2015). La salute delle vittime di torture, in *Libro Bianco Malattie Infettive, Infezioni ed Immigrazione, Società Italiana di Malattie Infettive e Tropicali*, Retrieved from: https://www.superabile.it/cs/superabile/salute-e-ricerca/simit-ecco-il-libro-bianco-delle-malattie-infettive.html

Conferenza delle Regioni e delle Provincie Autonome, Immigrati: Studio SIMM, Puglia la più "friendly" sul fronte sanitario, Retrieved from: http://www.regioni.it/ Migrazioni/ 2011/ 05/18/immigrati-studio-simm-puglia-la-piu-friendly-sul-fronte-sanitario-50520/

Convenzione sui Diritti del Fanciullo, New York, 20.11.1989, Retrieved from: https://www.minori.gov.it/it/minori/convenzione-onu-sui-diritti-del-fanciullo

Dalla Zuanna, T., Cacciani, L., Barbieri, G., Ferracin, E., Zengarini, N., Di Girolamo, C., Caranci, N., Petrelli, A., Marino, C., Agabiti, N. & Canova, C. (2020). Avoidable hospitalisation for diabetes mellitus among immigrants and natives: Results from the Italian Network for Longitudinal Metropolitan Studies, *Nutrition, Metabolism and Cardiovascular Diseases*, 30(9), 1535-1543.

Di Napoli, A., Ventura, M., Spadea, T., Giorgi Rossi, P., Bartolini, L., Battisti, L., Cacciani, L., Caranci, N., Cernigliaro, A., De Giorgi, M., Fanolla, A., Lazzeretti, M., Mininni, M., Mirisola, C. & Petrelli, A. (2022). Barriers to accessing primary care and appropriateness of healthcare among immigrants in Italy, *Frontiers in Public Health*, 10: 817696, Retrieved from: https://www.ncbi.nlm.nih.gov/pmc/articles/PMC8864157/

EUROSTAT (2020). Retrieved from: https://ec.europa.eu/eurostat/web/products-euro-indicators/-/3-20032020-ap

Fennelly, K. (2007). The "healthy migrant" effect, *Minnesota Medicine*, 90(3), 51-53.

Gambino, S. (2015). Crisi economica e diritti sociali (con particolare riguardo a salute, assistenza sociale e istruzione), In S. Gambino (Ed.), *Diritti sociali e crisi economica. Problemi e prospettive, Diritto Pubblico Comparato ed Europeo (DPCE) Dossier – VI. (*pp. 43-105)*,* Torino: G. Giappichelli Editore.

Hiam, L., Orcutt, M. & Yates, R. (2019). Universal health coverage in the UK, *BMJ* 367, l7054.

INMP (2020). *Indagine nazionale Covid-19 nelle strutture del sistema di accoglienza per migranti, Istituto Nazionale per la Promozione della Salute delle Popolazioni Migranti e per il Contrasto delle Malattie della Povertà*, Retrieved from: https://www.inmp.it/index.php/ita/Pubblicazioni/ Libri/ Indagine-nazionale-CoVid-19-nelle-strutture-del-sistema-di-accoglienza-per-migranti

INMP, ISS & SIMM (2017). *Linee guida I controlli alla frontiera. La frontiera del controllo. Controlli sanitari all'arrivo e percorsi di tutela per i migranti ospiti nei centri di accoglienza*, Roma: Eurolit.

IOM (2021). *IOM Strategic Response and Recovery Plan COVID-19*, Retrieved from: https://www.iom.int/covid19

ISTAT (2022). *Cittadini non comunitari in Italia. Anni 2021-2022, Statistiche Report*, Retrieved from: https://www.istat.it/it/files//2022/10/Report-cittadini-non-comunitari-2022.pdf

ISTAT Data Warehouse, Retrieved from: http://dati.istat.it/Index.aspx?lang=en&Sub SessionId=c72ed3e5-1cd8-4d1e-9158-393327544e2e

Listorti, E., Torbica, A., Cella, S.G., Fiorini, G., Corrao, G. & Franchi, M. (2022). Healthcare Services for Undocumented Migrants: Organisation and Costs from the Italian NHS Perspective, *International Journal of Environmental Research and Public Health*, 19(24), 1-10.

Marchetti, C. (2014). Rifugiati e migranti forzati in Italia. Il pendolo tra emergenza e sistema, REMHU – Rev. Interdiscip. Mobil. Hum. XXII, (43), 53-70, Retrieved from: https://www.academia.edu/84597817/Rifugiati_e_migranti_forzati_in_It%C3%A1lia_il _pendolo_tra_emergenza_e_sistema

Mastrorocco, N., Calò E. (2019). Il movimento migratorio in Puglia: policy e flussi, *Pace e diritti umani nel Mediterraneo*, Retrieved from: http://siba-ese.unile.it/index.php/paceediritti/ article/view/21726

Medici senza Frontiere (2018). *Insediamenti Informali: marginalità sociale, ostacoli all'accesso alle cure e ai beni essenziali per migranti e rifugiati, Secondo Rapporto*, Retrieved from: https://www.medicisenzafrontiere.it/news-e-storie/pubblicazioni/fuori-campo-secondo-rapporto/

Ministero dell'Interno, Dipartimento Libertà Civili e Immigrazione (2020). Retrieved from: http://www.libertaciviliimmigrazione.dlci.interno.gov.it/it/documentazione/statistica/i-numeri-dellasilo

Openpolis – ActionAid (2021). *Una mappa dell'accoglienza. Centri d'Italia 2021*, Retrieved from: https://www.openpolis.it/esercizi/limportanza-di-un-monitoraggio-dettagliato/

Pasini, N. (2011). (Ed.), *Confini irregolari. Cittadinanza sanitaria in prospettiva comparata e multilivello*,

Milano: FrancoAngeli.

Pellicani, M.C., Tafuri, S. (2020). (Ed.), *Migrazione e salute: un binomio da analizzare, Report dell'Indagine conoscitiva progetto FAMI "Prevenzione 4.0",* London: Transnational Press London.

Pellicani, M.C., Ince Beqo, G., Kushi, A. (2022). Emergency within emergency: the Impact of the Pandemic on Local Governance of Immigrant Health, In H. Faouzi, G.F. Dumont, C. Wihtol de Wenden (Ed.) *La Covid-19 est-elle un game changer géopolitique ?* (pp. 105-135). Paris: L'Harmattan.

Petrelli, A., Di Napoli, A., Perez, M. & Gargiulo, L. (2017). (Ed), *Lo stato di salute della popolazione immigrata in Italia: evidenza dalle indagini multiscopo ISTAT,* Epidemiologia e Prevenzione, 1-72.

Rinaldi, A., Civitelli, G., Marceca, M., Paglione, L. (2013). Le politiche per la tutela della salute dei migranti: il contesto europeo e il caso Italia, *REMHU,* 21(40), 9-26.

Seghieri, G., Seghieri, C., Policardo, L., Gualdani, E., Francesconi, P., Voller, F. (2019). Adherence to diabetes care process indicators in migrants as compared to non-migrants with diabetes: a retrospective cohort study, *International Journal of Public Health,* 64 (4), 595-601.

SIMM (2020). *Attuale legislazione sanitaria italiana per immigrati irregolari e attuale fruibilità di tale legislazione a livello regionale. Rapporto 2019,* Retrieved from: https://www.simmweb.it/973-attuale-legislazione-sanitaria-italiana-per-immigrati-irregolari-e-attuale-fruibilit%C3%A0-di%20-tale-legislazione-a-livello-regionale-rapporto-2019

Sulis, G., El Hamad, I., Fabiani, M., Rusconi, S., Maggiolo, F., Guaraldi, G., Bozzi, G., Bernardini, C., Lichtner, M., Stentarelli, C., Carenzi, L., Francisci, D., Saracino, A. & Castelli, F. (2014). Clinical and epidemiological features of HIV/AIDS infection among migrants at first access to healthcare services as compared to Italian patients in Italy: a retrospective multicentre study, 2000-2010, *Infection,* 42 (5), 859-67.

Tarricone, I., Stivanello, E., Ferrari, S., Colombini, N., Bolla, E., Braca, M., Giubbarelli, C., Costantini, C., Cazzamalli, S., Mimmi, S., Tedesco, D., Menchetti, M., Rigatelli, M., Maso, E., Balestrieri, M., Vender, S. & Berardi, D. (2012). Migrant pathways to community mental health centres in Italy, *Int J Soc Psychiatry,* 58 (5), 505-511.

UNHCR (2020). Retrieved from: *Global Trends. Forced displacement in 2019,* https://www.unhcr.org/media/unhcr-global-trends-2019

UNHCR (2022). Retrieved from: *Global Trends. Forced displacement in 2020,* https://www.unhcr.org/statistics/unhcrstats/60b638e37/global-trends-forced-displacement-2020.html

UNHCR (2023). Retrieved from: *Global Trends. Forced displacement in 2022,* https://www.unhcr.org/global-trends-report-2022

Villa, M. (2020). Fact Checking: migrazioni (e Covid-19), ISPI. Retrieved from: https://www.ispionline.it/it/pubblicazione/fact-checking-migrazioni-e-covid-19-27058

WHO - Regional Office for Europe (2018). *Report on the health of refugees and migrants in the WHO European Region. No public health without refugee and migrant health,* Retrieved from: https://apps.who.int/iris/handle/10665/311347

WHO (2022). Ensuring the integration of refugees and migrants in immunization policies, planning and service delivery globally, Retrieved from: https://www.who.int/publications/i/item/9789240051843

Zagrebelsky, V. (2016). *Diritto fondamentale alla salute: principi e realtà,* Atti del XIV Congresso Nazionale SIMM, Bologna: Pendragon.

EGO NETWORK ANALYSIS OF SOCIAL CAPITAL, GENERAL AND HEALTH-RELATED NETWORKS BETWEEN MIGRANTS AND NON-MIGRANTS IN PORTUGAL

Paulo Nascimento[1], Magda Sofia Roberto[2], Ana Sofia Santos[3]

Introduction

Migration is a dominant feature of human activity (Scott & Scott, 1989). Apart from a variety of reasons initiating transnational movements, the migratory experience is perpetuated across time and space: those who migrate will be involved in disrupted and reconstructed "sets of interpersonal ties that connect migrants, former migrants, and non-migrants in origin and destination areas through ties of kinship, friendship, and shared community of origin" (Massey et al., 1993, p. 448). Transnational movements can be perceived as social spaces, combining social and symbolic ties, positions in networks, and organizations: by encompassing more than physical features, social capital emerges as the resources inherent in social and symbolic ties (Faist, 1998). The concept of transnational social movements puts migrants at the centre of the social space, as nodes develop formal, informal, vertical, and horizontal ties with alters, in a specific time; being migration a process that considers multiple contexts (Levitt & Schiller, 2004; Lubbers et al., 2020).

In the field of migrations, the following recurring fundamental premise applies: migrants benefit from resources to attain goals by mobilising the former through social and symbolic ties, which are actively built (Volker, 2020). The social capital migrants mobilise from their networks may help them in several ways (e.g., finding a job, health, and well-being; Adedeji, 2019; Kindler et al., 2015). However, the literature on social capital and social networks remains segmented, suggesting multiple patterns and effects

[1] Paulo Nascimento, CICPSI (Centro de Investigação em Ciência Psicológica), Faculdade de Psicologia, Universidade de Lisboa, Alameda da Universidade, 1649-013 Lisbon, Portugal.
[2] Magda Sofia Valadas Dominguez Roberto, CICPSI (Centro de Investigação em Ciência Psicológica), Faculdade de Psicologia, Universidade de Lisboa, Alameda da Universidade, 1649-013 Lisbon, Portugal.
[3] Ana Sofia Correia dos Santos, CICPSI (Centro de Investigação em Ciência Psicológica), Faculdade de Psicologia, Universidade de Lisboa, Alameda da Universidade, 1649-013 Lisbon, Portugal.

Acknowledgements: The authors would like to thank all participants who took part of this study and Fundação para a Ciência e Tecnologia (FCT), for supporting this study [Grant of Paulo Nascimento – (PD/BD/150564/2020)].
We have no conflicts of interest to disclose.

(Volker, 2020), and a deeper characterization of migrant's social interactions is required (Munshi, 2020). To realize how social capital is mobilised, a better understanding of migrants' social networks dynamics is also needed, one that incorporates specificity and time.

That said, evidence indicates human migration continues to increase and is accompanied by a growing burden of disease disproportionately affecting migrant groups (Bempong et al., 2019; Mladovsky, 2007). Because social networks are central determinants of migration (Munshi, 2020), an analysis of the network component may contribute to bringing together literature on social capital as a social determinant of migrants' health. In this study, we rely on the need to reconcile the social network approach and migrations to understand better how social capital resources are mobilised among the Community of Portuguese Language Countries (CPLC) immigrants (with the largest communities being from Brazil, Cape Verde, Angola, and Bissau-Guinea), and non-migrants living in Portugal. We aim to contribute to this body of research by exploring different types of personal networks (general and health-specific networks), paying attention to their composition, and understand how those differences allow migrants to access social capital. We additionally extend these aims by looking at how the length of time spent by migrants at the destination shapes their networks and social capital to capture whether migrants' ties are rearranged according to time.

In the literature review, we begin by addressing the roots of social capital and how this concept is framed on social networks, followed by existing literature on general and specific networks. Finally, we funnel the attention to the interconnections between social capital, social networks and health in the field of migrations.

Social Capital and Social Networks

Theoretical insights on social capital may be translated by an evolving yet diverse literature; however, the premise that social capital reflects investments in social relations with expected returns is consistent across different scholars and states the network theory of social capital (Lin, 2001). That said, social capital is captured through social relations and works as a social asset due to the individuals' network connections (Lin, 2001), leading them to access resources (e.g., jobs, promotions, mental health; Hyyppä, 2010). Social capital can also depict an inward and outward perspective: when bonds connect similar people, bonding social capital occurs, but when networks tie different individuals, bridging social capital remains (Putnam, 2000; Putnam & Goss,

2002). While the former promotes reciprocity, solidarity, and strong ties, the latter connects individuals to external resources, expands the network flow of information, and uses weak ties to help people get ahead (Häuberer, 2011; Putnam, 2000).

Despite the agreement on a social capital metaphor embedded in social structures, where advantages occur for better-connected individuals, defining what exactly a "better" connection means remains a challenge (Burt, 2000). The hypothesis of structural holes as social capital, where better connections require brokerage opportunities, was advanced by Burt (1992; 2000). Specifically, whenever social structures present holes, nonredundant sources of information emerge, creating advantages for individuals whose relationships span the holes. Redundant information is provided by cohesive and equivalent ties, while brokerage occurs when networks are rich in structural holes, strengthening the information flow and providing nonredundant benefits (e.g., creativity, higher performance; Burt, 2000).

The ego network analysis approach has mainly addressed social capital and interpersonal ties because these networks and their structural qualities can impact individuals' behaviours, attitudes, and social outcomes (Perry et al., 2020). However, several authors have remarked on the importance of collecting nonoverlapping networks (Marsden, 2005; Perry & Pescosolido, 2010) by moving beyond the traditional general networks' perspective. By doing so, specific network functions will access additional ties egos may have, allowing better monitoring of how social capital is mobilised (Perry et al., 2018).

General and Specific Networks

Knoke (1990) discussed the role of activated ties in the social network theory, representing the contacts egos use whenever they face a specific problem to amplify the impact of microenvironments embedded in networks and disentangle ties relevant to egos rely on for specific issues. According to Pescosolido (2007), research on egonets should promote the ability to understand how individuals choose ties from their list of potential alters and what circumstances contribute to activating all ties, or just some ties but not the others. The discussion around general matters and specific networks highlights the lack of empirical evidence on the use of both approaches and the need to change the focus of the research to the match between problems and accessible ties (Perry & Pescosolido, 2010). Individuals have different resources available through distinct interpersonal ties, meaning that embedded social capital depends on each alter's social and relational characteristics because specific people provide relevant resources to certain purposes at different moments (e.g., Perry & Pescosolido, 2010; Wellman & Frank, 2001).

Health is an example of a domain in which the potential of specific networks can be determinant. For instance, Helliwell and Putnam (2004) considered that individuals with supportive networks tend to experience more subjective well-being and less sadness. The pathway by which social capital affects individual health has already been documented by the literature (e.g., Berkman, 1984); however, consistent empirical evidence is still lacking (Hyyppä, 2010). By addressing the selective activation of ties (e.g., health-specific networks), we can overcome the limitation of using a general network activation because ties will start matching specific resources.

The literature already pointed to some differences between general and specific-health networks worth noting. For instance, health discussion networks may have strong ties, but fewer alters because individuals tend to discuss their health problems, particularly with health confidants (Wellman, 2000). Moreover, family members and health professionals play a relevant role as health confidants (Wellman, 2000), leading to health networks composition characterised by less friendship and older ties (Perry & Pescosolido, 2010).

The differentiation between general and specific-health networks can provide a twofold contribution. First, by disentangling network resources, the association between social capital and health outcomes may be clarified. Second, although personal networks define individuals, their value is prominent on migrations, as disruption and reconstruction of networks systematically characterise migrant's experiences. Thus, a better understanding of which ties are more relevant during the migratory process is required.

Migrations: Interconnecting Social Capital, Social Networks and Health

Despite the importance of researching the relations between migrations, social capital, and social networks, literature remains segmented, bringing it challenging to capture convergences of patterns and effects (Volker, 2020). For instance, the literature on migrations from Latin America to the United States revealed that social capital differs across communities (e.g., urban vs. rural; Garip, 2012) and that both strong and weak ties promote and sustain international migration (Massey & Aysa-Lastra 2011). However, while some research suggests that co-ethnic communities attract migrants (Goodwin-White, 2007), other results reinforce the role of family ties as facilitators of mobility with co-ethnic communities in the host places perceived as interfering (Sue et al., 2019).

Literature diversity on social capital and social networks also depicts migration movements for destinations in Europe. Lubbers et al. (2010) discovered that personal networks of Argentinean immigrants in Spain were stable but with considerable variation: closest ties occurred with alters living in Argentina; contact frequency was higher with Spaniards, but fellow migrants had a central role in their networks. In contrast, Kim (2014) found that the Koreans living in Uzbekistan, who had networks with more structural holes, were more likely to anticipate access to social capital. Also, Roggeveen and Van Meeteren (2013), who studied Brazilian immigrants residing in Amsterdam, discovered the relevance of weak ties instead of co-ethnic communities. A similar pattern was found by Padilla (2006), illustrating that Brazilian immigrants in Portugal had strong transnational ties, but weak ties played a role in their access to social capital. In contrast, other research suggests that networks with the closure property are more relevant for immigrant communities, facilitating transactions, trust, and cooperation through shared norms and values (Levanon, 2011; Sanders et al., 2002). Nevertheless, Kindler et al. (2019), when addressing the Ukrainian migrants in Poland, suggested that better knowledge arises if attention is paid to how migrants' ties change over time due to their needs and circumstances.

Empirical inconsistencies remain when the look turns to the interconnections between social capital, social networks, and health. For instance, Lecerof et al. (2016) discussed an absent effect of social capital on health, probably because recently settled migrants generally have weak social networks and take time to build up social capital. However, the varied role of ties strength continues to contribute to literature discrepancies. While Zhu et al. (2019) found that strong ties provide support and health benefits, others (Lecerof et al., 2016; Uslaner & Conley, 2003) revealed those ties could also increase the association with the in-group, promoting social withdrawing and restricting the migrants' networks. Overall, research is still advancing in this regard, but a closer look at intra-networks characteristics and how they develop is essential to overcome significant gaps.

Research Context: Aims and Hypotheses

According to Bilecen et al. (2018), the relevance of social networks in migrations is essential, but studies relying on this approach are scarce and mainly adopt a qualitative approach. Portugal is considered a country of immigration, and according to the annual report of immigration in 2020, 662.095 legal immigrants were living in Portugal (Oliveira, 2021). The largest communities of immigrants are from CPLC countries, due to language proximity. Brazilian immigrants constitute the largest immigrant community in Portugal, with a total of 183.933 immigrants, representing a total of 27.8% of the immigrant community living in Portugal. When it comes to the Portuguese-speaking African Countries (PALOP)[4], a total of 36.609 immigrants were from Cape Verde (5.5%), 24.449 immigrants were from Angola (3.7%) and 19.700 immigrants were from Bissau-Guinea (Oliveira, 2021). Yet, significant gaps in the literature remain regarding these communities' social capital, social networks, and health.

To our knowledge, there are no studies that specifically focus on the approach of social networks among CPLC immigrants in Portugal. Our study was carried out during the COVID-19 pandemic, where both immigrants and non-migrants' social networks changed, but conducting the study during this timeframe informed us of the impact that disruptive events have on both immigrants and non-migrants' social networks and how they mobilise and activate the resources in their networks during this critical period. Thus, we aim to take a social network approach to clarify the segmented literature on social capital by analysing how CPLC immigrants mobilise resources and explore whether social networks and activated ties change according to these immigrants time in the country. Besides that, because most research on social networks focuses on general networks, which can impair social capital and health associations, we will bring this discussion to the field of migrations and compare the ties activated for the former with the ties captured by the specific-health networks. By doing so, we intend to bring light to the diverse literature connecting social capital and health. Table 1 illustrates the study research questions and hypotheses.

---

[4] PALOP: Angola, Cape Verde, Equatorial Guinea, Guinea-Bissau, Mozambique, São Tomé and Príncipe.

Table 1. Study Goals, Research Questions and Hypotheses

Mains Goals	Research Questions	Hypotheses
1. To understand how CPLC immigrants' networks differ from non-migrants' networks (general and health-specific).	a.2 What are the differences in general and health-specific networks regarding their composition and structure between CPLC immigrants and non-migrants? b.2 Are there any social capital changes between general and health-specific networks between CPLC immigrants and non-migrants? c.2 What are the differences in efficiency, constraint, and ties strength between CPLC immigrants and non-migrants' networks?	a.2.1 CPLC immigrants and non-migrants' networks have a higher degree on general networks. b.2.1 CPLC immigrants have less social capital on both networks than non-migrants.
2. To explore CPLC immigrants' networks (general and health-specific) according to immigrant's length of time in Portugal.	a.3 What are the differences in general and health-specific networks regarding their composition and structure between CPLC immigrants according to the length of time in Portugal? b.3 Are there any social capital changes between general and health-specific networks between CPLC immigrants according to the length of time in Portugal? c.3 What are the differences in social networks structural holes (density, efficiency, constraint) and ties strength between CPCL immigrants considering their length of time in Portugal?	a.3.1 CPLC immigrants living in Portugal for more than five years have general and specific networks with a higher degree. a.3.2 CPLC immigrants living in Portugal for more than five years have more non-migrants in their networks (migrant status heterophily). b.3.1 CPLC immigrants living in Portugal for more than five years have more social capital.

Method

Participants

The sample comprised 71 participants (egos). The following inclusion criteria were defined: i) being a CPLC immigrant living in Portugal, ii) being a non-migrant living in Portugal, iii) having more than 18 years of age. As indicated in Table 2, both groups had more ego females, high educational attainment, and the majority lived in urban areas. Urban areas are usually the residence area where most immigrants live since they perceive more job opportunities and fast insertion in the labour market, contributing to more robust social networks helping in their integration (Oliveira, 2021). The CPLC immigrant group was skewed towards Brazilian citizens, with other two immigrants from a Portuguese-speaking African Country (PALOP). A snowball strategy was used, divulging the survey through the author's professional and informal contacts to all immigrants from CPLC countries and to non-migrants.

Table 2. Egos Sociodemographic Characteristics (N = 71)

	Egos (*N* = 71)		CPLC Immigrant Egos (*n* = 18)		
	Immigrants (*n* = 18)	Non-migrants (*n* = 53)	<2 years (*n* = 6)	2-5 years 2-6 (*n* = 8)	>5 years (*n* = 4)
	n (%)	*n* (%)	*n* (%)	*n* (%)	*n* (%)
Gender					
Male	2(11.1)	13(24.5)	1(16.7)	1(12.5)	-
Female	16(88.9)	40(75.5)	5(83.3)	7(87.5)	4(100)
Other	-	-	-	-	-
Age					
<= 25	7(38.9)	34(64.2)	4(66.7)	2(25)	1(25)
26-35	6(33.3)	14(26.4)	1(16.7)	4(50)	1(25)
36-50	3(16.7)	4(7.5)	1(16.7)	1(12.5)	1(25)
>50	2(11.1)	1(1.9)	-	1(12.5)	1(25)
Marital Status					
Single	9(50)	43(81.1)	4(66.7)	3(37.5)	2(50)
Cohabitation	1(5.6)	5(9.4)	-	1(12.5)	-
Married	8(44.4)	5(9.3)	2(33.3)	4(50)	2(50)
Widower	-	-	-	-	-
Divorced/ Separated	-	-	-	-	-
Education					
Basic	1(5.6)	-	-	1(12.5)	-
Secondary	7(38.9)	23(43.4)	4(66.7)	1(12.5)	2(50)
Higher	10(55.6)	30(56.6)	2(33.3)	6(75)	2(50)
Professional Status					
Employed	5(27.8)	15(28.3)	1(16.7)	1(12.5)	3(75)
Student	9(50)	36(67.9)	4(66.7)	4(50)	1(25)
Unemployed	3(16.7)	2(3.8)	1(16.7)	2(25)	-
Inactive	-	-	-	-	-
Retired	1(5.6)	-	-	1(12.5)	-
Residence Area					
Urban	15(83.3)	33(62.3)	5(83.3)	7(87.5)	3(75)
Suburban	2(11.1)	15(28.3)	1(16.7)	1(12.5)	-
Rural	1(5.6)	5(9.4)	-	-	1(25)
CPLC Immigrant					
Brazil	16(88.9)	-	6(100.0)	7(87.5)	3(75.0)
PALOP	2(11.1)	-	-	1(12.5)	1(25.0)

Procedures and Data Collection

This study was approved by the Ethics Committee of the Faculty of

Psychology of Lisbon University and was conducted following the ethical code of the American Psychological Association (APA) (2002; 2010). A convenience sampling strategy was used, with data being collected through the Qualtrics Surveys platform (version 1.2020; Qualtrics, 2005) between July–December 2020. The participants had access to the informed consent to learn about the study's aims and procedures. Detailed information was provided, and the confidentiality and anonymity of their responses were granted. Because data were collected online, we only considered responses coming from unique IP addresses. We also analysed completion time and progress as quality strategies, with only responses with 100% completion progress being included in the analysis (Aust et al., 2013). The information regarding the networks (e.g., alters) was collected using text entry boxes. By doing so, we aimed to facilitate the detection of random answers, spam, or the use of autofill software (Dewitt et al., 2018). No compensation was offered to the participants. The questionnaires took an average of 20 minutes to finish.

Measures

a. Socio-demographic Questionnaire

A self-report questionnaire was used to collect information on the egos' gender, age, marital status, educational attainment, professional status. The questionnaire also collected information about whether egos were CPLC immigrants or non-migrants living in Portugal, and if so, for how long (less than two years, two to five years, more than five years).

b. Egocentric Network Questionnaire

b.1. Name Generators

The egocentric network data was collected using the name generator strategy (Marsden, 2005), with alter names activated for two networks. Specifically, we asked participants to think of the people they recently discussed important matters for the general network. We also asked participants to think of the people they recently discussed health problems with for the specific-health network. Then, participants had to write the name or the first letters of the names of the activated alters (up to 10 alters). The order of the networks was randomized to account for order effects.

b.2. Alters' Attributes

The egos provided alters' attributes for each network through the name interpreter (Marsden, 2005). The following information was collected: alters' age, gender, occupation, educational attainment (primary, secondary, higher), migrant status (CPLC immigrant vs. non-migrant residing in Portugal), relationship type, tie-closeness (five-point Likert scale ranging from 1 "not close" to 5 "extremely close") and face-to-face contact frequency (five-point Likert scale ranging from 1 "never" to 5 "daily"). Additionally, the egos determined alter-alter relationships by answering the following question for both networks: "Think for example about the relationship between (Name 1) and (Name 2) that you elicited before. Would you say that they know each other?" Three answers were possible: yes, no, and don't know.

b.3. Position Generators

Social capital was measured through the position generator instrument; a commonly used social capital instrument, by measuring the alters' status composition (Lin et al., 2001; Schulz et al., 2017). The egos provided for each alter, for both networks, their professional occupation and salary. We ranked the occupations from low-status and low-salary (e.g., housekeeper) to high-status and higher salary (e.g., engineers) and converted the ranking on a five-point Likert scale ranging from 1 "Extremely low social capital" to 5 "Extremely high social capital." Thus, the higher the status, the higher the social capital of ego. By collecting this data from alters, we were able to extract the levels of social capital that egos had access to through their social networks. This instrument allows to capture ties that have social advantages (e.g., higher education, better jobs and salaries) and that may contribute to egos social mobility, by providing resources (e.g., expertise, economic resources) and be a source of social support in stressful times or when their health is compromised (Meanley et al., 2020).

Statistical Analyses

First, we performed descriptive statistics to characterise the egos and the alters. Next, we computed personal network variables using the E-NET software (Borgatti, 2006) to assess the structure of the egos networks. The egos' position in the networks was evaluated using degree centrality (Borgatti et al., 2013). At the same time, the structural holes measures were computed to characterise the pattern of ties among egos' networks (Burt, 1992; Borgatti et al., 2013). Specifically, we collected networks efficiency and constraint. The structural holes measures were in the range of 0 to 1 and are related to each other: networks tend to be more efficient when lower constraints exist.

We assessed the extent of the egos being like their alters on the following categorical attributes: age, educational attainment, and migrant status. In terms of the ego-alter similarity, we computed the EI index (Krackhardt & Stern, 1988) as an inverse measure of homophily. This measure ranges from -1 (complete homogeneity) to 1 (complete heterogeneity). Visual representations of the networks were extracted from the E-NET software. The additional graphs to display descriptive data were computed using ggplot2 (Wickham, 2016) designed for the R environment (R Core Team, 2020).

Results

Descriptive results considering each research question are presented in this section. We summarized the main empirical highlights in Table 3.

Table 3. Main Results: Empirical Highlights

	Main results
CPLC immigrants and non-migrants general and specific networks' structure	- Both groups general networks have higher degree and comprised more non-migrants. - CPCL immigrants specific-health networks comprised more migrants. - CPCL immigrants had a higher degree on general and specific-health networks than non-migrants. - CPLC immigrants both networks were less efficient. - CPLC immigrants had less social capital on both networks.
CPLC immigrants general and specific networks structure across time living in Portugal	- Networks of CPCL immigrants living in Portugal for more than five years comprised fewer family ties. - CPCL immigrants living in Portugal for more than five years had less constrained, and more efficient networks, with more social capital embedded and more bridging ties (non-migrants) as alters.

CPLC Immigrants and Non-migrants General and Specific Networks Structure

Descriptive data on the networks of CPLC immigrants and non-migrants are reported in Table 4.

Table 4. General and Health Networks Alters Characteristics for CPLC Immigrants (n = 18) and Non-Migrants (n = 53)

	General Network		Health-Specific Network	
	Immigrants	Non-migrants	Immigrants	Non-migrants
Composition (*n; %*)				
Gender				
Male	25; 33.3	69; 31.1	18; 33.3	51; 29.5
Female	50; 66.7	151; 68.0	36; 66.7	122; 70.5
Other	-	1; 0.5	-	-
Age (*n; %*)				
<= 25	21; 28.0	88; 39.6	8; 14.8	43; 24.9
26-35	19; 25.3	48; 21.6	28; 51.9	72; 41.6
36-50	18; 24.0	34; 15.3	-	-
>50	16; 21.3	51; 23.0	18; 33.3	54; 31.2
Education (*n; %*)				
Basic	1; 1.3	25; 11.3	1; 1.9	24; 13.9
Secondary	26; 34.7	90; 40.5	15;27.8	60; 34.7
Higher	48; 64.0	107; 48.2	36; 66.7	87; 50.3
Migrant (*n; %*)				
Yes	30; 40.0	7; 3.2	26; 48.1	2; 1.2
No	45; 60.0	210; 94.6	27; 50.0	168; 97.1
Relationship Type (*n; %*)				
Family Members	38; 50.6	101; 45.5	37; 68.6	99; 57.2
Friends	28; 37.3	110; 49.5	13; 24.1	59; 34.1
Co-workers	4; 5.3	4; 1.8	2; 3.7	3; 1.7
Neighbours	-	1; 0.5	-	1; 0.6
Other (e.g., healthcare)	5; 6.7	6; 2.7	2; 3.7	11; 6.4
Structure (*M±SD*)				
Degree	4.50±0.73	4.21±1.07	4.00±1.04	3.59±1.28
Efficiency	0.49±0.22	0.51±0.22	0.49±0.23	0.54±0.24
Constraint	0.62±0.14	0.66±0.18	0.69±0.22	0.74±0.26
Similarity (*M±SD*)				
Gender	-0.15±0.54	-0.17±0.59	-0.04±0.78	-0.17±0.63
Age	0.09±0.55	-0.09±0.56	0.28±0.74	0.35±0.65
Education	-0.08±0.72	-0.14±0.58	-0.04±0.85	-0.07±0.69
Migrant	0.17±0.69	-0.89±0.40	-0.03±0.83	-0.95±0.17
Strength (*M±SD*)				
Closeness	4.24±0.90	4.32±0.74	4.37±0.73	4.24±0.90
Contact Frequency	3.03±1.63	3.65±1.26	3.52±1.68	4.00±1.29
Social Capital (*M±SD*)	2.60±1.35	2.78±1.22	2.67±1.30	2.94±1.34

CPLC immigrants' networks had more qualified alters, while non-migrants alter educational attainment was diverse. However, networks remained similar on this attribute. Regarding age, for CPLC immigrants, age homophily occurred for the health-specific network, while the opposite was verified for general networks (Figure 1).

Figure 1. General and Health Networks Age, School Attainment and Gender Homophily between CPLC Immigrants and Non-Migrants

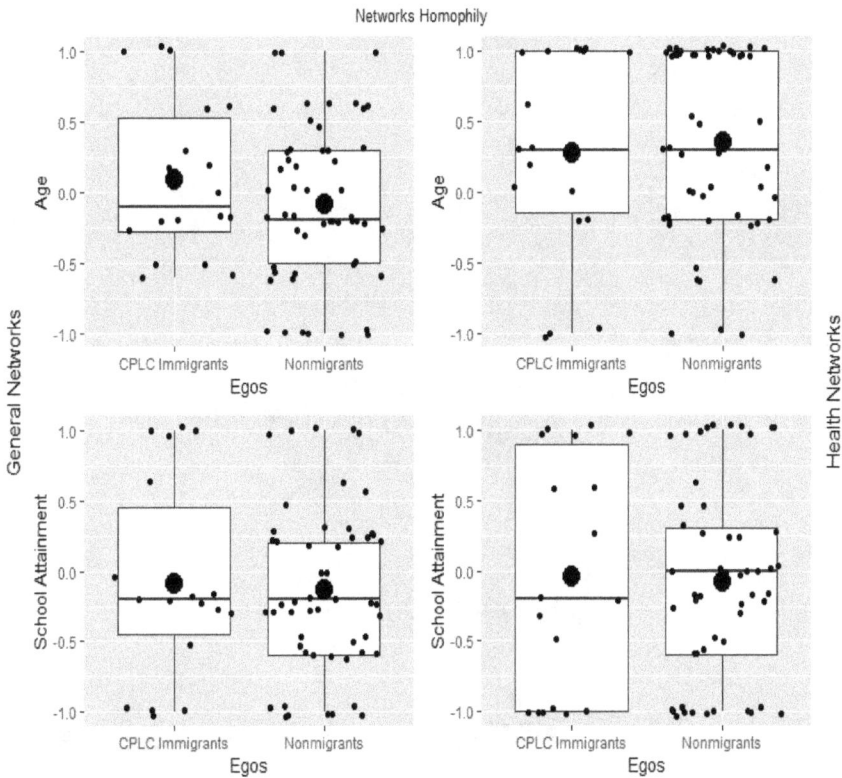

Also, both groups general networks had more non-migrants as alters; but, this trend changed for CPLC immigrants' health networks which, despite dispersion, were reshaped to comprise more migrants (Figure 2). The networks composition pattern was similar: while family alters increased from general to health networks, the relevance of friends followed the opposite direction, particularly for CPLC immigrants. The contact frequency revealed a positive trend for general networks, increasing from never to daily for non-migrants. For CPLC immigrants, a curvilinear trend was depicted, with the contact frequency occurring mostly never or daily.

Figure 2. General and Health Networks Migrant Status Homophily between CPLC Immigrants and Non-Migrants

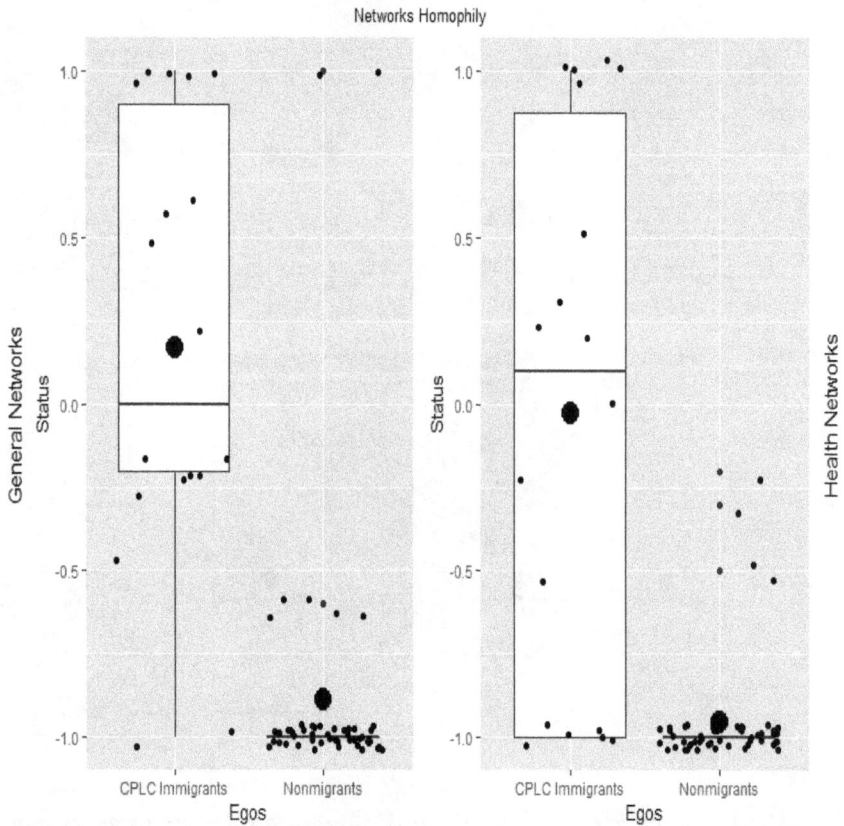

A similar result was found for health networks, but with a percentual decrease among those who never contacted alters and increased weekly and daily contacts (Figure 3)

Figure 3. General and Health Networks Composition and Frequency of Contact between CPLC Immigrants and Non-Migrants

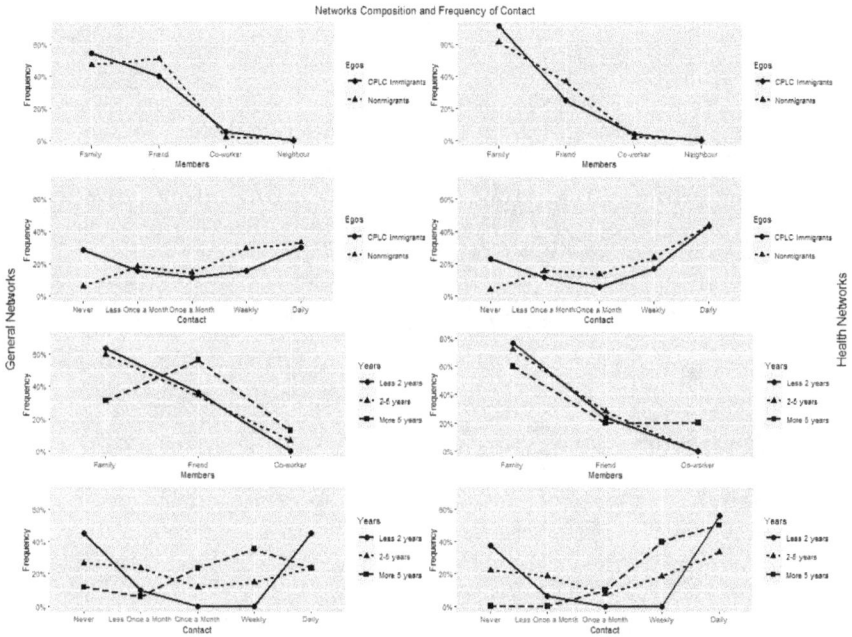

Networks Composition and Frequency of Contact

General and health networks of CPLC immigrants had a higher degree than non-migrant networks: overall, the constraints increased, but the CPLC networks were less efficient than the non-migrants. Also, CPLC immigrants had less social capital on both networks (Figure 4).

Figure 4. General and Health Networks Social Capital between CPLC Immigrants and Non-Migrants

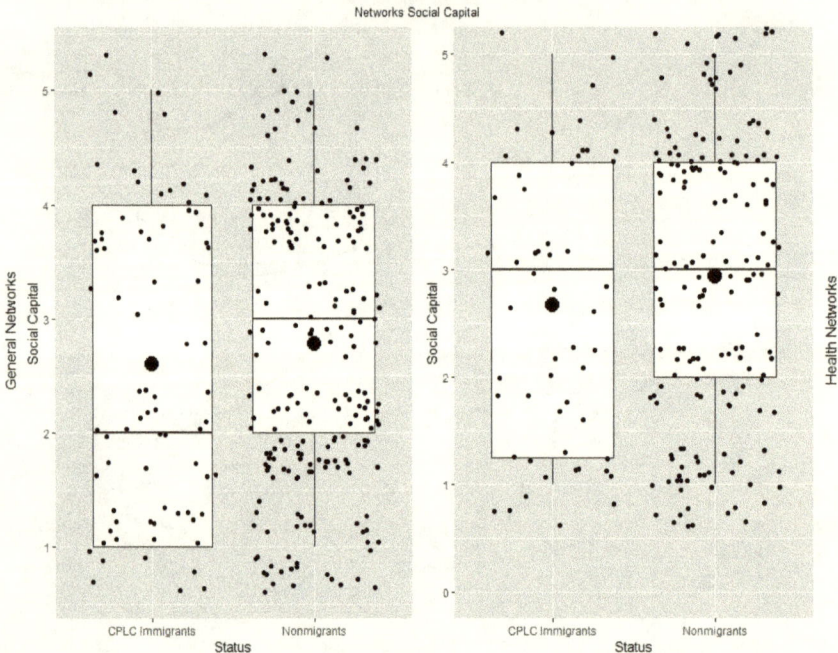

Networks Social Capital

CPLC Immigrants General and Specific Networks Structure across Time Lived in Portugal

Table 5 presents the results depicted for CPLC immigrants. Regarding age, the networks were heterophilic, except for general networks of those living in Portugal for less than five years. Both networks were also homophilic regarding educational attainment but only for CPLC egos living in Portugal for two to five years. CPLC immigrants living in Portugal for more than five years had more non-migrant alters in their networks. In the opposite direction, the health networks of CPLC egos living in Portugal for less than five years had more migrant alters. Family ties were higher for those living in Portugal for less than five years but decreased for egos living in the country for more than five years, particularly for general networks.

Table 5. General and Health Networks Characteristics according to the Time spent by CPLC Immigrants in Portugal (n = 18)

	General Network			Health-Specific Network		
	< 2 years	2-5 years	> 5 years	< 2 years	2-5 years	> 5 years
Composition (*n*; %)						
Gender						
Male	9; 39.1	10; 28.6	6; 35.3	7; 41.2	8; 29.6	3; 30.0
Female	14; 60.9	25; 71.4	11; 64.7	10; 58.8	19; 70.4	7; 70.0
Other	-	-	-			
Age (*n*; %)						
<= 25	12; 52.2	5; 14.3	4; 23.5	5; 29.4	1; 3.7	2; 20.0
26-35	2; 8.7	12; 34.3	5; 29.4	9; 52.9	14; 51.9	5; 50.0
36-50	8; 34.8	5; 14.3	5; 29.4	-	-	-
>50	1; 4.3	13; 37.1	2; 11.8	3; 17.6	12; 44.4	3; 30.0
Education (*n*; %)						
Basic	-	1; 2.9	-	-	1; 3.7	-
Secondary	13; 56.5	7; 20.0	6; 35.3	8; 47.1	5; 18.5	2; 20.0
Higher	10; 43.5	27; 77.1	11; 64.7	9; 52.9	19; 70.4	8; 80.0
Migrant (*n*; %)						
Yes	10; 43.5	16; 45.7	4; 23.5	8; 47.1	15; 55.6	3; 30.0
No	13; 56.5	19; 54.3	13; 76.5	9; 52.9	11; 40.7	7; 70.0
Relationship Type (*n*; %)						
Family	13; 60.8	19; 54.3	5; 29.4	13; 76.5	18; 66.6	6; 60.0
Friends	8; 34.8	11; 31.4	9; 52.9	4; 23.5	7; 25.9	2; 20.0
Co-workers	-	2; 5.7	2; 11.8	-	-	2; 20.0
Neighbours	-	-	-	-	-	-
Other (e.g., healthcare)	1; 4.3	3; 8.6	1; 5.9	-	2; 7.4	-
Structure (*M±SD*)						
Degree	4.40±0.89	4.71±0.49	4.25±0.96	3.75±0.96	4.17±1.17	4.00±1.41
Efficiency	0.39±0.17	0.45±0.21	0.68±0.23	0.34±0.08	0.49±0.20	0.80±0.28
Constraint	0.69±0.16	0.62±0.11	0.53±0.16	0.81±0.15	0.70±0.23	0.42±0.13
Similarity (*M±SD*)						
Gender	0.03±0.65	-0.24±0.53	-0.25±0.40	0.23±0.66	-0.11±0.81	-0.30±0.95
Age	-0.03±0.60	0.26±0.56	-0.08±0.51	0.23±0.76	0.30±0.73	0.30±0.95
Education	0.05±0.79	-0.29±0.76	0.13±0.60	0.02±0.91	-0.14±0.89	0.08±0.90
Migrant	0.18±0.81	-0.04±0.63	0.58±0.57	-0.03±0.93	-0.19±0.76	0.30±0.95
Strength (*M±SD*)						
Closeness	4.52±0.67	4.20±0.83	3.94±1.20	4.47±0.80	4.37±0.69	4.20±0.79
Contact Frequency	2.90±1.97	2.85±1.56	3.53±1.28	3.47±2.04	3.22±1.63	4.40±0.70
Social Capital (*M±SD*)	2.26±1.10	2.77±1.52	2.77±1.52	2.65±1.32	2.56±1.34	3.00±1.25

The curvilinear trend for contact frequency was explained by the CPLC egos living in Portugal for less than two years. Among the egos living in Portugal

101

for at least five years, the contact frequency was higher and more pronounced among the health networks (Figure 3). The structural holes analysis revealed that the networks efficiency increased with the duration of residency: egos living in Portugal for more than five years had less constrained and more efficient networks (Figure 5).

Figure 5. General and Health Networks Degree and Structural Holes among CPLC Immigrants

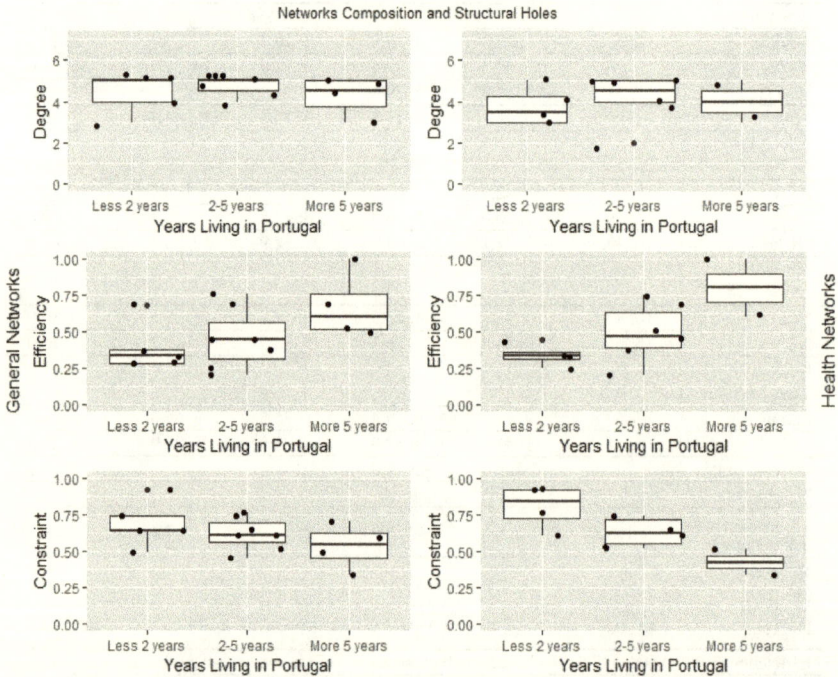

Networks Composition and Structural Holes

Social capital showed a tendency to be higher among this group. Figures 6 and 7 provides an example of high and low-constrained networks, respectively.

Figure 6. Example of General and Health Egocentric Networks with Low Efficiency from a CPLC Immigrant living in Portugal for less than 2 Years

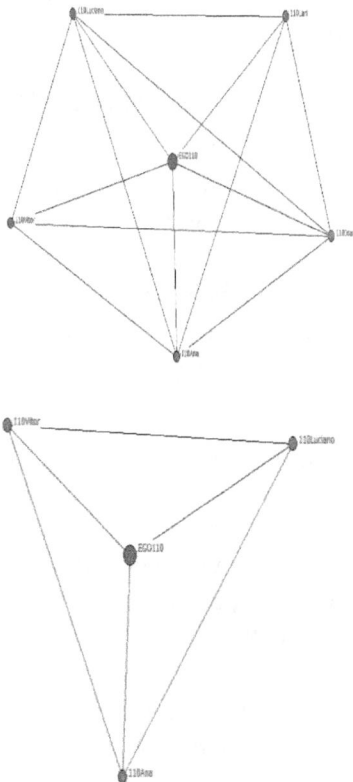

Figure 7. Example of General and Health Egocentric Networks with High Efficiency from a CPLC Immigrant living in Portugal for more than 5 Years

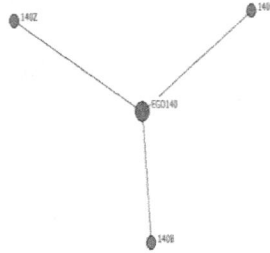

Note. Ego140 presented the same structure for both

Note. Top image (general network). Bottom image (health network).

Discussion

Theoretical and empirical segmentation describes the entanglement between social capital, social networks, and health. This entanglement becomes even more salient in the field of migrations, where despite the recognised role of social networks, the application of this approach is scarce. We intended to contribute to this literature by exploring the interconnections between these concepts and expanding the insufficient knowledge regarding Portugal migration flows by funnelling the attention to CPLC immigrants residing in the country. We started by analysing whether CPLC immigrants and non-migrants' general and specific-health networks capture different ties and how similar are their network structures, to understand better whether egos activate different ties according to the network specificity. Then, by looking at immigrants' length of time in Portugal, we inspected how their networks changed and whether time played a role in different social capital levels. In this section, the results are discussed accordingly.

CPLC Immigrants and Non-Migrants General and Specific-Health Networks

CPLC ego networks had a higher degree, and most alters were non-migrants, particularly those recalled for general networks. As for health networks, an inverse pattern occurred: the networks degree decreased, and alter migrants were recalled. For non-migrants, ties were mainly built with non-migrants. Thus, for CPLC immigrants, the role of bonding ties seems to be more relevant among health networks, while non-migrant ties act as bridging ties in general networks linking egos to resources.

The reason for CPLC immigrants recalling more non-migrant alters and having more degree among general networks may be explained by the role these ties play. The heterogeneity of the ties can broaden the immigrants' opportunities and give them access to relevant information that can be advantageous for multiple needs (e.g., job-seeking; Seibel & van Tubergen, 2013). Because the study sample is skewed to Brazilian egos, our finding resembles the conclusion provided by Roggeveen and Van Meeteren's (2013) qualitative work, highlighting Brazilian immigrants living in Amsterdam are mostly connected with Dutch individuals to mobilise resources better.

However, despite general networks of CPLC immigrants having more bridging alters, their social capital was lower than non-migrants. Non-migrants had more social capital, which increased from general to health networks. However, the same did not happen to CPLC egos, where social capital values remained low and quite similar across networks. Our results depicted a curvilinear contact frequency trend, illustrating that migrants' networks take time to build. This lack of sustained social embeddedness, when compared to non-migrants, can explain CPLC immigrants lower social capital values, as suggested by Arpino and de Valk (2018).

In addition, because non-migrants activated more health professionals' confidants in their networks, which did not happen among CPLC egos, the former seems to mobilise better resources to generate social capital among health networks. Linhas et al. (2019) revealed that about one-third of sampled immigrants do not have an assigned general practitioner in Portugal, suggesting that immigrants have difficulties accessing healthcare resources. The same challenges have also been reported elsewhere (e.g., Raphael, 2014), illustrating inequalities and higher dependency immigrants have on bonding ties. These ties, particularly transnational, may not always be available for the egos as presented by the contact frequency curvilinear trend.

Compared to non-migrants, CPLC immigrants' networks were also less efficient. Even though CPLC immigrants presented networks with higher degree and had more access to bridging ties, particularly among general networks, their networks were less efficient. It appears that non-migrants do not need higher degree networks to mobilise resources, particularly among health networks, even when redundancy and network constraint is high due to bonding ties. Because of the relationship between networks efficiency and constraint, it would be expected that non-migrants, with higher network constraints, presented a decrease in the efficiency of their networks. In the opposite direction, CPLC immigrants with less constrained networks would present more network efficiency. Perhaps, redundancy does not harm all well-established social networks, as those non-migrants have, but impairs the networks still evolving when trying to access more capital and novel resources. In the next section, a closer look at the role of time in networks structures and social capital can reinforce the knowledge on this topic.

CPLC Immigrants General and Specific-Health Networks: Considering Length of Time in Portugal

When network specificity was explored considering time, disentanglement between social capital and the functioning of social networks emerged. CLPC immigrants living in Portugal for more than five years had both networks embedded with non-migrants, particularly among general networks, illustrating the role of bridging ties. However, the same does not hold for those living in Portugal for two to five years, who had more migrants in their general and health networks, and for those living for less than two years, who had more migrants in their health networks. If the health networks result seems interpretable because access to healthcare and specialized healthcare confidants requires surpassing cultural and social barriers (Ledoux et al., 2018), which may only decrease with time, the results for general networks appear inconsistent. CPLC migrants change from general networks comprising more non-migrant bridging ties to slightly starting to incorporate more migrants and returned to having more non-migrants as bridging ties.

Facchini et al. (2015) found a similar U-shape pattern in Germany, where higher probabilities of acquiring non-migrant ties polarised at the extremes. Immigrants who recently arrived at the destination country and those who lived there for longer had higher probabilities of connecting to non-migrants. Variables such as getting into work and having children were positively associated with that probability. However, as this study result shows, despite both groups having more access to bridging non-migrant ties, only those staying at the destination for longer translate those ties into more social capital.

Structural holes revealed a positive trend intersecting those who live in the country for longer and network efficiency and a negative one between time and network constraints, contributing to increases in social capital. Those who live in Portugal for more than five years have more efficient and less constrained networks and can mobilise general and health resources without increasing their networks degree. Also, ties' strength decreased with the length of time in Portugal. At the same time, the contact frequency increased, suggesting the change from networks with more transnational ties, at the arrival, lacking face-to-face interaction, to more local ties and cultural assimilation patterns among those who live in Portugal for longer.

Conclusion, Limitations and Future Research

By adopting a social network approach, this study tackles a limitation on the migration literature and an empirical void in the research regarding CPLC immigrants in Portugal. Our study adds to the literature by illustrating the role of bridging ties instead of bonding because whenever networks have more tie strength, their efficiency and social capital decrease. Without considering time and neglecting how egos activate different ties according to their needs, social capital contributions as a social determinant of health may remain sparse in migrations.

Besides that, this study results go beyond the data usually extracted by qualitative approaches by providing quantitative details on how social networks function. Results reveal different ties are activated for distinct networks, highlighting the need to address health-specific networks, instead of general, when linking social capital, a social determinant of migrants' health, and health outcomes. The present study also discusses the role of bonding and bridging ties in accessing social capital and how bonding ties limit networks efficiency, emphasising the role of bridging ties in social capital. However, network efficiency is only clarified when time at the destination country enters the equation. Thus, by considering time as a relevant variable, the knowledge regarding networks structure expands, contributing to disentangle how social capital is mobilised at different moments in immigrants' lives. These variables and their interconnections should continue to be explored while looking at migrants' networks. Also, interventions should consider the need to be designed by taking into account the role of social networks to boost the resources migrants need at different times.

The current study also presents several limitations. First, the sampling strategy was non-probabilistic and imbalanced regarding egos gender, immigrant status, and immigrants' years spent in Portugal. Collecting social network data is time-consuming and exhausting to the participants, contributing to a reduced number of participants that completed the survey. The study was also conducted during COVID-19, and health networks may have faced additional disruptions than general networks, facing more interpersonal and institutional disruptions. Consequently, egos may have generated fewer health practitioners' alters. Thus, it is not our intention to generalize the results for the population. Also, a broad understanding of social networks requires analysing different immigrant trajectories and comparing distinct CPLC immigrant groups to check if different network patterns emerge.

Further, because the data were cross-sectional, networks were static depictions of relations CPLC immigrants have, which may change and be better understood with a longitudinal design. Finally, data collection occurred during the COVID-19 pandemic, which changed social interactions. Because disruptive events can modify social networks (Perry & Pescosolido, 2012), we do not know how the pandemic impacted the perceptions of the ego on their networks.

Due to the complexity of social interactions, much more work is required to understand what drives migrant choices to develop, sustain and change bonding and bridging ties. However, the clarification of social capital, particularly as a social determinant of health in migrations, requires a network perspective, addressing the specificity of ties activation and the years migrants spent in the destination country.

References

Adedeji, A. (2019). Social capital and migrants' quality of life: A systematic narrative review. *Journal of International Migration and Integration*, *22*, 87–101. https://doi.org/10.1007/s12134-019-00724-6

American Psychological Association (APA). (2002, as Amended 2010). *Ethical principles of psychologists and code of conduct.* Retrieved from: https://www.apa.org/ethics/code/

Arpino, B., & de Valk, H. (2018). Comparing life satisfaction of immigrants and natives across Europe: The role of social contacts. *Social Indicators Research*, *137*, 1163–1184. https://doi.org/10.1007/s11205-017-1629-x

Aust, F., Diedenhofen, B., Ullrich, S., & Musch, J. (2013). Seriousness checks are useful to improve data validity in online research. *Behavior research methods, 45*(2), 527-535. https://doi.org/10.3758/s13428-012-0265-2

Bempong, N., E., Sheath, D., Seybold, J. et al (2019). Critical reflections, challenges and solutions for migrant and refugee health: 2nd M8 Alliance Expert Meeting. *Public Health Review, 40*, 3. https://doi.org/10.1186/s40985-019-0113-3

Berkman, L. F. (1984). Assessing the physical health effects of social networks and social support. *Annual Review of Public Health, 5,* 413-432. https://doi.org/10.1146/annurev.pu.05.050184.002213

Bilecen, B., Gamper, M., & Lubbers, M. J. (2018). The missing link: social network analysis in migration and transnationalism. *Social Networks*, 53, 1-3. https://doi.org/10.1016/j.socnet.2017.07.001

Borgatti, S.P. [Computer software]. (2006). *E-Network software for ego-network analysis.* Analytic Technologies: Lexington, KY.

Borgatti, S. P., Everett, M. G., & Johnson, J. C. (2013). *Analyzing social networks.* London: SAGE.

Burt, R. S. (1992). *Structural holes: The social structure of competition.* Cambridge, Mass: Harvard University Press.

Burt, R. S. (2000). The network structure of social capital. In Sutton, R., & Staw, B. (Eds.) *Research in Organizational Behavior,* 22. Greenwich, CT: JAI press.

Dewitt, J., Capistrant, B., Kohli, N., Rosser, B. S., Mitteldorf, D., Merengwa, E., & West, W. (2018). Addressing participant validity in a small internet health survey (The Restore Study): Protocol and recommendations for survey response validation. *JMIR research protocols, 7*(4), e96. https://doi.org/10.2196/resprot.7655

Facchini, G., Patacchini, E., & Steinhardt, M. (2015). Migration, friendship ties, and cultural assimilation. *Scandinavian Journal of Economics*, *117*(2), 619-649. https://doi.org/10.1111/sjoe.12096

Faist, T. (1998). Transnational social spaces out of international migration: evolution, significance, and future prospects. *European Journal of Sociology, 39*(2), 213-247.

Garip, F. (2012), Discovering diverse mechanisms of migration: The Mexico–US Stream 1970–2000. *Population and Development Review, 38*(3), 393-433. https://doi.org/10.1111/j.1728-4457.2012.00510.x

Goodwin-White, J. (2007), Dispersion or concentration for the 1.5 generation? Destination choices of the children of immigrants in the US. *Population, Space and Place, 13*(5), 313-331. https://doi.org/10.1002/psp.466

Häuberer, J. (2011). Social capital theory: Towards a methodological foundation. Springer VS.

Helliwell, J. F., & Putnam, R. D. (2004). The social context of well-being. *Philosophical transactions of the Royal Society of London. Series B, Biological sciences, 359*(1449), 1435–1446.

https://doi.org/10.1098/rstb.2004.1522

Hyyppä, M. (2010). Healthy ties: Social capital, population health and survival. Springer.

Kim, H. (2014). Immigrant network structure and perceived social capital: A study of the Korean ethnic enclave in Uzbekistan. *Development and Society, 43*(2), 351-379. http://www.jstor.org/ stable/deveandsoci.43.2.351

Kindler M., & Wójcikowska-Baniak K. (2019). (Missing) bridging ties and social capital? The creation and reproduction of migrants' social network advantages: The Case of Ukrainian Migrants in Poland. *Central and Eastern European Migration Review, 8*(1), 95-116. https://doi.org/10.17467/ceemr.2019.02

Kindler, M., Ratcheva, V., & Piechowska, M. (2015). Social networks, social capital and migrant integration at local level. European literature review. *IRiS Working Paper Series, No. 6.* Birmingham: Institute for Research into Superdiversity.

Knoke, D. (1990). Political networks: The Structural Perspective. Cambridge University Press.

Krackhardt, D., & Stern, R.N. (1988). Informal networks and organizational crises: An experimental simulation. *Social Psychology Quarterly, 51*(2), 123–140. https://doi.org/10.2307/2786835

Lecerof, S. S., Stafström, M., Westerling, R., & Östergren, P. O. (2016). Does social capital protect mental health among migrants in Sweden? *Health Promotion International, 31*(3), 644–652. https://doi.org/10.1093/heapro/dav048

Ledoux, C., Pilot, E., Diaz, E., & Krafft, T. (2018). Migrants' access to healthcare services within the European Union: a content analysis of policy documents in Ireland, Portugal and Spain. *Global Health, 14*, 57. https://doi.org/10.1186/s12992-018-0373-6

Levanon, A. (2011). Ethnic social capital: Individual and group level sources and their economic consequences. *Social Science Research, 4*(1), 77-86. https://doi.org/10.1080/10410236.2016.1242032

Levitt, P., & Schiller, N. (2004). Conceptualizing simultaneity: A transnational social field perspective on society. *The International Migration Review, 38*(3), 1002-1039. https://www.jstor.org/ stable/ 27645424

Lin, N. (2001). Social capital: A theory of structure and action. Cambridge University Press.

Lin, N., Fu, Y. C., & Hsung, R. M. (2001). The position generator: Measurement techniques for investigations of social capital. In N. Lin, K. Cook, & R. S. Burt (Eds.), *Social capital: Theory and research* (pp. 57-81). New York: Aldine de Gruyter

Linhas, R., Oliveira, O., Meireles, P., Oliveira, P., de Melo, M. B., Lourenço, J., Ferreira, F., Gaio, R., & Duarte, R. (2019). Immigrants' access to health care: Problems identified in a high-risk tuberculosis population. *Pulmonology, 25*(1), 32–39. https://doi.org/10.1016/j.pulmoe.2018.04.002

Lubbers, M. J., Verdery, A. M., & Molina, J. L. (2020). Social networks and transnational social fields: A review of quantitative and mixed-methods approaches. *International Migration Review, 54*(1), 177–204. https://doi.org/10.1177/0197918318812343

Lubbers, M., Molina, J., Lerner, J., Brandes, U., Ávila, J., & McCarty, C. (2010). Longitudinal analysis of personal networks. The case of Argentinean migrants in Spain. *Social Networks, 32*(1), 91-104.https://doi.org/10.1016/j.socnet.2009.05.001

Marsden, P. (2005). Recent developments in network measurement. In P. J. Carrington, J. Scott, & S. Wasserman (Eds.), *Models and methods in social network analysis* (pp. 8–30). Cambridge, UK: Cambridge University Press.

Massey, D. S., & Aysa-Lastra, M. (2011). Social capital and international migration from Latin America. *International Journal of Population Research,* (834145), 1–18. https://doi.org/10.1155/2011/834145

Massey, D., Arango, J., Hugo, G., Kouaouci, A., Pellegrino, A., & Taylor, J. (1993). Theories of international migration: A review and appraisal. *Population and Development Review, 19*(3), 431-466. https://doi.org/10.2307/2938462

Meanley, S., Biernesser, C., O'Malley, T., Bear, T., & Trauth, J. (2021). Employing Position Generators to Assess Social Capital and Health: A Scoping Review of the Literature and Recommendations in Future Population Health Surveillance. *Journal of Health Disparities Research and Practice, 13*(3), 16-45. https://pubmed.ncbi.nlm.nih.gov/34721948

Mladovsky, P. (2007). *Migrant health in the EU*. Brussels: Commission of the European Communities. Available at: http://mighealth.net/eu/images/3/3b/ Mlad.pdf

Munshi, K. (2020). Social Networks and Migration. *Annual Review of Economics*, 12, 503-524. http://dx.doi.org/10.1146/annurev-economics-082019-031419

Oliveira, C. R. (2021). *Indicadores de Integração de Imigrantes: relatório estatístico anual*. Lisboa: Observatório das Migrações. Retrieved from:
https://www.om.acm.gov.pt/documents/58428/383402/Relat%C3%B3rio+Estat%C3%A Dstico+Anual+2021.pdf/e4dd5643-f282-4cc8-8be1-92aa499bb92f

Padilla, B. (2006). Brazilian migration to Portugal: social networks and ethnic solidarity. *CIES e-Working Papers*. https://repositorio.iscte-iul.pt/handle/10071/175

Perry, B. L., & Pescosolido, B. A. (2010). Functional specificity in discussion networks: The influence of general and problem-specific networks on health outcomes. *Social Networks, 32*(4), 345–357. https://doi.org/10.1016/j.socnet.2010.06.005

Perry, B. L., & Pescosolido, B. A. (2012). Social network dynamics and biographical disruption: The case of "first-timers" with mental illness. *American Journal of Sociology, 118*(1), 134–175. https://doi.org/10.1086/666377

Perry, B. L., Pescosolido, B. A., & Borgatti, S. P. (2018). Egocentric network analysis: Foundations, methods, and models. Cambridge University Press.

Perry, B. L., Pescosolido, B. A., Small, M. L., & McCranie, A. (2020). Introduction to the Special Issue on Ego Networks. *Network Science, 8*(2), 137–141. https://doi.org/10. 1017/nws.2020.18

Pescosolido, B. (2007). Sociology of social networks. In C. D. Bryant and D. L. Peck (eds), *21st Century Sociology: A Reference Book* (pp. 208–217). Sage Publications

Putnam, R. D. (2000). Bowling alone: The collapse and revival of American community. Simon & Schuster, New York, NY.

Putnam, R., & K.A. Goss (2002). Introduction. In R. Putnam (ed.) *Democracies in flux. The evolution of social capital in contemporary society* (1–19). Oxford University Press.

Qualtrics (2005). Qualtrics Labs, Inc. (version 1.2020) [computer software]. Provo, Utah, USA. Retrieved from: https://www.qualtrics.com/1

R Core Team. [Computer software]. (2020). *R: A language and environment for statistical computing.* R Foundation for Statistical Computing, Vienna, Austria. URL https://www.R-project.org/

Raphael, D. (2014). Challenges to promoting health in the modern welfare state: The case of the Nordic nations. *Scandinavian Journal of Public Health, 42*(1), 7–17. https://doi.org/10.1177/1403494813506522.

Roggeveen, S., & Van Meeteren, M. (2013). Beyond community: An analysis of social capital and the social networks of Brazilian migrants in Amsterdam. *Current Sociology, 61*(7), 1078–1096. https://doi.org/10.1177%2F0011392113495862

Sanders, J., Nee, V., & Sernau, S. (2002). Asian immigrants' reliance on social ties in a multiethnic labor market. *Social Forces, 81*(1), 281-314. http://www.jstor.org/stable/3086535

Schulz, B., Horr, A., & Hoenig, K. (2017). *The position generator in the NEPS (NEPS Survey Paper*

No. 23). Bamberg, Germany: Leibniz Institute for Educational Trajectories, National Educational Panel Study.

Scott, W. A., & Scott, R. (1989). International series in experimental social psychology (vol. 18). Adaptation of immigrants: Individual differences and determinants. Pergamon Press.

Seibel, V. & van Tubergen, F. (2013). Job-search methods among non-Western immigrants in the Netherlands. *Journal of Immigrant & Refugee Studies, 11*(3), 241-258. https://doi.org/10.1080/15562948.2013.801727

Sue, C., Riosmena, F., & LePree, J. (2019). The influence of social networks, social capital, and the ethnic community on the U.S. destination choices of Mexican migrant men. *Journal of Ethnic and Migration Studies, 45*(13), 2468-2488. https://doi.org/10.1080/ 1369183X. 2018.1447364

Uslaner, E. M., & Conley, R. S. (2003). Civic Engagement and Particularized Trust: The Ties that Bind People to their Ethnic Communities. *American Politics Research, 31*(4), 331–360. https://doi.org/10.1177/1532673X03031004001

Volker, B. (2020). Social capital across the life course: Accumulation, diminution, or segregation? *Network Science, 8*(3), 313-332. https://doi.org/10.1017/nws.2020.26

Wellman, B. (2000). Partners in illness: who helps when you are sick? In M. Kelner, B. Wellman, B. A. Pescosolido and M. Saks (Eds.), *Complementary and Alternative Medicine: Challenge and Change* (pp. 143-162). Harwood Academic Publishers.

Wellman, B., & Frank, K. (2001). Network capital in a multilevel world: Getting support from personal communities. In N. Lin, K. Cook and R.S. Burt (Eds.), *Social Capital: Theory and Research* (pp. 233-273). Aldine de Gruyter.

Wickham, H. (2016). *ggplot2: Elegant graphics for data analysis.* Springer-Verlag New York.

Zhu, W., Li, H., Xia, H., Wang, X., & Mao, C. (2019). Inequalities in Structural Social Capital and Health between Migrant and Local Hypertensive Patients. *Annals of Global Health, 85*(1), 48. http://doi.org/10.5334/aogh.2398

"WE'RE CONSTANTLY FIGHTING FOR THAT OPPORTUNITY":

A QUALITATIVE STUDY OF ACCESS BARRIERS TO SEXUAL AND REPRODUCTIVE HEALTH FOR HISPANIC IMMIGRANT WOMEN IN THE UNITED STATES

Jessica Merone[1], Rossella De Falco[2], Paola Degani[3]

Introduction

Immigrant women in the United States (US) face overlapping difficulties when accessing sexual and reproductive health (SRH) services (Althoff, et al., 2017; Center for Reproductive Rights, 2014; Hasstedt, Desai, & Ansari-Thomas, 2018; Jain, LaHote, Samari, & Garbers, 2022; National Women's Law Center (NWLC), 2017; Smith & LeVoy, 2016; Alarcão, et al., 2019). This is due to several factors, such as difficulties in navigating immigration healthcare policies, language difficulties, gender, socioeconomic inequalities, and cultural barriers (Hasstedt, Desai, & Ansari-Thomas, 2018). Due to the feminisation of migration, female immigrants are considered "a formidable presence" in the US and have slightly surpassed the total number of male immigrants (American Immigration Council, 2020). Although immigrant women – including naturalised US citizens, lawful permanent residents (LPR), and undocumented immigrants – represent a substantial portion of the US immigration population, they are considered more vulnerable than men and continue to suffer from various human rights violations (Kawar, 2004). These human rights violations include lack of access to comprehensive and affordable healthcare, in particular SRH services (Hasstedt, Desai, & Ansari-Thomas, 2018). Sexual and reproductive health and rights (SRHR) encompass universal access to a wide range of reproductive health services,

[1] Jessica Merone, Human Rights Centre 'A. Papisca', University of Padova, Italy.
[2] Rossella De Falco, Human Rights Centre 'A. Papisca', University of Padova, Italy.
[3] Paola Degani, Department of Political Science, Law, and International Studies, University of Padova, Italy.
Acknowledgements: The authors thank the participants who kindly agreed to be interviewed and Guadalupe Mendez and Kimberly Quintero, who acted as cultural and linguistic translators for the interviews conducted with undocumented immigrant women. Guadalupe Mendez is a student at the Cabrini University, studying Political Science and Kimberly Quintero has her Master of Science in Global Affairs from New York University.
Funding: This research did not receive any specific grant from funding agencies in the public, commercial, or not-for-profit sectors.
Declaration of Competing Interests: The authors declare that they have no known competing financial interests or personal relationships that could have appeared to influence the work reported in this paper.

including family planning, safe pregnancy and delivery services, abortion where legal, prevention and treatment of sexually transmitted infections, information and counselling on sexuality, and elimination of harmful practises against women (such as female genital mutilation/cutting and forced marriage) (Alarcão, et al., 2019).

Despite the centrality of SRH in the context of human rights, Hispanic immigrant women in the US continue to experience healthcare inequalities. A large amount of literature has demonstrated the significant barriers undocumented immigrant women face in accessing SRH, but little has explored the needs, uses of services, and outcomes among different groups of women (Alarcão, Stefanovska-Petkovska, Virgolino, Santos, & Costa, 2021; Funge, Boye, Johnsen, & Nørredam, 2020; Hasstedt, Desai, & Ansari-Thomas, 2018; López-Domene, et al., 2019; Swartz, Hainmueller, Lawrence, & Rodriguez, 2017; Wolff, et al., 2008). Therefore, to help to reduce the gap in the literature, this research study aims to explore how Hispanic immigrant women in Philadelphia, Pennsylvania (US), with various immigration status, access and utilise SRH services and describe the barriers they face.

The article is structured as follows: first, we define the terminology and the context of our study; second, we present the theoretical and analytical framework; lastly, we ground our analysis on intersectionality theory and international human rights law. We analyse SRH as an essential component of the universal right to the highest attainable standard of physical and mental health, enriched in the Universal Declaration of Human Right and in other international human rights conventions, declarations, and agreements (United States Census Bureau, 2019). We then discuss inequalities in accessing healthcare as potentially deriving from structural discrimination for immigrant women, linking the discussion to the US context. After presenting the methodology used to conduct the study, we present the results through thematic analysis undertaken through the software NVivo. The thematic analysis also includes the policy recommendations made by women based on their lived experiences of barriers in accessing their right to SRH.

Context and Terminology

The term immigrant is generally referred to people who leave their country of origin to settle or reside in another country, usually as permanent residents (US Immigration: An Online Software Company, 2021). In 2018, census data estimated that 44.8 million people who were born in another country were living in the US (Budiman, 2020). Most of these immigrants are in the country legally, where 45% are naturalised US citizens, 27% are LPRs, and 5% are temporary residents. An estimated 14% of the immigration population is undocumented (Budiman, 2020). Assuming current immigrant trends continue to move forward, immigrants and their descendants - first- and second-generation immigrants – are predicted to account of 88% of the overall population growth in the US through 2065 (United States Census Bureau, 2019). Hispanic immigrants are estimated to account for 31% of all immigrants arriving in 2065 in the US (Budiman, 2020). Since immigrant women represent half of these numbers as described previously, addressing the healthcare needs of immigrant Hispanic women in the US is not an academic and political process that affects a small number of people (Schenker, Castañeda, & Rodriguez-Lainz, 2014).

Therefore, this study focuses on immigrant Hispanic women with various types of immigration statuses (United States Census Bureau, 2019). The definition of each status and other key terminology are explained below (Table 1).

Table 1. Terminology

Generational status	First-generation refers to those who are foreign born. Second generation refers to those born in the US with at least one foreign parent.
Lawful Permanent Resident (LPR)	Non-citizens who are lawfully authorised to live permanently within the US; also known as "green-card holders".
Lawfully present immigrants	An individual who is considered a "qualified" immigrant or is not a citizen but have long-term permission to live and/or work in the US; examples LPRs, asylees, refugees.
Naturalized citizens	LPRs who have become US citizens through the naturalisation process.
Undocumented immigrants	Foreign-born non-US citizens residing in the country who are not "lawfully immigrants".

Sources: (Fortuny & Chaudry, 2011; Freedom for Immigrants, 2018; Passel & Cohn, 2018; United States Census Bureau, 2019)

Immigrants Eligibility for Healthcare Insurance in US

The US healthcare system is often referred to as a private-public hybrid system (Gerisch, 2018). The most common way of receiving health insurance in the US is through employer-based insurance (Ku & Jewers, 2013). Another form of receiving healthcare insurance is through federal and state programmes, such as Medicaid for low-income individuals and Children's Health Insurance Programme (CHIP) for low-income children in families with household incomes too high for Medicaid (Ku & Jewers, 2013). Then there is a group of individuals who either buy their own health insurance or are uninsured. For immigrants and their families, their immigration status and citizenship affect their access to health insurance and coverage.

Before 1996, lawfully present immigrants were eligible for public benefits based on the same terms as citizens (Fortuny & Chaudry, 2011). However, the Personal Responsibility and Work Opportunity Reconciliation Act (PRWORA) of 1996 significantly transformed the US welfare system, and welfare was no longer seen as an entitlement to individuals. Title IV of PROWRA specifically makes it difficult for immigrants to access welfare, stating that "self-sufficiency has been a basic principle of United States Immigration law since this country's earliest immigration statues" (Personal Responsibility and Work Opportunity Reconciliation Act, 1996). It further reads the eligibility rules are to assure "that individual aliens do not burden the public benefits system".

Immigrants who become citizens through the naturalisation process can access welfare and public benefits on similar terms as US born citizens (Fix, Capps, & Kaushal, 2009).

Lawfully present immigrants who have entered the country after 1966 are eligible to apply for Medicaid and CHIP. They must meet the eligibility restrictions under PRWORA, which include the qualified immigrant status and the five-year bar (National Conference of State Legislatures (NCSL), 2017). The "qualified" immigration status includes LPRs, refugees, asylees, and persons in various other immigration status (Fortuny & Chaudry, 2011). The five-year bar states that lawfully present immigrants must wait five years after obtaining their qualified status to enrol in federal means-tested benefits. In 2009, the Children's Health Insurance Programme Reauthorisation Act (CHIPRA) gave states the option to cover lawfully present children and pregnant women under Medicaid and CHIP during the first five years (Wherry, Fabi, Schickedanz, & Saloner, 2017).

In 2010, The Patient Protection and Affordable Care Act (PPACA) established the Health Insurance Marketplace that offers various types of health insurance plans (Entitled The Patient Protection and Affordable Care Act, 2010). ACA expanded the category of immigrants that are eligible for health insurance programmes by using the standard of "lawfully present" for eligibility.

Undocumented immigrants are systematically excluded from enrolling in federal health insurance programmes, including Medicaid, Medicare, the ACA Marketplaces, and CHIP. Therefore, undocumented immigrants in the

US have few options to obtaining health insurance coverage. Some undocumented immigrants are able to access employer-sponsored health insurance. However, evidence has shown undocumented immigrants are less likely to be offered employer-based insurance because they are often employed in low-wage industries (i.e., agriculture and construction) that most often do not offer health benefits (Artiga & Diaz, 2019). Another option is receiving health coverage through a spouse or a dependent who has employer-provided health plan. Additionally, undocumented immigrants are able to purchase private health insurance outside of the ACA Marketplace, since citizenship or a lawfully present status are not required for private insurance eligibility. But due to limited incomes and lack of ability to apply for subsidies, many are unable to afford the coverage (Fortuny & Chaudry, 2011).

The most common way undocumented immigrants are able to receive healthcare is through community health centres and emergency rooms (The Congress of the United States, 2007). The Emergency Medical Treatment and Labour Act (EMTALA) enacted by Congress in 1986 requires Medicare-participating hospitals with emergency departments to provide emergency care and active labour in a non-discriminatory manner, regardless of immigration status (Beck, Le, Henry-Okafor, & Shah, 2019). In some states, women have the option in receiving prenatal care regardless of their immigration status and health programmes are offered to undocumented children (Wherry, Fabi, Schickedanz, & Saloner, 2017).

The Right to Health under International Law and the US Law

Having discussed migration health policies at the domestic level in the US, we now introduce the notion of sexual and reproductive health and rights (SRHR) as social entitlements under international human rights law, highlighting implications for the US. SRHR are an essential component of the right to health. Enshrined by Article 12 of the International Covenant on Economic, Social, and Cultural Rights (ICESCR) (2000) the right to health obliges states to progressively diminish health inequalities, protect individuals from medical debt, and eliminate barriers in accessing healthcare. Under international human rights law, everyone is entitled to timely, affordable, accessible and high-quality healthcare, as well as the underlying determinants of health (Hunt, 2016). The right to health is also warranted by several other treaties, including the Convention on the Rights of the Child (CRC), the Convention on the Elimination of All Forms of Discrimination Against Women (CEDAW), and Art. 25 of the Convention on the Rights of Persons with Disabilities (CRPD).

First notions of SRH emerged in 1994, in the context of the Cairo Programme of Action adopted at International Conference on Population and Development (ICPD) which, at section 7.2, underlines that individuals are entitled to a 'satisfying and safe sex life and that they have the capability to reproduce and the freedom to decide if, when and how often to do so'; that everyone has a right to 'decide freely and responsibly the number, spacing and timing of their children and to have the information and means to do so'; that sexual health is 'a state of physical, emotional, mental, and social well-being' (United Nations Population Fund, 2004).

The US is also bound to respect the right to health under international law (Yamin, 2005). The US is a State party of the International Convention in the Elimination of all Forms of Racial Discrimination (ICERD) (1966), and it is thus obliged to eliminate racial disparities in public health and healthcare, providing equal access to healthcare for all, including all immigrants. In particular, the US government is obliged by ICERD Article 14 'to prohibit and to eliminate racial discrimination in all its forms and to guarantee the right of everyone, without distinction as to race, colour, or national or ethnic origin, to equality before the law, notably in the enjoyment of (….) the rights to public health, medical care, social security, and social services'. The US is obliged to both sanction discrimination and to proactively eradicate racial discrimination in health. The US has signed, even if not ratified, the ICESCR, the CRC, and the CEDAW. The federal government is thus bound not to contravene the object or purpose of these international conventions. At the domestic level, Title VI of the Civil Rights Act (1964) also prohibits discrimination in all healthcare activities funded by the federal government.

It is true that the US has historically been reluctant to conform domestic legislation to international human rights norms (Yamin, 2005). For instance, the US is the only country in the industrialised world not providing a plan for universal healthcare coverage as well as not showing any legal recognition of the right to care. However, discrete aspects of health are already framed in terms of judicially protected right, such as for the EMTALA and the protection of women in labour. Likewise, federal courts have been ensuring that treatments in psychiatric hospitals comply with constitutional standards (Wyatt v. Stickney, 1972), while some states have also been drafting affirmative obligations to provide services to underserved populations (Health Facilities v. Axelrod, 1991).

Concerningly, the Committee on the Elimination of Racial Discrimination

(CERD) (2008) blamed the US for the 'wide racial disparities continue to exist in the field of SRH and for failing to actively combat racial discrimination in reproductive healthcare'. These calls have been renewed in CERD's (2014) Concluding Observations, where CERD reiterated "previous concern at the persistence of racial disparities in the field of SRH, particularly about the high maternal and infant mortality rates among African American communities", while urging the US to "eliminate racial disparities in the field of SRH". CERD (2014) also called on the US to "take concrete measures to ensure that all individuals, in particular (…) undocumented immigrants and immigrants and their families who have been residing lawfully in the United States for less than five years, have effective access to affordable and adequate health-care services (…)".

Conceptual Framework: Intersectionality and Human Rights

This article uses intersectionality as a theoretical framework. Intersectionality has recently been acknowledged as a transformative theoretical framework in analysing social inequality and discrimination in healthcare, especially in the context of marginalised groups (Hankivsky, 2012). Intersectionality theory was first conceptualised by Kimberly Crenshaw, who argued that the US legal definition of discrimination was monistic and viewed sex and gender has mutually exclusive categories (Crenshaw, 1989). While intersectionality theory was originally developed to examine discrimination based on the "intersection" of race and gender in Black women in the US, other groups of people took their own identities and discussed how they too were "impacted by a multiped of social justice and human rights issues" (Coaston, 2019). Social identities such as gender, race, ethnicity, disability, sexuality, class and nationality have enhanced the complexity of intersectionality there and demonstrated the transition of identities (Knudsen, 2006). Therefore, intersectionality has been drawn upon to more effectively articulate injustices and advocate for positive social change in contemporary marginalised groups of people (Hankivsky & Jordan-Zachery, 2019). The movement of intersectionality has not been limited to research within the US but has moved into global spheres, such as in Europe and human rights international discourses (Yuval-Davis, 2006; Knudsen, 2006; Lutz, Herrera Vivar, & Supik, 2011). In fact, various UN human rights treaty bodies have been increasingly applying intersectionality in their monitoring practices, exposing how different grounds of discrimination have created multiple forms of disadvantage (Sekalala, et al., 2021). In her article Yuval-Davis (2006), specifically explores intersectionality in contemporary public international discourse. The author underscores how the UN CERD Committee (2000) adopted General Recommendation 25 on the gender-related dimensions of racial discrimination, which recognises "that certain groups of women, in addition to suffering from discrimination directed against them as women, may also suffer from multiple forms of discrimination based on additional grounds such as race, ethnic, or religious identity, disability, age, class, caste or other factors".

Connected to the concept of intersectionality is power, specifically to the mechanisms of exclusion and inclusion (Knudsen, 2006). Intersectionality is used to analyse the production of power and processes between different social locations and is involved in examined the different social and cultural hierarchies that are thus created in different discourses and institution (Knudsen, 2006; Lykke, 2010). Therefore, intersectionality investigates how the minority cultural becomes "the other" in and normative setting, thus being viewed as "troublesome" and being marginalized by the majority cultural (Knudsen, 2006).

Intersectionality is particularly appropriate in investigating the social determinants of health as it recognises that individual experiences are influenced by multiple social characteristics that overlap and intersect. Furthermore, intersectionality assumes that individual social identities intersect with inequalities at the structural level, while also emphasising the necessity of exploring the lived experiences of oppressed groups. Coherently, intersectionality theory is used in this study to both explore and explain how gender, language, socioeconomic status, and health status interact to create unique experiences of marginalisation and oppression in interviewed immigrant women in the context of access to SRH services.

From an analytical point of view, this article also understands SRH services as a social right under international law. Conceiving healthcare and its determinants as a right, transforms inequality in accessing care from matters of medical quality to issues of social justice (Yamin, 2005), and health policies become driven by legal obligations rather than charity or political will. The right to health framework builds on social epidemiology (Bambra, et al., 2010), implicitly suggesting that determinants of health or ill-health are not solely biological or natural, but also dependent upon laws, policies, social relations, and inequalities. By grounding intersectionality theory in international human rights law, it is possible to analyse the systemic failures of the US healthcare system in fulfilling equitable access to healthcare for all immigrant women.

Materials and Methods

In 2016, the latest census data available for this article demonstrated that an estimated number of 390,000 residents in Philadelphia were either immigrants or US natives with immigrant parents (Ginsberg, 2018). According to research conducted by Pew Research Centre (a nonpartisan American Think Tank) more undocumented immigrants live in Philadelphia than in any of the largest Northeast American cities, in addition to New York City (Kopp, 2017).

Figure 1. Foreign-born Population: Share of total population (%) in US states

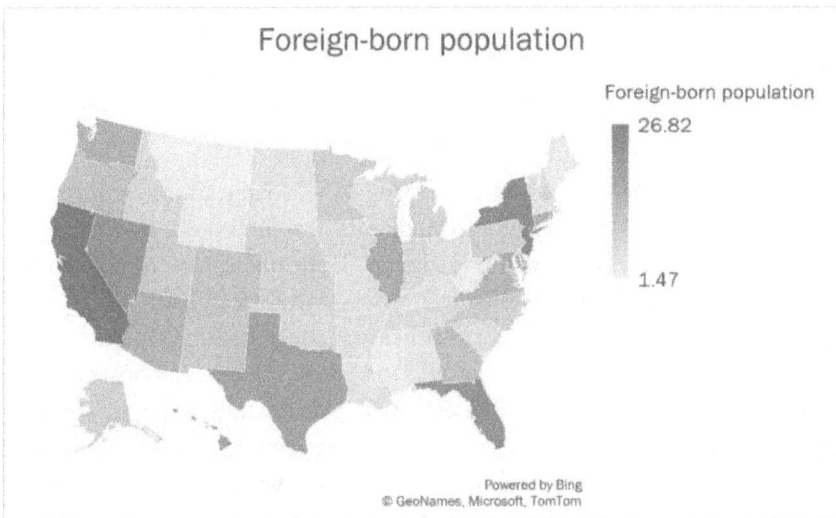

Source: Own elaboration, data available at:
https://www.pewresearch.org/hispanic/2020/08/20/facts-on-u-s-immigrants-current-data/

An exploratory qualitative study[4] was conducted through semi-structured narrative interviews of 18 Hispanic women with various immigration statuses, including first- and second-generation immigrants, LPRs, naturalised citizens, and undocumented immigrants (Table 2).

Snowball sampling was employed, with multiple strategies to recruit participants. Eligibility criteria were for participants to identify themselves as Hispanic immigrants, speak Spanish or English, be between the ages of 18 and 55 years old, and have accessed SRH services in the Philadelphia area.

---

[4] The ethical approval for this study was obtained from the Ethical Review Board of Cabrini University (EXT20-01). Cabrini University is a Catholic, liberal-arts university located in Radnor, Pennsylvania (US) and dedicated to academic excellence, leadership development, and a commitment to social justice.

Through the collaboration of community healthcare centres, undocumented immigrant women who met the eligibility criteria were identified and then telephoned to provide additional information of the study, including the benefits and risks of participation. Other participants in the study were then identified through chain-referral. It is important to note that despite the numbers of interviews (18) were limited and not statistically representing the different categories of group of women by their legal status, the analysis of this study is nevertheless useful to highlight the important issues and to detect further research paths needed.

Once a participant gave permission to be part of the study, written information regarding the study's objectives, confidentiality, and recordings of the interviews were emailed or messaged to them in their preferred language. Due to the COVID-19 pandemic, all interviews were only conducted online between June and August 2020 and lasted between 30 to 60 minutes.

Two community members self-identifying as Hispanic immigrant women served as translators and cultural mediators for interviews conducted in Spanish and the recruitment of participants. Both translators completed the online Tri-Council Policy Statement 2: Course on Research Ethics TCPS 2: CORE[5]. Interviews were conducted either in Spanish or English. Prior to the interviews, participants were asked for oral informed consent. The participants' names and other identifying information were omitted to protect their confidentiality. Due to fear of being deported and being known by authorities, many identifying information were not answered by undocumented migrant women, such as education level and employment status. Consequently, in the Table 2. certain identifying information of irregular migrant women are listed as "unassign". All interviews were fully transcribed and then thematically coded using the qualitative analysis software NVivo.

---

[5] Course on Research Ethics (TCPS: CORE) is an online tutorial that provides an in-depth review of issues relating to the conduct of safe and ethical research with humans. For more information refer to the original webpage: http://tcps2core.ca/welcome.

Table 2. Characteristics of Participants

	Age	Immigration Status	Place of Birth	Language	Education Level	Employ Status
1	22	Native Born	Mexico	English	Tertiary	Working Student
2	22	Native Born	Mexico	English	Tertiary	Student
3	19	Native Born	Ecuador	English	Tertiary	Student
4	19	LPR	Dominican Republic	English	Tertiary	Student
5	50	Naturalised Citizen	Colombia	English	Unassign	Employed
6	55	Naturalised Citizen	Colombia	English	Unassign	Employed
7	28	Naturalised Citizen	Mexico	English	Tertiary	Employed
8	30	Naturalised Citizen	Ecuador	English	Tertiary	Employed
9	46	Undocumented	Mexico	Spanish	Unassign	Unassign
10	36	Undocumented	Mexico	Spanish	Unassign	Unassign
11	34	Undocumented	Mexico	Spanish	Unassign	Unassign
12	50	Undocumented	Mexico	Spanish	Unassign	Unassign
13	37	Undocumented	Guatemala	Spanish	Unassign	Unassign
14	24	Undocumented	Honduras	Spanish	Unassign	Unassign
15	25	Undocumented	Guatemala	Spanish	Unassign	Unassign
16	36	Undocumented	Mexico	Spanish	Unassign	Unassign
17	29	Undocumented	Guatemala	Spanish	Unassign	Unassign
18	36	Undocumented	Mexico	Spanish	Unassign	Unassign

Results

All the participants presented barriers in accessing healthcare, suggesting interconnected and mutually reinforcing sources of marginalisation.

The four main themes that emerged are: i) historical cultural beliefs, practises and languages; ii) fear, stigma, and negative self-perception; iii) the positive role of community and social services; and iv) influence of socioeconomic status.

Historical cultural beliefs, practises, and language

All women identified themselves as Hispanic, with family origins from Central or South America. The undocumented immigrant women stated that their primary language was Spanish, while the other participants spoke both Spanish and English.

Several women compared their experiences in accessing SRH services with past experiences in their country of origin. One undocumented migrant woman, for instance, recounted her experience in refusing to change her intra-uterine device because she was unable to receive the same treatment as in Mexico:

> *I have a, a, contraceptive method that is this, it is a device, made of metal, so I asked the doctor to change it, and she told me, she told me that I had one that was going to be that I would not have menstruation. But I told him no, that I wanted him to use the same method that I have (translation of Participant 10).*

Another common theme was the delay in seeking healthcare treatment due to negative opinions towards the US healthcare system. A native-born immigrant woman with undocumented immigrant parents stated:

> *I was taught that the doctors don't do anything. They just, they are not going to give anything, you are going to go and tell them your problems, but you are just going to leave like the same (Participant 1).*

Likewise, an immigrant woman with LPR status additionally stated that, despite thinking that heath care in the US was more advanced than in her home country, she still had adverse feelings in seeking healthcare:

> *I feel like in this country it is way better than in my country in terms of resources, but at the same time, it's like you go to the emergency room and all they give you is Tylenol. It is not worth it (Participant 4).*

Moreover, many of the women expressed their preference in using natural herbs as alternative healthcare methods, rather than seeking aid through conventional medicine. A woman born in the US with undocumented parents stated that: "Where my parents are from in Mexico, it's very rural. They still believe in curanderos, like in medicine people (…) the ones that take care of them more than like doctors" (Participant 1). She further said that "I also believe in the natural remedies, and like, you can wait it out".

Other women identified as first- and second- generation immigrant additionally stated that, while they believed that healthcare was more advanced in the US, they more often used natural medicines from their countries of origin:

> *I take medication and I also do like, this thing my mom has, like, from Ecuador that she knows can help. At times it does help, but it's like a mix of both (Participant 3).*

> *I only take medication when it's extremely necessary. We don't take medicine for everything in our culture. A lot of times when I am sick, it's always natural remedies (Participant 4).*

Natural remedies included taking hot showers to "sweat out the toxins", drinking herbal teas, and performing certain practices such as "praying to the water":

Yeah, like hot showers like really, really as hot as you can take them with like, herbal tea, like, kind of like the like, kind of make the bathroom feel like a sauna. Like, the toxin you have, like you'll sweat out. They'll do like rosemary tea and like, oregano (Participant 1).

So, we were part of a very, very, very small town in Mexico, where people are very superstitious and people, you know, believe in something like praying to the water (....) I mean, here's some tea, I might put some, some baking soda in the new tea and some lemon and maybe some baking soda, you should be good to go (Participant 7).

Lastly, language constituted a severe access barrier for women coming to the US and seeking care for the first time:

When I came, I didn't know what to say. When I came to the United States, not a lot of people spoke Spanish, they were not either hospitals or medical centres that spoke Spanish (Participant 5).

I couldn't understand what the doctors they were saying as soon as I came here. My mom was taking us to the doctor. Her English is broken. When I was 18, I was able to talk to the doctors. I learned English (Participant 8).

The only time I've had a translator [at the hospital] was only when they did the biopsy. But after, I don't have translators. So, I have to go back to ask my doctor [at the community clinic] to explain to me (translation from Participant 18).

Fear, stigma, and negative self-perception

When seeking SRH services for the first time, a US Born women described herself as a "villain".

I grew up and became a villain, I know I needed to get the services (Participant 2).

When asked further why she described herself as a "villain", she further explained that she felt "like a burden on the government and family".

Other women described feelings of mistrust and fear when seeking healthcare:

It is uncomfortable because you are not sure that they will provide you with medical services (translation of Participant 9).

We have kind of been forgotten. We are afraid of asking because we don't want to be deported (Participate 7).

This fear and embarrassment were also seen during the beginning of the interviews, where some women were self-conscious in speaking about certain services they had received. Once the women gained confidence and trust in the research team, they were more open to share their experiences and difficulties. Another common theme that emerged was the fear of being stigmatised when seeking SRH services:

> *I had to find access by myself, and I was really young, like embarrassed to access those types of services (Participant 2).*

Many of the women who reported feeling shamed or embarrassed in seeking SRH services associated it to widespread taboos found in their culture of origin:

> *I think for women, like women needs, like birth control and seeing a gynecologist is very taboo, like you can't talk about that kind of stuff. I feel like that kind of made it difficult, like I don't really ask for help. I kinda just have to figure it out on my own. My mom never really had any experience with birth control we just don't talk about that kind of stuff (Participant 3).*

When discussing the theme of culture, some of the women additionally commented on the traditional social role of women in their culture, and the influence this had in accessing and discussing women's health.

> *Especially for women, not only immigrant, in Latin America countries, women are not viewed at the same way of men, there is a sense of machismo, women are not encouraged or empowered to make decisions for healthcare, women should take care of the house, if you a women they will be like no we have been told not to do that, they are not self-efficient, there is a cultural thing, difference men and women (Participant 7).*

> *It's kind of embarrassing for the mother in front of the child. And for the child in front of the mother too (Participant 6).*

Lastly, other sentiments of mistrust included the fear of being deported when seeking healthcare:

> *When you are an immigrant, you might be afraid of speaking the language and you might be afraid to be deported, or you might be afraid to be incarcerated, you might be afraid to die (Participant 6).*

The role of community and social support services

Faith-based organisations, social workers, and community members all played a fundamental positive role in unlocking access to healthcare, especially in regard to navigating the healthcare system and accessing information. For example, one undocumented immigrant women

(Participant 11) stated that she received information through her church of available healthcare centres in her community.

All the women reported that social workers played a key role in their access to healthcare, especially for undocumented immigrant women. For instance, two undocumented women described that after giving birth, a social worker at the hospital provided her information of a program that would cover the cost of her labour. She further stated that the social worker assisted her in filling out and submitting the application.

> *So, a social worker helped me, and I was able to obtain a, um, like an insurance, a temporary insurance, just to pay for the, um, for the maternity (translation of Participant 11).*

> *The doctor at the clinic helped me get the "baby insurance", so I did not have to pay at the birth at the hospital (translation of Participant 14).*

Participant 2 additionally declared that she was able to find a gynaecologist for the first time at age 13 due to information provided by a social worker.

Social workers were fundamental in overcoming barriers, especially language, embarrassment, and lack of information. Many of the women recounted moments when social workers helped them overcome the financial barriers they experienced:

> *I remember that when I went to the hospital, they tried to charge me a lot of money. I called an agency, like a social worker in the hospital, a Hispanic social worker, she told me like call this number and tell them that you can't pay your hospital bill. Because you're under-age. You don't have a job and the family doesn't have to take care of the bill for you (Participant 4).*

Finally, participants also described how community healthcare centres specifically aimed at assisting immigrants were crucial in filling in access gaps:

> *The clinic I go to is diverse. There's a good amount of people who speak Spanish. There's been a lot of people who speak other like Asian languages, for example, Indonesia and Malaysia (Participant 1).*

Many of the women expressed their preference in accessing health at centres that free or low-cost healthcare:

> *So, then we went to Planned Parenthood. It wasn't like super cheap, but like cheaper than most places and we could do all the check-ups and they care much about health (Participant 7).*

> *When I started going with a private doctor, I had to pay for each consultation, my medicine, the tests and I brought money that I save but it is very expensive*

> *when it is a private individual. Someone informed me of this clinic. I started going there, that's where they have done almost all the tests I need (translation of Participant 12).*

Socioeconomic status

Most women described how factors linked to their socioeconomic status, such as financial availability or education levels, could either unlock or constitute a barrier for accessing SRH services.

First, many women reported delaying or going without medical care due to fear of high financial costs. For example, one participant explained that cost was determinant in her not following-up with the healthcare treatment she needed:

> *That will cost you a lot of money. Like just to see this specialist cost me $500 just for the appointment (Participant 6).*

> *If you have just a normal job, you're going to have extra money to pay and you got one, if you go once, you didn't go back. Because you cannot pay although you need to do a follow up (Participant 5).*

Likewise, all three undocumented immigrants in the study reported not having health insurance. They reported to seek healthcare only in emergency situations, due to fear of high medical bills. To overcome lack of insurance or high co-payments, some women described returning to their home countries to seek healthcare:

> *Yes, even without having insurance it costs less than here. But a lot of people do that. For Mexican. Of course, you need to have documents to be able to get out of the United States and come back. Right. But it would be a lot cheaper to even get a flight to travel and do these procedures than doing that in the US (Participant 6).*

In addition to cost, many women outlined transportation barriers, explaining that community-based centres were easier to access:

> *Like, transportation is an issue. Since you don't have a car and then also something that is quick (Participant 3).*

> *Transportation was sort of an issue because we didn't have a car for a long time. So, most of the time, I have to walk to places (Participant 4).*

> *I always suffer to go to appointments; I have to pay for taxis (translation of Participant 17).*

Finally, some women lamented excessive waiting times, although this was less frequently quoted than barriers regarding cost and distance.

> *It was the easiest thing to do for me, because I couldn't even get appointment or anything because it was too long (Participant 3).*

One woman could not access any SRH services due to her immigration status:

> *When I was 17 I had to have my green card for five years in order to get help from the government. If I wanted to get health insurance, I had to pay for it (Participant 4).*

Participant 4 was on inability to purchase health insurance due to the fact that she possessed her green card for less than five years.

For all the women interviewed, health insurance was linked to having a good job. They further connected suitable employment to one's immigration status. Inability to have health insurance was a significant deterrent in seeking SRH services:

> *I think because I didn't have any insurance. Everywhere we go I would always get asked like, 'Oh, do you have insurance' (Participant 4).*

Many women described the fear of using reproductive health treatments and check-ups due to its potential cost, showing an overlapping lack-of-information barrier:

> *I think that's, that's a lot of other things, I think a lot of people are like survival mode, so though they just prefer on because they know that no one's going to take better care of them than them (Participant 2).*

Some women described how digitalisation of healthcare services, especially when it comes to reservation and access, is an access barrier for those lacking basic technological skills:

> *That you don't have money to buy a computer or to somebody who can teach you to use a computer, suppose you know English, but women of my generation in our country, they don't know how to use computers, they don't know how to type, they are afraid of technology (Participant 6).*

> *Everything is with a robot; everything is with automatic answer machine (Participant 6).*

Other women interviewed lamented lack of technological skills when reserving healthcare treatments or finding SRH information, while being ashamed of asking for help to their children:

> *Maybe they don't want to explain those things. First of all, they are children,*

and it's kind of embarrassing for the mother in front of the child. And for the child in front of the mother too (Participant 6).

Technology barriers were connected to education levels:

I was lucky, when I was very young, to learn how to use computer when I came to the United States, I entered to school to study that (Participant 6).

Education by itself was connected to higher barriers by another woman:

Just to say that people that stay in their communities, don't go to college, don't graduate in high school, they stay in their community, are really stuck in a mentality that I can't go to doctors, and they try to use home remedies for whatever. But those who have gone to college, they graduated, they had healthcare, they, you know, they figure out what they need from medical care, and they take it seriously. So, I think education plays a big part, kind of like getting the same experiences of those that are American, that is fairly available to them (Participant 7).

Finally, lack of information and unclear processes were also described as a considerable barrier in accessing SRH:

I have no idea how that work. It was just complicated (…) I wasn't even explained really well, it was just really complicated (Participant 3).

Policy Recommendations

In this section we critically describe the policy recommendations women made as regards to improving access to healthcare for immigrant women in the US. This is crucial as, under a human rights framework, health policies must be informed through participatory and inclusive dialogue, taking into account the perspectives of women on their bodies and their needs. In fact, having a right to health also implies being warranted a right to participate in decisions affecting one's health, with public health and social citizenship being intertwined (Yamin, 2005). Participation is an essential component of rights-inspired health policies, as well as one of the most difficult to realise (Sekalala, 2017). The lack of use of systematic surveys by official bodies (e.g., thematic surveys conducted by statistic institutes) to include actors directly involved in the migration experience, makes the survey we conduct valuable. We take a little step forward by conveying the voices of the women in regard to healthcare policies in the US.

Most women recommended that there should be a way to make healthcare more affordable, especially for undocumented immigrants and those who are unemployed. In the case of undocumented immigrants, two women recommended that undocumented immigrants should be given the option to attain health insurance, even if by payment.

> *She wasn't able to because he was undocumented. Yeah. And he was like, either die or you don't get it. You know, you just can't, so I would say that for life. I would say that. For undocumented migrants to get it (Participant 8).*

> *Well, allow to get health insurance that we can pay for (translation of Participant 16).*

Another crucial theme was the empowerment of women in the community by creating awareness about health programmes and opportunities:

> *Creating awareness, awareness specifically in talking in the community about programmes that are available to them to help them (Participant 7).*

> *The information is not on our language. We are misinformed. We as immigrants are misinformed. The other thing is that we are embarrassed and afraid to ask (translation of Participant 12).*

Addressing stigma stemming from perceived gender roles and machismo was also raised as a recommendation:

> *Specifically for women, girls have different means from men, of course. I think it's really influent to have one designated group that helps educated young immigrant women, once they need healthcare, I guess, I would. A healthcare policy for immigrant women to help them get the healthcare that they need because right now ~~you~~ we are forgotten (Participant 7).*

Many women recommended a policy that addressed the delay in accessing healthcare due to fears of deportation:

> *I think the first thing I would say is creating a policy that allows illegal immigrants to get healthcare without being in fear of repercussion like being deported (Participant 7).*

Additionally, there were policy recommendations on inclusivity:

> *Treat everyone with equality. That is, I believe immigrants are the ones who come to work the most in this country and are the ones who have the least benefits (translation of Participant 13).*

The hope for universal healthcare policy in the US was a recurring theme:

> *So, healthcare for everyone, not just the privileged (Participant 7).*

Discussion and Conclusion

From a thematic analysis, this study is based on the following results.

First, the naming of immigrants as a "burden", "alien", or "illegal" has had negative consequences on the women, not only on the willingness to seek healthcare but additionally on their individual self-perception.

Second, we found that women preferred the use of herbs, traditional medicine, self-healing either due to self-perceived cultural identification with their country of origin or to fill access gaps. Machismo and gender roles, instead, are connected to stigma and taboo surrounding women's health.

Third, in regard to socioeconomic status, we find that financial availability or access to coverage through employment is a key social determinant of healthcare access. Likewise, women might be disadvantaged in accessing SRH because of lack of information, difficulties in interacting with technology, transportation, waiting lists, and problems in navigating the healthcare system. These difficulties stem from educational levels or broader class status and might combine with material deprivation. Women in a precarious or unsecured job setting might have difficulties taking days off, while others might be discouraged by long and expensive trips to healthcare facilities.

Fourth, we find that social services and social capital is fundamental in overcoming healthcare barriers in the short term. Social services can help overcome the language and lack of information barriers, while communities can help in overcoming stigma, mistrust, and fear of being deported.

Finally, differences in migration status make a difference. Undocumented immigrant had considerably higher barriers in accessing healthcare in comparison to other immigrants.

In comparison to other studies, our study adds the needs and uses of services among different groups of immigrant women in the US. Future research should include larger samples with participants with various immigration statuses. In addition, we encourage the use of intersectionality theory to understand and recognise the unique lived experiences of marginalised groups of people. It is the belief of this article, that intersectionality theory is not only a theoretical tool, but an instrument necessary for advocacy, interventions, and policy development.

All the factors emerged combined, creating unique experiences of isolation and marginalisation. The result on healthcare access is that women might delay healthcare, foregoing prevention and follow-up, and use healthcare only in emergency situations. In conclusion, the results showed that, while women's immigration status impact their access to healthcare, there are also other interconnected barriers. Such barriers act as mutually reinforcing sources of marginalisation. Therefore, there is a need to overcome the narrow sole focus on women's immigration status and gender in their access to SRH, confirming the usefulness of intersectionality in analysing the discriminatory processes through a gender lens. This is evidence in the case of the US, a developed country with relatively low legs of discrimination against women, where there are yet significant barriers in accessing healthcare when all other factors are taken into account, in accordance with a human rights-aligned intersectional analysis.

Appendix A: Abbreviations

CHIP	Children's Health Insurance Programme
CHIPRA	Children's Health Insurance Programme Reauthorization Act
CESCR	Committee on Economic, Social, and Cultural
CERD	Committee on the Elimination of Racial Discrimination
CEDAW	Convention on the Elimination of All Forms of Discrimination Against Women
CRPD	Convention on the Rights of Persons with Disabilities
CRC	Convention on the Rights of the Child
EMTALA	Emergency Medical Treatment and Labour Act
ICPD	International Conference on Population and Development
ICERD	International Convention in the Elimination of all Forms of Racial Discrimination
ICESCR	International Covenant on Economic, Social, and Cultural Rights
LPR	Legal Permanent Residents
PPACA	Patient Protection and Affordable Care Act
PRWORA	Personal Responsibility and Work Opportunity Reconciliation Act
SRH	Sexual and Reproductive Health
SRHR	Sexual and Reproductive Health and Rights
UDHR	Universal Declaration of Human Rights
UN	United Nations
US	United States

References

Alarcão, V., Stefanovska-Petkovska, M., Virgolino, A., Santos, O., & Costa, A. (2021). Intersections of Immigration and Sexual/Reproductive Health: An Umbrella Literature Review with a Focus on Health Equity. *Soc. Sci., 10*(2), 63. doi:10.3390/socsci10020063

Alarcão, V., Stefanovska-Petkovska, M., Virgolino, A., Santos, O., Ribeiro, S., Costa, A., . . . Machado, F. L. (2019). Fertility, Migration and Acculturation (FEMINA): a research protocol for studying intersectional sexual and reproductive health inequalities. *Reproductive Health, 16*(140). doi:10.1186/s12978-019-0795-5

Althoff, M. D., Theall, K., Schmidt, N., Hembling, J., Gebrekristos, H. T., Thompson, M., ... Kissinger, P. (2017). Social support networks and HIV/STI risk behaviors among Latino immigrants in a new receiving environment. *AIDS Behav, 21*(12), 3607-3617. doi:10.1007/s10461-017-1849-8

American Immigration Council. (2020). *Immigrant Women and Girls in the United States: A Portrait of Demographic Diversity*. Washington, DC. Retrieved from https://www.american immigrationcouncil.org/sites/default/files/research/immigrant_women_in_the_united_states.pdf

Artiga, S., & Diaz, M. (2019). *Health Coverage and Care of Undocumented Immigrants*. San Francisco, CA: Henry J. Kasier Family Foundation (KFF). Retrieved from https://files.kff.org/attachment/Issue-Brief-Health-Coverage-and-Care-of-Undocumented-Immigrants

Bambra, C., Gibson, M., Sowden, A., Wright, K., Whitehead, M., & Petticrew, M. (2010). Tackling the wider social determinants of health and health inequalities: evidence from systematic reviews. *J Epidemiol Community Health*, 284-291. doi:10.1136/jech.2008.082743

Beck, T. L., Le, T.-K., Henry-Okafor, Q., & Shah, M. K. (2019). Medical Care for Undocumented Immigrants: National and International Issues. *Physician Assist Clin, 4*(1), 33-45. doi:10.1016/j.cpha.2018.08.002

Budiman, A. (2020). *Key findings about U.S. immigrants*. Washington, DC: Pew Research Center. Retrieved from https://www.pewresearch.org/short-reads/2020/08/20/key-findings-about-u-s-immigrants/

Center for Reproductive Rights. (2014). *Reproductive Injustice: Racial and Gender Discrimination in U.S. Health Care [A Shadow Report for the UN Committee on the Elimination of Racial Discrimination]*. New York, NY. Retrieved from https://reproductiverights.org/wp-content/uploads/2020/12/CERD_Shadow_US_6.30.14_Web.pdf

CESCR General Comment No. 14: The Right to the Highest Attainable Standard of Health (Art. 12), E/C.12/2000/4) (2000). Retrieved from https://www.refworld.org/ pdfid/4538838d0.pdf

Coaston, J. (2019). *The intersectionality wars*. Vox. Retrieved from https://www.vox.com/the-highlight/2019/5/20/18542843/intersectionality-conservatism-law-race-gender-discrimination

Crenshaw, K. (1989). Demarginalizing the Intersection of Race and Sex: A Black Feminist Critique of Antidiscrimination Doctrine, Feminist Theory and Antiracist Politics. *University of Chicago Legal Forum, 1989*(1), 139-167. Retrieved from https://chicagounbound.uchicago.edu/cgi/viewcontent.cgi?article=1052&context=uclf

Entitled The Patient Protection and Affordable Care Act, 124 STAT. 119 (2010). Retrieved from https://www.congress.gov/111/plaws/publ148/PLAW-111publ148.pdf

Evans, E. (2016). Intersectionality as feminist praxis in the UK. *Women's Studies International Forum, 59*, 67-75. doi:https://doi.org/10.1016/j.wsif.2016.10.004

Examination and treatment for emergency medical conditions and women in labour, 42 USC 1395dd (1994). Retrieved from https://uscode.house.gov/ view.xhtml?req= granuleid: USC-1994-title42-section1395dd&num=0&edition=1994

Fix, M. E., Capps, R., & Kaushal, N. (2009). Immigrants and Welfare: Overview. In M. Fix, *Immigrants and Welfare: The Impact of Welfare Reform on America's Newcomers* (pp. 1-36). Russell Sage Foundation.

Fortuny, K., & Chaudry, A. (2011). *A Comprehensive Review of Immigrant Access to Health and Human Services*. Urban Institute. Retrieved from https://www.urban.org/sites/ default/files/publication/27651/412425-A-Comprehensive-Review-of-Immigrant-Access-to-Health-and-Human-Services.PDF

Freedom for Immigrants. (2018). *Glossary of Immigration Terms*. Retrieved from https://www.freedomforimmigrants.org/terminology

Funge, J. K., Boye, M. C., Johnsen, H., & Nørredam, M. (2020). "No Papers. No Doctor": A Qualitative Study of Access to Maternity Care Services for Undocumented Immigrant Women in Denmark. *International Journal of Environmental Research and Public Health*,

17(6503). doi:10.3390/ijerph17186503

Gerisch, M. (2018). Health Care As a Human Right. *Human Rights Magazine, 43*(3), 2-9. Retrieved from https://www.americanbar.org/ groups/crsj/publications/human_ rights_magazine_home/the-state-of-healthcare-in-the-united-states/health-care-as-a-human-right/

Ginsberg, T. (2018). *Philadelphia's Immigrants: Who they are and how they are changing the city.* Philadelphia: The Pew Charitable Trusts'. Retrieved from https://www.pewtrusts.org/-/media/assets/2018/06/pri_philadelphias_immigrants.pdf

Hankivsky, O. (2012). Women's health, men's health, and gender and health: implications of intersectionality. *Social Science & Medicine, 74*(11), 1712-1720. doi:10.1016/j.socscimed.2011.11.029

Hankivsky, O., & Jordan-Zachery, J. S. (2019). *The Palgrave Handbook of Intersectionality in Public Policy.* Palgrave Macmillan Cham. doi:https://doi.org/10.1007/978-3-319-98473-5

Hasstedt, K., Desai, S., & Ansari-Thomas, Z. (2018). Immigrant Women's Access to Sexual and Reproductive Health Coverage in the United States. *Issue Brief (Commonwealth Fund), 1*(2018), 1-10.

Health Facilities v. Axelrod, 77 N.Y.2d 340 (1991). Retrieved from https://law. justia. com/cases/new-york/court-of-appeals/1991/77-n-y-2d-340-0.html

Hunt, P. (2016). Interpreting the International Right to Health in a Human Rights-Based Approach to Health. *Health and Human Rights Journal, 18*(2), 109-130.

International Convention on the Elimination of All Forms of Racial Discrimination, A/RES/2142) (1966). Retrieved from https://www.ohchr.org/ sites/ default/ files/ cerd.pdf

International Convention on the Elimination of all Forms of Racial Discrimination, CERD/C/DEU/CO/18 (2008). Retrieved from https://www2.ohchr.org/ english/ bodies/cerd/docs/co/cerd.c.deu.co.18.pdf

International Convention on the Elimination of All Forms of Racial Discrimination, CERD/C/USA/CO/7-9 (Committee on the Elimination of Racial Discrimination 2014). Retrieved from https://docstore.ohchr.org/SelfServices/FilesHandler.ashx? enc= 6QkG1d%2FPPRiCAqhKb7yhspzOl9YwTXeABruAM8pBAK1Q%2FDZ6XAqlyobgts 1zwlHPkQhsSqMrVxuS6brQbHYpDYGXBUCX1bgRtTg3HaweAr5PBs9soaesD5KdB yekI9OS

Jain, T., LaHote, J., Samari, G., & Garbers, S. (2022). Publicly-Funded Services Providing Sexual, Reproductive, and Maternal Healthcare to Immigrant Women in the United States: A Systematic Review. *Journal of Immigrant and Minority Health, 24*(3), 759-778. doi:0.1007/s10903-021-01289-2

Kawar, M. (2004). Gender and Migration: Why are Women more Vulnerable? In *Femmes en mouvement: Genre, migrations et nouvelle division internationale du travail* (pp. 71-87). Genève: Graduate Institute Publications. Retrieved from http://books. openedition.org/ iheid/ 6256

Knudsen, S. V. (2006). Intersectionality - A theoretical inspiration in the analysis of minority cultures and identities in textbooks. In É. Bruillard, B. Aamotsbakken, S. V. Knudsen, & M. Horsley, *Caught in the Web or Lost in the Textbook?* (pp. 61-76). Jouve.

Kopp, J. (2017). *Pew Center research puts a number on Philly's undocumented immigrants.* Philadelphia: Philly Voice. Retrieved from https://www.phillyvoice.com/pew-center-research-puts-a-number-on-phillys-undocumented-immigrants/

Ku, L., & Jewers, M. (2013). *Health Care for Immigrant Families: Current Policies and Issues.* Washington, DC: Migration Policy Institute. Retrieved from https://www.migration

policy.org/pubs/COI-HealthCare.pdf

López-Domene, E., Granero-Molina, J., Fernández-Sola, C., Hernández-Padilla, J., del Mar López-Rodríguez, M., Fernández-Medina, I., . . . del Mar Jiménez-Lasserrrotte, M. (2019). Emergency Care for Women Irregular Migrants Who Arrive in Spain by Small Boat: A Qualitative Study. *16*(3287). doi:10.3390/ijerph16183287

Loprest, P., & Zedlewski, S. (2006). *The Changing Role of Welfare in the Lives of Low-Income Families with Children.* Washington, DC: The Urban Institute.

Lutz, H., Herrera Vivar, M., & Supik, L. (2011). *Framing Intersectionality: Debates on a Multi-Faceted Concept in Gender Studies.* New York, NY: Routledge.

Lykke, N. (2010). *Feminist Studies: A Guide to Intersectional Theory, Methodology, and Writing.* New York, NY: Routledge.

National Conference of State Legislatures (NCSL). (2017). *Immigrant Eligibility for Health Care Programs in the United States.* Washington, DC. Retrieved from https://www.ncsl. org/ immigration/immigrant-eligibility-for-health-care-programs-in-the-united-states#:~:text=In%20general%2C%20permanent%20resident%20immigrants,meet%20 all%20other%20program%20requirements

National Women's Law Center (NWLC). (2017). *Immigrant Rights and Reproductive Justice: How Harsh Immigration Policies Harm Immigrant Health.* Retrieved from https://nwlc.org/wp-content/uploads/2017/04/Immigrant-Rights-and-Reproductive-Justice.pdf

Passel, J. S., & Cohn, D. (2018). *U.S. Unauthorized Immigrant Total Dips to Lowest Level in a Decade.* Pew Research Center. Retrieved from https://www.pewresearch.org/ hispanic/ 2018/ 11/27/u-s-unauthorized-immigrant-total-dips-to-lowest-level-in-a-decade/

Personal Responsibility and Work Opportunity Reconciliation Act, 110 STAT. 2105 (1996). Retrieved from https://www.congress.gov/104/plaws/publ193/PLAW-104publ193.pdf

Schenker, M. B., Castañeda, X., & Rodriguez-Lainz, A. (2014). *Migration and Health: A Research Methods Handbook.* Oakland, California: University of California Press.

Sekalala, S. (2017). Who gets to sit at the table? Interrogating the failure of participatory approaches within a right to health framework. *The International Journal of Human Rights, 21*(7), 976-1001. doi:https://doi.org/10.1080/13642987.2017.1322066

Sekalala, S., Perehudoff, K., Parker, M., Forman, L., Rawson, B., & Smith, M. (2021). An intersectional human rights approach to prioritising access to COVID-19 vaccines. *BMJ Global Health, 6*(2). doi:10.1136/bmjgh-2020-004462

Smith, A. C., & LeVoy, M. (2016). *The Sexual and Reproductive Health Rights of Undocumented Migrants: Narrowing the Gap between their Rights and the Reality in the EU.* Brussels, Belgium: Platform for International Cooperation on Undocumented Migrants (PICUM). Retrieved from http://picum.org/wp-content/uploads/2017/11/Sexual-and-Reproductive-Health -Rights_EN.pdf

Swartz, J. J., Hainmueller, J., Lawrence, D., & Rodriguez, M. I. (2017). Expanding Prental Care to Unauthorized Immigrant Women and the Effects on Infant Health. *Obstet Gynecol., 130*(5), 938-945. doi:10.1097/AOG.0000000000002275

The Congress of the United States. (2007). *The Impact of Unauthorized Immigrants on the Budget of State and Local Governments.* Congressional Budget Office. Retrieved from https://www.cbo.gov/sites/default/files/110th-congress-2007-2008/reports/12-6-immigration.pdf

Title VI of the Civil Rights Act of 1964, 42 U.S.C. § 2000 (1964). Retrieved from https://www.dol.gov/agencies/oasam/regulatory/statutes/title-vi-civil-rights-act-of-1964#:~:text=No%20person%20in%20the%20United,activity%20receiving%20Federal %20financial%20assistance.

UN CERD (Commission on the Elimination of Racial Discrimination). (2000). *General Recommendation 25, adopted on 25 March*. Retrieved from http://sim.law.uu.nl/ SIM/ %20%20CaseLaw/Gen_Com.nsf/0/4696490f7608080ac12568bf00509b83?OpenDoc% 20%20ument

United Nations Population Fund. (2004). *Programme of Action adopted at the International Conference on Population and Development Cairo, 5-13 September 1994*. UNFPA. Retrieved from https://www.unfpa.org/sites/default/files/event-pdf/PoA_en.pdf

United States Census Bureau. (2019). *Frequently Asked Questions (FAQs) About Foreign Born*. Retrieved from https://www.census.gov/topics/population/foreign-born/ about/ faq. html

US Immigration: An Online Software Company. (2021). *Immigrant Definition: U.S. Immigration Glossary*. Retrieved from https://www.usimmigration.org/glossary/immigrant

Wherry, L. R., Fabi, R., Schickedanz, A., & Saloner, B. (2017). State And Federal Coverage For Pregnant Immigrants: Prenatal Care Increased, No Change Detected For Infant Health. *Health Affairs, 36*(4), 607-615. doi:https://doi.org/10.1377/hlthaff.2016.1198

Wolff, H., Epiney, M., Lourenco, A. P., Costanza, M. C., Delieutraz-Marchand, J., Andreoli, N., . . . Irion, O. (2008). Undocumented migrants lack access to pregnancy care and prevention. *BMC Public Health, 8*(93). doi:10.1186/1471-2458-8-93

Wyatt v. Stickney, 344 F. Supp. 373 (US District Court for the Middle District of Alabama 1972). Retrieved from https://law.justia.com/ cases/ federal/ district-courts/ FSupp/ 344/373/2303083/

Yamin, A. (2005). The Right to Health Under International Law and Its Relevance to the United States. *American Journal of Public Health, 95*(7), 1156–1161. doi:10.2105/ AJPH. 2004.055111

Yuval-Davis, N. (2006). Intersectionality and Feminist Politics. *European Journal of Women's Studies, 13*(3). doi:https://doi.org/ 10.1177/ 1350506 806 065752

CHANGES IN HEALTH POLICY AND MIGRANTS, REFUGEES AND ASYLUM SEEKERS IN NEW ZEALAND

Grace Wong[1], Padmapriya Saravanakumar[2],
Jagamaya Shrestha-Ranjit[3]

Introduction

New Zealand has a long history of migration, driven by the need for an able workforce. As well as economic migrants, the government operates a refugee quota system and has policy provisions for asylum seekers and undocumented migrants. The proportion of NZ's population who were born overseas increased from 25.2% in 2013 to 27.4% in 2018 (Statistics NZ, 2013, 2019). More recent migrants originate from Asia and Europe than Middle Eastern, Latin American, and African (MELAA) countries, or the Pacific Islands.

Migrants from non-Western countries are highly diverse. Pacific Island peoples are less likely to be born overseas than other non-European migrants. They comprise 8.1% of the total NZ population (34% born offshore). In contrast, people who identify as Chinese comprise 5.1% (73.3% born offshore) and Indian 5.1% (76% born offshore) of the total population. Migrants from multiple other Asian countries comprise the remainder of the NZ Asian population. The proportion of MELAA peoples is small but growing (2013: 1.2% versus 2018: 1.5%). Most (77%) were born overseas (Statistics NZ, 2018, 2019). Migrants with European, Chinese, Indian, and Pacific backgrounds join well-established communities (McKinnon, 1996).

The health of Asian migrants is often described as 'good' overall, perhaps reflecting the healthy migrant effect whereby economic migrants have a younger, healthier profile on average than the overall resident population (Hajat et al, 2010; Zhou & Bennett, 2017). Such migrants are at risk of acculturation to less healthy Western lifestyles (Di Cosmo et al., 2011; Rudmin, 2009). In contrast, the overall health of Pacific Island peoples in NZ is poor in comparison with the whole population (Ministry of Health, 2012).

Aggregation into categories such as 'Asian', 'Pacific' or MELAA disguises the unique needs among the different sub-populations which each category

---

[1] Grace Wong, Auckland University of Technology, New Zealand.
[2] Padmapriya Saravanakumar, University of Technology Sydney, Australia.
[3] Jagamaya Shrestha-Ranjit, Auckland University of Technology, New Zealand.

includes. For example, in the Asian category, cardiovascular disease is a significant issue for South Asian, but not Chinese people in NZ (Mehta, 2012; Scragg, 2016). Aggregation of data also reduces the degree to which health issues may be identified among older migrants, refugees, asylum seekers, and undocumented migrants. Their mental and physical health needs may be worse than average since they may reflect the difficult circumstances under which they migrate, their challenging journeys, and/or adjustment to Western cultural values and health services. In addition, their proficiency in English may limit their access to and use of health services.

Political context

The health of vulnerable people is critically determined by public policy - the choices that governments make on behalf of people living under their jurisdiction (Mintrom, 2012, p. 1). Health policies are courses of action and inaction that affect the sets of institutions, organizations, services, and funding arrangements of the health system (Buse et al, 2012). They include laws, regulations, codes, strategies, standards of practice, operational guidelines, plans, and audit and quality frameworks. They reflect the ideologies of the governments in power when they are created or operationalised.

In 2014, the centre-right National Party governed NZ. Their policies emphasise personal freedom, and individual responsibility, merit and entrepreneurship to create wealth. This government discriminated against older migrants by suspending the parent residence visa which allows overseas-born parents to permanently join children who are NZ citizens or residents. Ostensibly, the aim was to reduce future public health spending on aging older adults. It is effectively a migrant health policy because of the toll on the mental health of children and grandchildren of not having the frequent, regular, in-person contact with family elders which is central to collective societies. The policy was partially rescinded in 2019[4], two years after a centre-left Coalition of Parties came into power, led by the Labour Party in 2017[5].

---

[4] Conditions for what is now known as the 'Parent Retirement Resident Visa' include an 'investment period' of four years as follows: Applicants need an annual income of NZ$60,000 plus NX$1 million to invest for 4 years, and another $500,000 to live on. Once they have completed the 4-year investment period, they are eligible for permanent residence.
[5] In 2017, a centre-left Coalition of Parties came into power led by the Labour Party. They lean towards a more collective approach to ensuring equality of access, human rights and fair distribution of resources than the centre-right National Party. The Labour government in the 1930s humanely allowed family

Currently, policy analyses do not consider the nuances of different policies for different migrant ethnic subgroups separately, or the political context of policy change from data sweep to data sweep. This paper uses the MIPEX health policy indicator questions to compare NZ policy about entitlement, access, and responsiveness to health services for legal migrants, refugees, asylum seekers and undocumented migrants in 2014 and 2019. There is a consideration of differences in health policy for different migrant ethnic subgroups and of how the 2017 change in government affected health policy for migrants.

Data and methodology

The Migration Policy Index (MIPEX) is a robust, comprehensive tool used to evaluate public policy trends across multiple domains which are critical to the humane and equitable settlement of immigrants. It reveals policy strengths, as well as areas of concern, and allows comparisons among countries. MIPEX recognises the vital role that policy plays in the availability of, access to, and requirements for opportunities to be healthy for documented and undocumented migrants, refugees and asylum seekers. MIPEX added health to other policy areas such as labour market mobility, political participation and education in 2014. A limitation of policy indexes is that they do not measure how policies are implemented or their outcomes. Nevertheless, policy is a starting point, signalling intent, and often determining the distribution of resources, how they should be used, and the evaluation of their effect. Policy indexes are also a means by which the level of migrant input into policies affecting their own wellbeing can be gauged (Scipioni & Urso, 2017; Solano & Huddleston, 2020).

The methodology for the MIPEX health indices is described in-depth elsewhere (Solano & Huddleston, 2020). In brief, 23 key questions (comprising 41 indicators) were created to review migrants' entitlements to health care, accessibility to health services, and the responsiveness of these services. Each indicator is scored from 1 – 3, with three indicating the best standard for equitable treatment of migrants in comparison with non-

---

reunification of Chinese families in NZ. In 2001, the Party issued a formal apology for a long-standing poll tax on Chinese arrivals to NZ from 1881 to 1944. The Labour–led 2017 Coalition of Parties doubled the refugee quota in NZ. They were in power during the March 15, 2019, mosque attacks in Christchurch perpetrated by an extreme right-wing migrant from Australia against many Muslim former refugees and migrants. This disastrous event prompted soul-searching into the effectiveness of NZ's policy actions supporting migrants, refugees and NZ-born peoples of different ethnic groups and faiths. For example, it is forcing a re-think about police surveillance away from a sole focus on possible Muslim terrorist migrants to dangerous alt-right people. It is unclear if this re-think includes the effects of health policy on migrant well-being.

migrants. In 2019, MIPEX collapsed the indicators into 12 core migrant health indicators in response to results of analyses of the 2014 data. These demonstrated that the correlation (r) between all 41 indicators used in 2014 and the averages of 12 core indicators was 0.95. The core indicators accounted for 90% of the variance in the full scores. It provided a shorter, reasonably accurate version of the full MIPEX tool (Solano & Huddleston, 2020).

Policies related to health services and legal migrants, refugees, asylum seekers and undocumented migrants in NZ were accessed from international, government and other websites in 2014 and 2019. Policies included laws, regulations, codes, strategies, standards of practice, operational guidelines, plans, and audit and quality frameworks. The information was entered into the MIPEX indicator matrix and scored using MIPEX criteria. The data were reviewed by national migration policy experts and migrant health service leaders. The central Migration Policy Group team independently reviewed the data and corresponded with country experts to establish consensus on ratings where there were questions or omissions.

Results

The overall scores for the core indicators for 2014 and 2019 for NZ are provided in Table 1. There are also comments in italics where policies differ for different ethnic sub-groups and about any changes. The data, including the references and justifications for each score, are available on the MIPEX website.

NZ scored 'A' for all questions about Entitlement for Health Services, on a par to nationals in all but three instances. Full cover for health care (the same as for nationals) only applies to permanent residents and not to those on visas such as student visas or work visas for less than two years. By 2019, aged migrant parents were specifically named as having to live in NZ for over two years before receiving full cover. Undocumented migrants were only eligible for Accident Compensation Corporation (ACC) care[6].

Policy Measures to Facilitate Access scored less well with half of the questions receiving 'A' ratings and half receiving 'B'. This mainly reflected a more concerted use of policy instruments to address Pacific Island people's needs whereas policies and services to address specific health access needs of other migrant such as Asians and MELAA people were more ad hoc. Asylum

---

[6] The Accident Compensation Corporation (ACC) provides comprehensive, no-fault personal injury cover for all NZ residents and visitors to NZ regardless of their migration status http://www.acc.co.nz/

seekers sometimes encountered difficulties proving their eligibility for care at the face-to-face service level.

The scores for Responsiveness of Health Services in NZ were all 'As'. In part, this reflected policy provision of interpreters for an extensive range of languages and high-level policy supporting respect for cultural diversity.

For Measures to Achieve Change the national strategy to advance Pacific people's health but absence of similar tools for Asian and MELAA people was noted, as was the lack of a health in all policies directive.

Table 1. NZ MIPEX health policy scores

Entitlement to health services		2014	2019
1a	Legal migrants: conditions for inclusion in a system of health care coverage		
	A. Inclusion is unconditional	B	B
	B. Some conditions for inclusion		
	C. No inclusion (costs must be paid in full by the user or by a commercial insurance policy)		
	Comment: 'B' – 2014 and 2019 - Holders of work visas which are for less than two years are not eligible for services except Accident Compensation Corporation (ACC) cover. *2019 - Aged migrant parents who migrated as permanent residents are now named specifically in terms of having to live in NZ 2 years or more as a condition of inclusion.*		
1b	Legal migrants: extent of coverage		
	A. Same coverage as nationals	A	A
	B. More than emergency care, but less than for nationals		
	C. Emergency care only		
2a	Asylum seekers: conditions for inclusion in a system of health care coverage	A	A
	A. Inclusion is unconditional		
	B. Some conditions for inclusion		
	C. No inclusion (costs must be paid in full by the user or by a commercial insurance policy)		
2b	Asylum seekers: extent of coverage		
	A. Same coverage as nationals	A	A
	B. More than emergency care, but less than for nationals		
	C. Emergency care only		
3a	Undocumented migrants: conditions for inclusion in a system of health care coverage	C	C
	A. Inclusion is unconditional		
	B. Some conditions for inclusion		
	C. No inclusion (costs must be paid in full by the user or by a commercial insurance policy)		

	Comment: NZ has a special arrangement with some South Pacific countries under the 'Medical Treatment Scheme' and medical visas and NZ public funding apply in certain instances including ACC cover[7].		

4	Special exemptions from restrictions on entitlement: Antenatal and/or perinatal and/or postnatal care; infectious disease (e.g. TB, HIV/Aids); care for minors (or for unaccompanied minors if other minors are covered); care for vulnerable groups (e.g. victims of torture, trafficking or traumatisation); other (NB. If an exemption is not necessary because the migrant group in question is already entitled to this form of care, it should not be counted here).
	  A. Three or more exemptions
	  B. One or two exemptions
	  C. No exemptions (or none needed)
		A	A

5	Administrative demands for documents which may be difficult for migrants to produce. Examples: proof of low income on the basis of tax returns; identity documents available only from the police; proof of address from local authority records.
	  A. Does not apply to any group
	  B. Applies to only one group
	  C. Applies to two or three migrant groups
		A	A

6	Administrative discretion in granting coverage
	Coverage for migrants may depend on decisions with uncertain outcome, made for example by administrators (receptionists, managers or committees), health workers making clinical judgements about criteria for entitlement such as 'urgency', financial departments deciding how rigorously to pursue unpaid bills, etc.
	  A. Does not apply to any group
	  B. Applies to only one group
	  C. Applies to two or three migrant groups
	Comment: 'B'- sometimes applies to asylum seekers who are seeking care
		B	B

Policies to facilitate access	2014	2019

7 Information for service providers about migrants' entitlements
Service provider organisations receive up-to date information on migrants' entitlements.
Organisations pass on up-to-date information about these entitlements to their employees.
  A. Both
  B. One of these
  C. Neither
Comment: 'B' - While service providers may receive information in entitlements at the highest level, they may not pass this information on to contractors or employees
	B	B

8a Information for migrants concerning entitlements and use of health services Method of dissemination: Websites; brochures in public places; 'one-stop shops'; classes or individual instruction; other	A	A

---

[7] Ibid

	A. More than one of these		
	B. One of these		
	C. None of these		

8b	Number of languages in which information for migrants concerning entitlements and use of health services is available (not including the official languages of the country or English) A. 4 or more languages B. 1 – 3 languages C. No languages	A	A
8c	Groups reached by information for migrants on entitlements and use of health services: Legal migrants; Asylum seekers; Undocumented migrants A. All three groups B. 1 or 2 groups C. No groups	A	A
9a	Health education and health promotion for migrants Method of dissemination: Websites; brochures in public places; 'one-stop shops'; classes or individual instruction; other A. More than one of these B. One of these C. None of these	A	A
9b	Number of languages in which health education and health promotion are available (not including the official languages of the country or English) A. Four or more languages B. 1 – 3 languages (specify) C. No languages	A	A
9c	Groups reached by health education and health promotion Legal migrants; asylum seekers; undocumented migrants A. All three groups B. Only two groups C. Only one group	A	A
10	Where practical obstacles to access have been reported, have policy measures been taken to tackle them? Provision of services is inadequate (e.g. mental health services) Services are difficult for migrants to reach (using public transport) Opening hours are inconvenient for migrants (e.g. because of long hours of work and precarious conditions of employment). Other practical obstacles (specify) A. No such obstacles have been reported without measures being taken to tackle them B. One such obstacle has been reported without measures being taken to tackle it C. Two or more of obstacles have been reported without measures taken to tackle them *Comment: 'B' - There is a concerted effort to reduce practical obstacles to access for Pacific peoples but not Asian or MELAA peoples.*	B	B

11a	Provision of 'cultural mediators' or 'patient navigators' to facilitate access for migrants
	   A. Guaranteed across the system or in major immigrant areas
	   B. On a smaller or ad hoc basis
	   C. Not available
		B	B

11b	Groups for which cultural mediators are provided
	   A. All three groups
	   B. Only two groups
	   C. Only one group
	Comment: 'B' Pacific Island and a limited range of Asian only
		B	B

12a	No obligation to report undocumented migrants
	Are healthcare professionals or organisations required to report undocumented migrants to the police or immigration authorities?
	   A. Explicitly forbidden in law and/or professional codes of conduct
	   B. No relevant legislation or professional codes of conduct
	   C. Explicitly required in law
		B	B

12b	No sanctions against helping undocumented migrants
	Are there legal or organisational sanctions against healthcare professionals or organisations assisting undocumented migrants?
	   A. No legal sanctions or other pressures on professionals to deter them from helping migrants who cannot pay
	   B. Only organisational sanctions exist (organisations discourage carers from helping migrants who cannot pay)
	   C. Legal sanctions exist against helping undocumented migrants
		B	B

Responsive health services		2014	2019

13a	Availability of qualified interpretation services for patients with inadequate proficiency in the official language(s)
	   A. Interpreters are available free of charge to patients
	   B. Interpreters are available but patients must pay all (or a substantial part) of the costs
	   C. No interpretation services available
		A	A

13b	Methods used for interpretation: Face-to-face; telephone interpretation; interpretation by video link; credentialed volunteers; employment of 'cultural mediators'; employment of competent bilingual or multilingual staff
	   A. Three or more methods are available
	   B. One or two methods are available
	   C. No methods are available
		A	A

14	Requirement for 'culturally competent' or 'diversity-sensitive' services Standards or guidelines require that health services take account of individual and family characteristics, experiences and situation, respect for different beliefs, religion, culture, competence in intercultural communication.	A	A

	A.	Standards or guidelines exist on "culturally competent' or 'diversity-sensitive' services plus Compliance with these standards or guidelines is monitored by a relevant authority.	
	B.	Standards or guidelines exist on "culturally competent' or 'diversity sensitive' services	
	C.	Neither	

Comment: 'A' – compliance with standards is monitored for Pacific Island peoples only.

15	Training and education of health service staff Policies exist to support training of staff in providing services responsive to the needs of migrants. Training may be part of basic professional education and/or in-service professional development.	A	A
	A. At national level		
	B. At local or organisational level		
	C. Neither of these		

16	Involvement of migrants in information provision, service design and delivery (mention only forms of migrant involvement that are explicitly encouraged by policy measures at any level) Migrants are involved in service delivery e.g., through the employment of 'cultural mediators' Migrants are involved in the development and dissemination of information Migrants are involved in research (not only as respondents) Migrant patients or ex-patients are involved in the evaluation, planning, and running of services. Migrants in the community are involved in the design of services.	A	A
	A. Three to five of these		
	B. One or two of these		
	C. None of these		

Comment: 'A' – refers largely to Pacific Island peoples

17	Encouraging diversity in the health service workforce Recruitment measures (e.g., campaigns, incentives, support) to encourage participation of people with a migrant background in the health service workforce (this question does not concern policies aimed at recruiting or employing health care professionals from abroad because of a national shortage of staff)	A	A
	A. At national level		
	B. At local or organisational level		
	C. Neither of these		

18a	Development of capacity and methods Diagnostic procedures and treatment methods are adapted to take more account of variations in the sociocultural background of patients	A	A
	A. Policies exist to encourage the adaptation of diagnostic procedures and treatment methods to sociocultural diversity		
	B. Adaptation of diagnostic procedures and treatment methods is to a limited extent tolerated, but not encouraged		

		2014	2019
	C. Policies are exclusively focused on standardising diagnostic procedures and treatment methods		
18b	Specific forms of the above Policies exist to encourage: Development of treatments for health problems specific to certain migrant communities (e.g., female genital mutilation, effects of torture, rare important diseases, genetic risk factors) Adaptation of standard treatments for routine health problems to better serve migrant communities Use of complementary and alternative 'non-Western' treatments for physical and mental health problems A. All three of these B. One or two of these C. None of these	A	A

Measures to achieve change		**2014**	**2019**
19	Collection of data on migrant health Data on migrant status, country of origin or ethnicity is included in medical databases or clinical records. Choose B if linkage between medical databases and national databases containing the above personal information is practically possible. A. Inclusion of such information is mandatory B. Inclusion of such information is optional C. Such information is never included *Comment: 'A' - collection of data is limited to ethnicity and here, it is limited to broad categories such as 'South-East Asian'.*	A	A
20	Support for research on migrant health Funding bodies have in the past five years supported research on the following topics: Occurrence of health problems among migrant or ethnic minority groups Social determinants of migrant and ethnic minority health Issues concerning service provision for migrants or ethnic minorities Evaluation of methods for reducing inequalities in health or health care affecting migrants or ethnic minorities A. Three or four topics B. One or two topics C. None of these topics *Comment: 'A' Research support for research supporting Pacific people's health but rarely for Asian or MELAA peoples or refugees*	A	A
21	'Health in all policies' approach Attention to the health impact of all policies A. Mandatory consideration of the impact on migrant or ethnic minority health of policies in other sectors than health B. Ad hoc consideration of the impact on migrant or ethnic minority health of policies in other sectors than health	B	B

	C.	No consideration taken of the impact on migrant or ethnic minority health of policies in sectors other than health		
22	Whole organisation approach			
	A.	Migrant or ethnic minority health is a priority throughout service provider organisations and health agencies ('integrated' versus 'categorical' approach). Commitment to providing equitable health care for migrants or ethnic minorities is present in all departments of service provider organisations and health agencies	A	A
	B.	Concern for migrant or ethnic minority health is regarded as a priority only for specialised departments or organisations		
	C.	No systematic attention is paid to migrant or ethnic minority health in any part of the health system. Measures are left to individual initiative		

Comment: 'A' – Pacific people's health is a priority which is integrated throughout service provider organisations and health agencies as required in the District Health Board Operational Framework and Health Service Specifications. This does not apply to Asian or MELAA peoples.

23	Leadership by government			
	A.	Government publishes an explicit plan for action on migrant health Policies are implemented to support these measures	B	B
	A.	Only ad hoc policies introduced on migrant health		
	B.	No policy measures introduced on migrant health		

Comment: 'B' – there is a national Pacific Health Strategy ('Ala Mo'ie) supported by policies, strategies, funding (population-based funding is partly on demographic characteristics related to health status with formulae and reporting requirements related to outputs and health gain for Pacific peoples. The same does not apply to Asian or MELAA peoples.

24a	What is the policy to involve stakeholders in the design of (national or regional) migrant health policies? Is there an advisory body or centre of expertise promoting cooperation amongst stakeholders on migrant health policy? Note: This can be led by government, service-providers, or NGOs/institutes. Stakeholders include administrative and health authorities at various levels of governance, service providers, health insurers, professional bodies, universities, accreditation agencies, NGOs and commercial organisations. (NB: participation at service provider level is covered by q. 16)		A	A
	A.	Through structural cooperation (e.g., via advisory body or centre of expertise)		
	B.	Through ad hoc cooperation (e.g., during consultations on new health strategy or law or through projects)		
	C.	None		

Comment: 'A' - There is a strong mandate to involve stakeholders in the design of national health policy for Pacific peoples ('Ala Mo'ue) and at the regional level for Pacific and other ethnic groups. There is national policy about the

	minimum requirements for the health of potential migrants (not refugees) determined on the likelihood of imposing significant costs or demands on NZ's health services or special education services and/or transmitting infectious diseases such as tuberculosis.		

24b	Migrants' contribution to health policymaking at national or regional level:
	How do migrant stakeholders (e.g., NGO's and CSO's) participate in national policymaking affecting their health? (NB: participation at service provider level is covered by q. 6)
	    A. Through structural cooperation (e.g., involvement in advisory body or regular review of health legislation, services, and outcomes)
	    B. Through ad hoc cooperation (e.g., during consultations on new health strategy or law or through projects)
	    C. Immigrant organisations are not explicitly consulted on health policy.
	Comment: 'A' - Pacific peoples participate in health policy making through structural cooperation as required in the Operational Policy Framework and the Service Coverage Schedule as well as 'Ala Mo'ui (Ministry of Health, 2014). This is not required for Asian or MELAA peoples.
		A	A

Discussion

While NZ ranked top in the Migration International Policy Index health policy index in 2014, and among the top five countries in 2019, there were significant gaps (Solano & Huddleston, 2020). In particular, the gaps relate to entitlements for undocumented migrants, barriers to service use by asylum seekers, and issues with aggregating policy ratings for Pacific peoples with policy ratings for different subgroups of Asian and MELAA migrants. The advent of the new centre-left government in 2017 did not have a discernible effect on health policy for migrants in the short time (one year) they were in power before the 2019 data were collected.

Huddleston et al (2015) compare NZ's health policies with those of other countries. They provide examples of best practice from other MIPEX countries. Areas for improvement include more humane health policy provision of services for undocumented migrants, better efforts to provide up-to-date information about health care entitlements to first-line staff for asylum seekers, and more consistent provision of efforts across NZ to address barriers to access for Asian and MELAA peoples. This includes providing cultural mediators. Currently services for these groups are ad hoc. They depend on where clients live.

While entitlement is important it is equally important to have policy assuring accessible, sufficient appropriate and responsive services which take ethnic, cultural and religious sub-group identity into account. Huddleston et al (2015) note that policy for Māori and Pacific Island peoples could serve as a model for improving policies for migrants overall. One major area for improvement would be a national health plan for Asian and MELAA peoples similar to plans for Pacific Island peoples (Ministry of Health, 2002, 2014). This would reduce the patchy nature of service and ensure that measures for change were systematically and equitably planned, operationalised, and evaluated.

Policy change is required for accountability. Accountability to funders drives service provision and practice change. There is little service without accountability. Explicit National Asian and MELAA inclusion in health policy development would prioritise need and shape lower-level strategy and accountability measures. More consistent disaggregation of ethnic and migrant specific data would identify troublesome health issues in sub-populations, and support research and policy action to address these. In conclusion, in 2019, there was still room for improvement so that high level policy entitling migrants to inclusion and equity will be reflected in policy about health service delivery, research and planning.

References

Buse, K., Mays, N., & Walt, G. (2012). *Making health policy*. United Kingdom: McGraw-Hill Education.

Di Cosmo, C., Milfont, T. L., Robinson, E., Denny, S. J., Ward, C., Crengle, S., & Ameratunga, S. N. (2011). Immigrant status and acculturation influence substance use among New Zealand youth. *Aust N Z J Public Health, 35*(5), 434-441. https://doi.org/10.1111/j.1753-6405.2011.00758.x

Hajat, A., Blakely, T., Dayal, S., & Jatrana, S. (2010). Do New Zealand's immigrants have a mortality advantage? Evidence from the New Zealand Census-Mortality Study. *Ethn Health, 15*(5), 531-547. https://doi.org/10.1080/13557858.2010.496479

Huddleston, T., Bilgili, Ö., Joki, A.-L., & Vankova, Z. (2015). *Migrant Integration Policy Index*. Barcelona/Brussels: CIDOB and MPG. http://www.mipex.eu

McKinnon, M. (1996). *Immigrants and citizens. New Zealanders and Asian immigration in a historical context*. Wellington: Institute of Policy Studies, Victoria University of Wellington.

Mehta, S. (2012). *Health needs assessment of Asian people living in the Auckland region*. Auckland: Northern DHB Support Agency. http://www.countiesmanukau.health.nz/assets/About-CMH/Performance-and-planning/health-status/2012-health-needs-of-asian-people.pdf

Ministry of Health. (2002). *He Korowai Oranga*. Wellington: Ministry of Health.

Ministry of Health. (2012). *Tupu Ola Moui: Pacific Health Chart Book 2012*. Wellington: Ministry of Health.

Ministry of Health. (2014). *'Ala Mo'ui: Pathways to Pacific Health and Wellbeing 2014–2018*. Wellington: Ministry of Health.

Mintrom, M. (2012). *Contemporary Policy Analysis*. New York: Oxford University Press.

Rudmin, F. W. (2009). Constructs, measurements and models of acculturation and acculturative stress. *International Journal of Intercultural Relations, 33*, 106-123. https://doi.org/10.1016/j.ijintrel.2008.12.001

Scipioni, M., Urso, G., *Migration Policy Indexes.* Joint Research Centre, Ispra, 2018, ISBN 978-92-79-77989-3 JRC109400. https://joint-research-centre.ec.europa.eu/ system/files/ 2018-05/jrc109400_migration_policy_indexes_online.pdf

Scragg, R. (2016). *Asian Health in Aotearoa in 2011 - 2013: Trends since 2002-2003 and 2006-2007.* Auckland. http://www.ecald.com/assets/Resources/Asian-Health-Aotearoa-2011.pdf

Solano, G., & Huddleston, T. (2020). *Migrant Integration Policy Index 2020.* Barcelona/Brussels: CIDOB and MPG. http://www.mipex.eu

Statistics New Zealand. (2013). *2013 census quickstats about culture and identity.* Wellington: Statistics New Zealand.

Statistics New Zealand. (2018). *Ethnic group summaries.* https://www.stats.govt.nz/tools/2018-census-ethnic-group-summaries

Statistics New Zealand. (2019). *New Zealand's population reflects growing diversity.* https://www.stats.govt.nz/news/new-zealands-population-reflects-growing-diversity

Zhou, L., & Bennett, S. (2017). *International Benchmarking of Asian Health Outcomes for Waitemata and Auckland DHBs.* Auckland: Waitemata District Health Board. http://www.waitematadhb.govt.nz/assets/Documents/health-needs-assessments/International-benchmarking-report-of-Asian-health-outcomes-FINAL.PDF

MIGRANTS AND DIGESTIVE PATHOLOGIES IN A PANDEMIC CONTEXT: A PRELIMINARY COMPARATIVE STUDY BETWEEN THE FRENCH AND THE SWEDISH HEALTHCARE SYSTEMS AND MIGRATION POLICIES

Fanny Christou[1] and Niki Christou[2]

Introduction

This paper stems from a current innovative research proposal in order to strengthen multidisciplinary research when it comes to the articulation between the Covid-19 and migrants' health issues through the scope of gastro-intestinal diseases. Indeed, based on an extensive literature review dealing with migrants' inequalities in accessing health, this paper aims to further reflect on the ways health promotion measures towards migrant populations can help in preventing the development of new pathologies in the current pandemic context based on two case studies. The original choice of France and Sweden to conduct this research can be explained by two main factors: 1/ their migration policies diverge, tracing the clear difference between the two that has emerged over time, 2/ these two countries have handled the spread of the Covid-19 very differently. Examining two countries such as France and Sweden can help to understand how discourses on immigration and the role of the welfare state are articulated but also to what extent their respective approaches to face the pandemic have resulted in a similar absence of effectiveness regarding the health situation of vulnerable population such as migrants.

In Sweden, immigrants (born abroad or with parents born abroad, that is to say 24.9% of the national population) represent 74% of Covid-19 cases recorded in the so-called vulnerable areas (Swedish Public Health Agency, 2020 & 2021). France is no exception to this trend with the Covid-19 epidemic affecting the most vulnerable and the poorest, both from a health and economic point of view, with an increase in the number of deaths twice

[1] Fanny Christou, South Denmark University, Odense, Denmark. Migrinter, University of Poitiers, France. Associate Researcher, Arab Center for Research and Political Studies in Paris (CAREP), France. Collaborative Institute on Migration, Paris, France.
[2] Niki Christou, Department of General, Digestive and Endocrine Surgery, University Hospital of Limoges – France. Laboratory INSERM U1308-CAPTuR.
"Control of Cell Activation in Tumor Progression and Therapeutic Resistance", Medical School, Limoges-France. Head of the Chair of Excellence in Colorectal Cancer Research (CECCR)

higher for immigrants compared to people who were born in France during the months of March and April 2020 (Papon & Robert-Bobée, 2020). This situation is worsened by the existence of barriers to accessing health care among migrants. In both Sweden and France, the conditions of access to health services may be even more complicated for undocumented migrants due to the presence of different factors[3].

Indeed, in Sweden, "fear of deportation and practical and psychosocial factors constitute hinderance of access to healthcare for undocumented migrants" (Mona et al., 2021). On the other hand, during the asylum process and until the asylum seeker leaves Sweden or is granted a residence permit, he or she is entitled to a free medical examination, emergency health care and urgent medical or dental care that cannot be "postponed", gynaecological and prenatal care. However, it seems to be no coherent national system for carrying out health assessments on asylum seekers in Sweden (Jonzon et al., 2018; Swedish Red Cross, 2018). In France, asylum seekers under the regular procedure have access to healthcare through the universal healthcare insurance (PUMA) system. Those who have no right to remain on the territory, including rejected asylum seekers, benefit from the PUMA for six months after the end of validity of the asylum claim certification, and after this period, State Medical Aid (AME) enables them to receive free treatments in hospitals as well as in any doctors' office. As many NGOs reports, although access to health insurance and healthcare are supposed to be universal, administrative obstacles, geographical fragmentation and discrimination are the main problems in accessing health services for migrants in France (Gosselin et al., 2020). More generally, in both Sweden and France, the evidence shows unmet healthcare needs, especially when it comes to migrants' mental health (Lebano et al., 2020).

The Covid-19 pandemic context exacerbates the fragility of the healthcare system as well as the reinforcement of health inequalities that many vulnerable people face. Migrants are at high risk of an increased precarious situation, lacking from necessary resources for treatments and primary prevention. In addition, among the most frequent health problems faced by refugees, migrants and asylum seekers, it is worth mentioning gastrointestinal illnesses as well as eating disorders due to stressful situations, sub-optimal hygiene as well as poor living conditions before, during and after the migration process (World Health Organisation, 2020). In this regard, the

---

[3] For more details regarding the case of detention conditions of asylum seekers, see the Asylum Information Database: https://asylumineurope.org

interruption of care is the main problem, due to the lack of access to health care systems, or the decimation of these services, and displacement.

The articulation between Covid-19, ethnic/racial disparities and spatial fragmentations

While migrant populations across the Europe are extremely heterogeneous, there is evidence that some migrant communities may be at high risk of exposure to, and infection with, Covid-19. The recent literature highlights the articulation between Covid-19 and ethnic/racial disparities (Chowkwanyun et al., 2020; Gruer et al., 2021; Webb Hooper et al., 2020), with minority ethnic groups at increased risk of death from Covid-19. Indeed, the few data available by origin usually show a significant over-representation of immigrants in the incidence of Covid-19 (OECD, 2020). For example, Denmark, Norway and Sweden have all seen higher than expected proportions of migrants amongst Covid-19 cases given their numbers in the population: 42% of all cases in Norway (to April 27, 2020), 32% in Sweden (to May 7, 2020) and 26% in Denmark (to September 7, 2020). The United Kingdom, Netherlands, France, and Sweden have reported significantly higher all-cause mortality in migrants from specific countries/regions in 2020 compared with the host population, and when compared to previous years.

Furthermore, being male, having less individual income, lower education, not being married all independently predict a higher risk of death from Covid-19 and from all other causes of death. The interaction of the virus causing Covid-19 and its social environment exerts an unequal burden on the most disadvantaged members of society (Drefahl et al., 2020). Studies that have been conducted in the United Kingdom and in the United States specifically show a tendency of ethnic minorities, Black people, and Asians being disproportionately affected by Covid-19 due to socioeconomic differences (Abuelgasim et al., 2020). A similar trend has affected French and Swedish neighbourhoods, where there is a high concentration of first and second generations migrants and where the population is more often exposed to critical work conditions. Both in Sweden and in France, various complex socio-economic factors have meant that vulnerable, low income and undocumented migrant groups have found themselves particularly at risk due to the pandemic. Amplifying and deepening existing inequalities (Goldin & Muggah, 2020), the impacts of the Covid-19 are racialised (Timothy, 2020) but also gendered, with the so-called "shadow pandemic" of rising gender-based violence (UNWOMEN, 2020).

Figure 1. Share of immigrants among deaths in France and Sweden, March-April 2020 compared with previous periods (OECD, 2020)

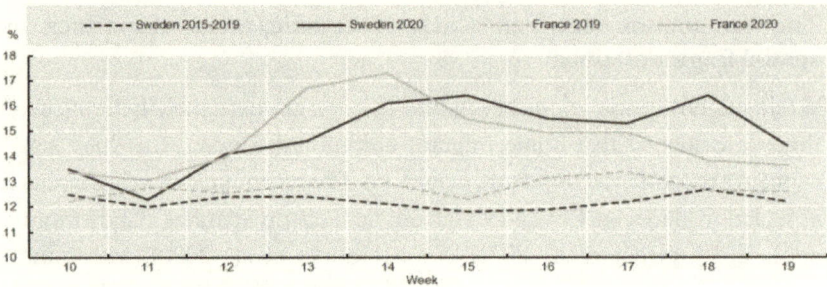

Note: The share of immigrant deaths in France in the weeks 10 to 19 2020 is compared with the share for the same period for the year 2019. The share of immigrant deaths in Sweden in the weeks 10 to 19 2020 is compared with the share for the same period for the years 2015-19. Source: OECD Secretariat calculations based on national sources.

France: available data

The collection of so-called "ethnic" statistics is prohibited in France and it is seldom discussed in research or the media, but it may be authorized on a case-by-case basis, particularly for scientific purposes. To date, the study published by the Institute of Statistics and Economic Studies (INSEE) in July 2020 (Papon & Robert-Bobée, 2020) is the only one that highlights the mortality figures by country of origin in France, showing that both poverty and ethno-racial discrimination have an impact on exposure of the Covid-19. As explained by Louarn (2020), "mounting evidence from the US, Britain and Canada pointing to greater Covid-19 mortality risks for non-white groups increased pressure on French researchers to do the same. While the study pointing to high death rates among their foreign-born parents suggest that minorities, especially from sub-Saharan African groups, were disproportionately affected by the pandemic, it shed no light on the situation among French-born children of immigrants."

The study conducted under the umbrella of the INSEE (Papon & Robert-Bobée, 2020) reveals that in France, Covid-19 death rates were twice and sometimes three times higher among foreign-born French nationals or residents compared to their French-born counterparts at the height of the pandemic. More precisely, between March and April 2020, excess mortality – the difference in mortality compared with the same period in 2019 – among the foreign-born was twice that of native-born (Papon and Robert-Bobée, 2020). The immigrant groups which were hit the worst by the excess mortality were from North Africa (+54% deaths compared to the same period in 2019), sub-Saharan Africa (+114%) and Asia (+91%), compared with 22%

excess mortality for the native-born (Melchior et al., 2021). Higher excess mortality for immigrants was even observed among the youngest cohorts. Immigrants' excess mortality remained twice to four times as much as that for the native-born, even after taking into account that foreign-born are more likely to live in densely populated areas that were more affected by the pandemic. The state of the art also highlights that this trend is reflected in geographic inequalities in mortality with the high death rate among migrants that can be explained in part by the fact that immigrant populations in France tend to settle in poorer, more densely populated areas, especially in the Paris metropolitan area of Île-de-France, home to impoverished banlieues, or suburbs.

For instance, between March and April 2020, there is "a 118% increase compared with the preceding year in Seine-Saint-Denis, a district North of Paris which is the poorest in France and where 30% of the population is immigrant, compared with a 96% increase in Paris itself" (Melchior et al., 2021). This excess mortality in Seine-Saint-Denis can be explained by three main factors (Brun and Simon, 2020): relatively precarious living conditions likely to facilitate virus spread, health inequalities affecting the department's immigrant and second-generation population, subaltern jobs with higher exposure to the virus (as immigrants are heavily overrepresented among the department's manual and lower-level office workers, endorsing jobs such as domestic employees, security guards, and cleaning workers making the greatest use of public transport to get to work), and unequal access to health system care and treatment.

Sweden: available data

A similar trend has affected specific Swedish neighbourhoods, where there is a high concentration of first and second generations migrants and where the population is more often exposed to critical work conditions such as working in public transportation, home care, and retirement homes caring for the elderly, without the possibility of working from home. Disadvantaged socioeconomic and living conditions may increase infection rates in migrants and contribute to their higher Covid-19 mortality risk (Rostila et al., 2020). These areas, that have specifically been affected by the pandemic, are also characterised by socio-economic deprivation, overcrowded living conditions, and linguistic obstacles in adopting preventative measures. Official data about the spread of Covid-19 among undocumented migrants are missing. But for the period up to May 19, 2020, in Spånga-Tensta (North-West Stockholm), where about 60% of inhabitants are foreign-born and come mostly from the Middle East, the local authority registered 71 cases and 12 deaths per 10 000 inhabitants, a number that is drastically higher than in the general Swedish population (Valeriani et al., 2020).

According to the Swedish Public Health Agency (2020), in Sweden (between 13 March to 7 May 2020), 32% of positive cases were migrants, despite their comprising only 19% of the population. In Sweden the incidence of Covid-19 was highest among migrants from Turkey, Ethiopia, and Somalia. In another comprehensive dataset from Sweden (period 13 March 2020-15 February 2021) the relative risk of being diagnosed with Covid-19 was higher for persons born in the Middle East, Southeast Europe, South America, Africa, Asia and Oceania compared to persons born in Sweden (Swedish Public Health Agency, 2021). The number of deaths among persons aged 40 years and more who were born in countries from which many refugees have migrated to Sweden in the last decades (Syria, Iraq and Somalia) was 220% higher in March-May 2020 compared to the average in 2016-19. In contrast, the respective increase during these three months was only 18% for those born in Sweden, European Union or North America, despite an older age composition (Hansson et al., 2020).

Other data collected under the umbrella of the Asylum Commission[4] also provide interesting insights regarding Sweden's migration-related detention centres, capturing the lack of measures taken by the authorities to safeguard migrants' health during the pandemic but also the virtual absence of public and political debate on the situation for detained and deportable migrants in Sweden (Lindberg et al., 2020, Lindberg et al., 2022). In this respect, while the ongoing pandemic has provided an opportunity to rethink the use of migration-related detention, based on the suspension of deportation, the choice for other alternatives to detention, or the regularisation of all people with precarious legal status to ensure their full access to healthcare, Sweden has not proposed such progressive initiatives. Contributing to the reinforcement of ethnic disparities as well as spatial fragmentations, "as a result, those who have been released from detention when their deportation order is not enforceable are excluded not only from legalisation options but also from social rights protections as a direct result of restrictive laws and legal praxis" (Lindberg et al., 2020).

---

[4] The Asylum Commission is a collaboration between Linköping University, the Swedish Network of Refugee Support Groups (FARR), people who sought refuge in Sweden, professional groups and researchers: https://liu.se/en/research/asylum-commission

Two different approaches of the Covid-19 management in 2020 but the entrenchment of migrants' health inequalities

As explained, there is evidence that Covid-19 is linked to ethnic/racial disparities as well as spatial fragmentations. France and Sweden have handled the spread of the Covid-19 very differently since March 2020 but the various health policies that have been adopted seem to produce the same effects on migrants who are facing greater challenges as well as socio-spatial inequalities in facing the current health crisis. The two respective approaches that have been adopted in France and in Sweden to face the pandemic highlights once again to what extent Covid-19 exposes and amplifies migrants' inequalities and vulnerability. Even before Covid-19 came along, there was evidence of growing inequality within and between countries (UNDESA, 2020) but the "pandemic has amplified these existing inequalities, pushing those already on the margins of society still further away from the rights and opportunities that many of us take for granted", including inequalities associated with migration (Crawley, 2021).

France: measures and discourses that do not take into account migrants

France was one of the European countries that was most severely affected by the Covid-19 pandemic in the first half of 2020. Despite the effective capacity of crisis management often ascribed to majoritarian democracies, the French centralised state-led health system is subject to rising critiques for the measures it has adopted and for the strategies it deployed to fight the Covid-19 (Hassenteufeul, 2020). In the face of the global spread of Covid-19 since March 2020, key population health protection measures have been promulgated in France. One of them was the containment, as a conventional public health measure in epidemic settings to prevent contagion (Campeau et al. 2018; Tognotti, 2013), aimed at reducing contact and movement of individuals to a minimum. With the watchword "stay at home", this measure came into force on 17 March 2020, at a time when the number of cases and deaths was increasing and the virus was circulating throughout the country (Santé Publique France, 2020).

In addition, as highlighted by the European Network Against Racism[5], preferring the expression "we are at war" to the terms "resistance", "struggle", or even "individual and collective resilience", political discourses

---

[5] ENAR is a network of over 150 NGOs working to combat racism everywhere in Europe: https://www.enar-eu.org

may reinforce a feeling of fear and of belonging to a national community that must be protected. Then, by opposing "the children of the nation" to those who do not belong to it, the government may exclude foreigners living in France, many of whom are in a vulnerable situation, from national containment measures.

The study conducted by Carillon et al. (2020) shows that confinement can affect individuals' abilities to act and generate a "disaffiliation process" to placing this precarious immigrant population even more on the margins of society, by tipping individuals towards "social non-existence". Thus, the Covid-19 crisis exacerbates pre-existing difficulties, generating not so new situations for migrants (Carillon et al., 2020), with a structural aggressiveness of a response to the epidemic that does not take social inequalities into account (Marmot and Allen, 2020). We could mention here different examples of how the Covid-19 pandemic has exacerbated the vulnerability of the displaced men, women and children in France. For migrants residing in Northern France, in Calais and Grande-Synthe, different NGOs (such as Choose Love/Help Refugees, Human Rights Observers HRO, L'Auberge des Migrants, Refugee Rights Europe) report that Covid-19 sheltering operations were insufficient across the time period, with many people still requiring safe accommodation (Paton and Boittiaux, 2020).

Sweden: towards the end of the welfare state?

Claeson and Hanson (2021) mention that in the second wave of the Covid-19 pandemic, the Swedish national response continues to be an outlier with cases and deaths increasing more rapidly than in its Nordic neighbours. According to these authors, "this difference between Nordic countries cannot be explained merely by variations in national cultures, histories, population sizes and densities, immigration patterns, the routes by which the virus was first introduced, or how cases and deaths are reported. Instead, the answers to this enigma are to be found in the national Covid-19 strategies, the assumptions on which it is based, and in the governance of the health system that has enabled the strategy to continue without major course corrections" (Claeson and Hanson, 2021).

In this respect, while France has adopted lockdown measures since the beginning of the pandemic, for months Swedish public health authorities have defended their controversial decision not to lock down the country in response to the global Covid-19 pandemic, in favour of a culture of trust, relying on the individual responsibility to deal with the Covid-19. At the heart of the government's strategy was the implicit and controversial idea that, rather than contain the spread of disease, a country could achieve herd immunity by allowing a proportion of the population to be infected—at the expense of deaths among the vulnerable. However, time has told a different story and Sweden recorded the most coronavirus deaths per capita in Europe in a seven-day average between 25 May and 2 June, 2020 (Habib, 2020).

While Sweden, with a record 163,000 asylum seekers arriving in the country of 10 million in 2015, has often been depicted as a model of welfare state with an openness solidarity towards migrants, recent restrictive measures have been adopted and the country reported no changes to its migration law due to the pandemic, with all requirements remaining the same. In May-June 2020, the Swedish government announced its intention to offer funding to civil society (non-governmental organisations) in order to ease the consequences of the pandemic for particularly vulnerable groups, including undocumented migrants. However, one particularly noteworthy aspect of Sweden's specific institutional set-up is the consequences in terms of who is most at risk – the newly arrived – with the indirect and long-term impacts that can prove to be politically, socially and economically unsustainable to Sweden as a society. Indeed, refugees in Sweden are already facing challenges such as poor health, difficulties with employment, crowded living conditions and difficulties obtaining health care as well as understanding health care information (Zdravkovic et al., 2020; Mangrio et al., 2018; Mangrio et al. 2020), that can exacerbate new challenges and worsen their conditions of life with the current pandemic (for instance domestic hardship due to mental and social struggles).

Gastro-intestinal illnesses: the common pattern between Covid-19 symptoms and migrants' experiences with post-traumatic stress disorders

As in many other crises, migrants may be particularly vulnerable to the direct and indirect impacts of Covid-19. Their ability to avoid the infection and to receive adequate health care can be articulated with various factors, including an exposure to crowded working, and living conditions without any possible social distancing, insufficient resources and limited access to key hygiene items, cultural and linguistic barriers due to their limited local knowledge and networks resulting in limited access to information, lack of consideration of their cultural and linguistic diversity in service provision. They are therefore less likely to seek medical care for suspected Covid-19 symptoms due to restrictive access to rights related to their status, financial constraints or fear.

But they may also be at risk of isolation, anxiety with being stranded, potentially arrested or victim of xenophobia acts (Liem et al., 2020; Guadano, 2020; Hennebry & Hari, 2020). In addition, migrants may face an inability to deal with pre-existing pulmonary and respiratory issues as well as digestive illnesses that are found to be a consequence of both the Covid-19 as well as post-traumatic stress disorders.

Covid-19 Can Create Gastro-Intestinal Symptoms

While the three symptoms of Covid-19 are currently well documented by the state of the art (fever, cough, respiratory distress), several studies report that half of patients who have been tested positive for the coronavirus also evoke digestive symptoms (Ungaro et al., 2020; Gu et al., 2020; Perisetti et al., 2020). Indeed, most studies show the SARS-CoV-2 virus enters intestinal cells, or enterocytes, and respiratory cells using the angiotensin-converting enzyme 2

Figure 2. Illustrative model of SARS-CoV-2 infection and its association with the lung-gut-brain axis and microbiome dysbiosis (Villapol, 2020)

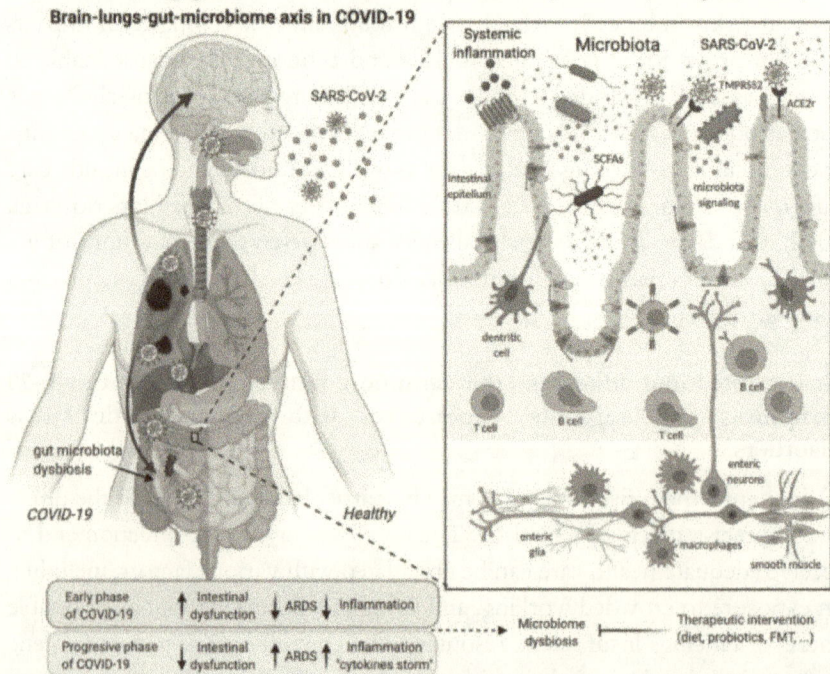

(ACE-2) protein as a receptor (Kopel et al., 2020). Covid-19 can attach itself to the ACE-2 receptors that sit in the cellular membranes of the cells lining many of the organs, including the gastrointestinal (GI) tract. Thus, when SARS-CoV-2 particles leave an infected cell, it triggers the release of cytokines, small proteins that play a role in inflammation. This process may cause GI symptoms that can also occur as viruses destroy or damage GI tissues. The most common GI symptoms associated with Covid-19 include: lack of appetite, lack of smell or taste, diarrhoea, nausea, vomiting up blood or GI bleeding, abdominal pain (Elshazli et al., 2021; Vespa et al., 2021).

Migration experiences and post-traumatic stress disorders can create gastro-intestinal issues

Mental and psychosocial illness is also a significant health problem for migrants and refugees, in particular newly arrived people, including depression, anxiety disorder, alcoholism and drug abuse as a result of traumatic experiences prior to dislocation or during the migration process which may be related to war, hunger, physical and sexual abuse (Priebe et al., 2016). Specific challenges in migrant mental health include communication difficulties because of language and cultural differences; racism and unemployment; new food habits and/or lack of access healthy food; the effect of cultural shaping of symptoms and illness behaviour on diagnosis, coping and treatment; differences in family structure and process affecting adaptation, acculturation and intergenerational conflict; and aspects of acceptance by the receiving society that affect employment, social status and integration (Kirmayer et al., 2011). Risk factors for mental illness in migrants and refugees also include age, gender, lower socio-economic status and lack of social support (Hermansson et al., 2003; Masman et al., 2008; Roth & Ekblad, 2006).

In this respect, the symptoms provoked by the Covid-19 can also be found in the post-traumatic stress disorder (PTSD) or complex post-traumatic disorder (cPTSD) that migrants experience all along the migration process (Schouler-Ocak, 2015). Post-traumatic stress, defined as "an adverse reaction to traumatic experiences which decreases daily functioning and quality of life", can induce the release of different hormones – cytokines – that lead to chronic inflammation and this status thus triggers different digestive disorders such as inflammatory bowel disorders with ulcerative colitis or Crohn's disease (Cámara et al., 2011).

Indeed, one of the most common reported health problems may be related to the pre-migration process, with a variety of diseases gastrointestinal and respiratory problems (Firenze et al., 2014; Eonomopoulou et al., 2017; Schilling et al., 2017). Then, the migration process itself including the period while on 'the move' and the time of arrival and later, during early settlement and the period of living in the host country may affect migrants' health. The duration of the migration journey that can be articulated with legal or illegal border crossing, exposure to physical dangers, and living in reception as well as detention centres can have a significant impact upon migrant health. Vulnerable groups specifically are prone to respiratory and gastrointestinal infections and dermatologic conditions due to sub-optimal hygienic and inadequate living conditions, but also nutritional deprivation with a lack of access to appropriate food and water during migration.

Conclusions

Against this analysis aiming at strengthening the link between migration post-traumatic stress disorders, Covid-19 and digestive issues, one can conclude that migrants have paid a higher toll with respect to the incidence of Covid-19, with higher infection risk and higher mortality, despite having a younger age on average, but also in creating deeper inequalities. Migrants face post-traumatic stress disorders, but they also suffer various impacts of the pandemic that has exceptionally bleak consequences on their health, such as a deterioration of mental health with greater levels of depression, worry, anxiety, and loneliness (WHO, 2020). Refugees and migrants are often exposed to the virus with limited tools to protect themselves and in many cases public health measures do not reach them. This group of refugees and migrants also reported being less likely to seek medical care for suspected Covid-19 symptoms because of financial constraints or fear of deportation. At the same time, they are less likely to comply with the safety directions given by the authorities.

However, there is a lack of study dealing with the articulation between the impacts of Covid-19 on migrants' health and their post-traumatic stress disorders they are suffering from, specifically looking at the digestive diseases they may face all along the migratory process. This paper aims at filling this gap by proposing a reflection on the scholarly need to highlight the existing inequalities in terms of prevention and primary access to healthcare for migrants in the context of a pandemic and in European countries that have adopted different approaches but with the similar way of keeping migrants invisible in accessing health. More specifically, through the scope of gastro-intestinal diseases, as an effect of both Covid-19 and migration experiences, this project seeks to bring synergies of medical sciences as well as humanities in order to strengthen research on migrants' inequalities. This involves setting up a series of intervention actions aimed at developing awareness, information and communication strategies to encourage primary prevention and ensure equitable access to care.

What has been done so far in both France and Sweden highlights that the specific health needs of migrants are not clearly understood and communication between health care practitioners and migrants remains poor. On the other hand, since migrant populations are often already subject to chronic gastrointestinal illnesses, these digestive disorders seem to worsen with the Covid-19, thus reflecting the urgent need to scholarly question the articulation between the precarious situation of migrants and pathologies such as chronic diseases linked to the digestive system. In addition, there is often inadequate responsiveness of health care systems due to poor preparedness which is enhanced by legal issues that migrants have to face in relation to health and other basic services. Approaches to manage migration health problems have not kept pace with increasing challenges associated with the size, speed, diversity and disparity of current migration patterns and factors such as barriers to access health services have not sufficiently been addressed.

Thus, throughout a comparative approach based on the French and the Swedish case studies, this paper calls for the need of a further scholarly investigation related to the analysis of the articulation between gastrointestinal pathologies that migrants are likely to develop due to the PTSD with the lack of services in accessing primary prevention and healthcare due to the existence of social and spatial fragmentation reinforced by the Covid-19. In this regard, while the current pandemic further accentuates already existing inequalities, the fragmentation of access to healthcare is also questioning, in particular for vulnerable populations such as migrants, in particular asylum seekers. It is therefore crucial to focus our attention on their access to health services, crucial during a pandemic, as well as their management of chronic pathologies linked to their migratory journey.

References

Abuelgasim, E., Saw, LJ., Shirke, M., Zeinah, M., Harky, A. (2020). COVID-19: unique public health issues facing Black, Asian and minority ethnic communities. *Current Problems in Cardiology, 45*(8), 100621. https://doi.org/10.1016/j.cpcardiol.2020.100621

Brun, S. and Simon, P. (2020). L'invisibilité des minorités dans les chiffres du Coronavirus: le détour par la Seine-Saint-Denis. Dossier « Inégalités ethno-raciales et pandémie de coronavirus », *De facto,* 68-78. HAL ID: hal-02887933.

Cámara, RJA., Gander, M., Begré, S., Von Känel, R. and Swiss Inflammatory Bowel Disease Cohort Study Group. (2011). Post-traumatic stress in Crohn's disease and its association with disease activity. *Frontline Gastroenterology, 2*(1), 2-9. https://doi.org/10.1136/ fg. 2010.002733

Campeau, L., Degroote, S., Ridde, V., Carabali, M., Zinszer, K. (2018). Containment measures for emerging and re-emerging vector-borne and other infectious diseases of poverty in urban settings: a scoping review. *Infectious Diseases of Poverty, 7*(95), 1-16. https://doi.org/10.1186/s40249-018-0478-4

Carillon, S., Gosselin, A., Coulibaly, K., Ridde, V., Desgrées du Loû, A. (2020). Immigrants facing Covid 19 containment in France: An ordinary hardship of disaffiliation. *Journal of Migration and Health, 1-2.* https://doi.org/10.1016/j.jmh.2020.100032

Chowkwanyun, M. and Reed, AL. (2020). Racial Health Disparities and Covid-19 — Caution and Context. *New England Journal of Medicine, 383*(3), 201-203. https://doi.org/10.1056/NEJMp2012910

Claeson, M. and Hanson, M. (2021). COVID-19 and the Swedish enigma. *The Lancet, 397*(10271), 259-261. https://doi.org/10.1016/S0140-6736(20)32750-1

Crawley, H. (2021). The Politics of Refugee Protection in a Post-COVID-19 World. *Social Sciences, 10*(3), 81-95. https://doi.org/10.3390/socsci10030081

Drefahl, S., Wallace, M., Mussino, E., Aradhya, S., Kolk, M., Brandén, M., Malmberg, B., & Andersson, G. (2020). A population-based cohort study of socio-demographic risk factors for COVID-19 deaths in Sweden. *Nature Communications,* 11(5097). https://doi.org/10.1038/s41467-020-18926-3

Elshazli, R.M., Kline, A., Elgaml, A., Aboutaleb, M. H., Salim, M. H., Omar, M., Munshi, R., Mankowski, N., Hussein, M. H., Attia, A. S., Toraih, E. A., Settin, A., Killackey, M., Fawzy, M. S., Kandil, E. (2021). Gastroenterology manifestations and COVID-19 outcomes: A meta-analysis of 25,252 cohorts among the first and second waves. *Journal of Medical Virology Wiley Periodicals, 93*(5), 2740-2768. https://doi.org/10.1002/jmv.26836

Eonomopoulou, A., Pavli, A., Stasinopoulou, P., Giannopoulos, LA., Tsiodras, S. (2017). Migrant screening: lessons learned from the migrant holding level at the Greek-Turkish borders. *Journal of Infection and Public Health, 10*(2), 177–184. https://doi.org/10.1016/j.jiph.2016.04.012

Firenze, A., Restivo, V., Bonanno, V., Aleo, N., Pace, S., Marsala, M. G. L., Palermo, M. (2014). Health status of immigrants arrived to Italian coast (Article in Italian). *Epidemiologia e Prevenzione*, vol. *38*(6 Suppl. 2), 78–82.

Goldin, I. and Muggah, R. (2020). COVID-19 is Increasing Multiple Kinds of Inequality. Here's What We Can Do about It. World Economic Forum. Available at: https://www.weforum.org/agenda/2020/10/covid-19-is-increasing-multiple-kinds-of-inequality-here-s-what-we-can-do-about-it/

Gosselin, A., Desgrées, du Loû, A., Casella-Colombeau, S., Vignier, N., Melchior, M. (2020). Situational Brief: The Health of Asylum Seekers & Undocumented Migrants In France during Covid-19. Available at: https://www.migrationandhealth.org/ files/ ugd/188e74_7e2e9164b7d74101aac2ffc6a5ea175f.pdf?index=true

Gruer, L., Agyemang, C., Bhopal, R., Chiarenza, A., Krasnik, A., Kumar, B. (2021). Migration, ethnicity, racism and the COVID-19 pandemic: A conference marking the launch of a new Global Society. *Public Health in Practice, 2*, 100088. https://doi.org/10. 1016/j.puhip.2021.100088

Gu, J., Han, B., Wang, J. (2020). COVID-19: Gastrointestinal Manifestations and Potential Fecal-Oral Transmission. *Gastroenterology*, 158(6), 1518-1519. https://doi.org/10. 1053/ j. gastro.2020.02.054

Guadagno, L. (2020). Migrants and the COVID-19 pandemic: An initial analysis, *Migration Research Series,* issue 60

Habib, H. (2020). Has Sweden's controversial covid-19 strategy been successful?. *BMJ: British*

Medical Journal, 369. https://doi.org/10.1136/bmj.m2376

Hansson, E., Albin, M., Rasmussen, M., Jakobsson, K. (2020). Stora skillnader i överdödlighet våren 2020 utifrån födelseland [Large differences in excess mortality in March-May 2020 by country of birth in Sweden], *Lakartidningen, 117,* 20113

Hermansson A-C, Timpka, T, Thyberg M. (2003). The long-term impact of torture on the mental health of war-wounded refugees: findings and implications for nursing programmes, *Scandinavian Journal of Caring* Sciences, 17(4), 317-324. https://doi.org/10.1046/j.0283-9318.2003.00241.x

Hassenteufeul, P. (2020). Handling the COVID-19 crisis in France: Paradoxes of a centralized state-led health system. *European Policy Analysis Wiley,* 6(2), 170-179, https://doi.org/10.1002/epa2.1104

Hennebry, J., & Hari, K. C. (2020). Covid-19 and the transformation of migration and mobility globally - Quarantined! Xenophobia and migrant workers during the COVID-19 pandemic. *IOM-UN Migration*

Jonzon, R., Lindkvist, P., & Hurtig, A-K. (2018). Structural and procedural barriers to health assessment for asylum seekers and other migrants - an explorative survey in Sweden. *BMC Health Services Research,* 18(1): 813. https://doi.org/10.1186/s12913-018-3588-6

Kopel, J., Perisetti, A., Gajendra, M., Boregowda, U., & Goyal, H. (2020). Clinical Insights into the Gastrointestinal Manifestations of COVID-19. *Digestive Diseases and Sciences,* 65(7), 1932-1939. https://doi.org/10.1007/s10620-020-06362-8

Kirmayer, L. J., Narasiah, L., Munoz, M., Rashid, M., Ryder, A. G., Guzder, J., Hassan, G., Rousseau, C., Pottie, K., & Canadian Collaboration for Immigrant and Refugee Health (CCIRH) (2011). Common mental health problems in immigrants and refugees: general approach in primary care. *CMAJ: Canadian Medical Association journal = journal de l'Association medicale canadienne,* 183(12), E959-E967. https://doi.org/10.1503/cmaj.090292

Lebano, A., Hamed, S., Bradby, H. *et al.* (2020). Migrants' and refugees' health status and healthcare in Europe: a scoping literature review. *BMC Public Health,* 20, 1039. https://doi.org/10.1186/s12889-020-08749-8

Liem, A., Wang, C., Wariyanti, Y., Latkin, C.A. and Hall, B.J. (2020). The neglected health of international migrant workers in the COVID-19 epidemic. *The Lancet. Psychiatry,* 7(4). https://doi.org/10.1016/S2215-0366(20)30076-6

Lindberg, A., Lundberg, A., Häyhtiö, S. and Rundqvist, E. (2020). Detained and Disregarded: How COVID-19 Has Affected Detained and Deportable Migrants in Sweden. Available at: https://www.law.ox.ac.uk/research-subject-groups/centre-criminology/centre border-criminologies/blog/2020/07/detained-and

Lindberg, A., Lundberg, A., Rundqvist, E., & Häythiö, S. (2022). Governing Through Ignorance: Swedish Authorities' Treatment of Detained and Non-deported Migrants during the COVID-19 Pandemic. *Feminist Legal Studies,* 30(3), 309–329. https://doi.org/10.1007/s10691-022-09495-5

Louarn, A-D. (2020). Death tolls show France's immigrants hardest hit by COVID-19, study finds. *InfoMigrants.* Available at: https://www.infomigrants.net/en/post/26034/death-tolls-show-frances-immigrants-hardest-hit-by-covid19-study-finds

Mangrio, E., Carlson, E., Zdravkovic, S. (2018). Understanding experiences of the Swedish health care system from the perspective of newly arrived refugees. *BMC research notes, 11*(1): 616. https://doi.org/10.1186/s13104-018-3728-4

Mangrio, E., Maneesh, P-S., and Strange, M. (2020). Refugees in Sweden During the Covid-19 Pandemic—The Need for a New Perspective on Health and Integration. *Frontiers in Public Health,* 8, 574334. https://doi.org/10.3389/fpubh.2020.574334

Marmot, M. and Allen, J. (2020). COVID-19: exposing and amplifying inequalities, *Journal of epidemiology and community health,* 74(9), 681-682. https://doi.org/10.1136/jech-2020-214720

Masmas, TN., Møller, E., Buhmannr, C., Buhmann, C., Bunch, V., Hald Jensen, J., Hansen, T. N., Møller Jørgensen, L., Nørregård, T., Kjær, C., Mannstaedt, M., Oxholm, A., Skau, J., Theilade, L., Worm, L., & Ekstrøm, M. (2008). Asylum seekers in Denmark: a study of health status and grade of traumatization of newly arrived asylum seekers. *Journal on Rehabilitation of Torture Victims and Prevention of Torture,* 18(2), 77-86

Melchior, M., Desgrées du Loû, A., Gosselin, A., Datta, G. D., Carabali, M., Merckx, J., & Kaufman, J. S. (2021). Migrant status, ethnicity and COVID-19: more accurate European data are greatly needed. *Clinical microbiology and infection: the official publication of the European Society of Clinical Microbiology and Infectious Diseases,* 27(2), 160–162. https://doi.org/10.1016/j.cmi.2020.10.014

Mona, H., Andersson, L. M. C., Hjern, A., & Ascher, H. (2021). Barriers to accessing health care among undocumented migrants in Sweden - a principal component analysis. *BMC health services research,* 21(1), 830. https://doi.org/10.1186/s12913-021-06837-y

OECD. (2020). What is the impact of the COVID-19 pandemic on immigrants and their children?, *OECD Policy Responses to Coronavirus (COVID-19)*

Papon, S. & Robert-Bobée, I. (2020). Une hausse des décès deux fois plus forte pour les personnes nées à l'étranger que pour celles nées en France en mars-avril 2020, *Insee focus,* issue 198.

Pavli, A. & Maltezou, H. (2017). Health problems of newly arrived migrants and refugees in Europe, *Journal of Travel Medicine,* 24(4). https://doi.org/10.1093/jtm/tax016

Paton, E. & Boittiaux, C. (2020). Facing Multiple Crises: On treatment of refugees and displaced people in northern France during the COVID-19 pandemic. Available at: https://resource-centre-uploads.s3.amazonaws.com/uploads/facing-multiple-crises-report.pdf

Perisetti, A., Goyal, H., Gajendran, M., Boregowda, U., Mann, R., & Sharma, N. (2020). Prevalence, Mechanisms, and Implications of Gastrointestinal Symptoms in COVID-19, *Frontiers in* Medicine, 7, 588711. https://doi.org/10.3389/fmed.2020.588711

Priebe, S., Giacco, D., & El-Nagib, R. (2016) *WHO Health Evidence Network Synthesis Report 47. Public health aspects of mental health among migrants and refugees: A review of the evidence on mental health care for refugees, asylum seekers and irregular migrants in the WHO European Region.* Copenhagen, Denmark: WHO Regional Office for Europe

Rostila, M., Cederström, A., & Wallace, M. (2020) Disparities in covid-19 deaths by country of birth in Stockholm, Sweden: A total population-based cohort study, *Stockholm Research Reports in Demography,* nº 2020: 39

Roth G. & Ekblad S. (2006). A longitudinal perspective on depression and sense of coherence in a sample of mass-evacuated adults from Kosovo, *The Journal of nervous and mental disease,* 194(5), 378-381. https://doi.org/10.1097/01.nmd.0000217882.70120.38

Santé Publique France (2020). Covid-19: point épidémiologique-Situation au 15 mars 2020 à minuit. Available at: https://www.santepubliquefrance.fr/maladies-et-traumatismes/maladies-et-infections-respiratoires/infection-a-coronavirus/documents/bulletin-national/covid-19-point-epidemiologique-du-15-mars-2020

Schilling, T., Rauscher, S., Menzel, C., Reichenauer, S., Müller-Schilling, M., Schmid, S. & Selgrad, M. (2017). Migrants and refugees in Europe: challenges, experiences and contributions. *Visceral* Medicine, 33(4), 295-300. https://doi.org/10.1159/000478763

Schouler-Ocak, M. (2015). *Trauma and Migration. Cultural Factors in the Diagnosis and Treatment of*

Traumatised Immigrants, Switzerland: Spring International Publishing.

Swedish Public Health Agency (2020). Demografisk Beskrivning av Bekräftade Covid-19 Fall i Sverige 13 Mars-7 Maj 2020, Stockholm. Available at: https://www.folkhalsomyndigheten.se/contentassets/d6538f6c359e448ba39993a41e111 6e7/covid-19-demografisk-beskrivning-bekraftade-covid-19-fall.pdf

Swedish Public Health Agency (2021). Utrikesfödda och covid-19: Konstaterade fall, IVA-vård och avlidna bland utrikesfödda i Sverige 13 mars 2020–15 februari 2021, Stockholm. Available at: https://www.folkhalsomyndigheten.se/publicerat-material/publikation sarkiv/u/utrikesfodda-och-covid-19/

Swedish Red Cross. (2018). Nedslag i verkligheten – tillgång till vård för papperslösa. Available at: https://bit.ly/3Px1nnE.

Tognotti, E. (2013). Lessons from the history of quarantine, from Plague to Influenza A. *Emerging Infectious Diseases, 19*(2), 254-249. https://doi.org/10.3201/eid1902.120312

Timothy, R. (2020). Coronavirus is not the Great Equalizer—Race Matters. Available at: https://theconversation.com/coronavirus-is-not-the-great-equalizer-race-matters-133867

UNDESA. (2020). *World social report 2020: inequality in a rapidly changing world*, New York, NY.

Ungaro, RC., Sullivan, T., Colombel, JF., & Patel, G. (2020). What Should Gastroenterologists and Patients Know About COVID-19? *Clinical Gastroenterology Hepatology, 18*(7), 1409-1411.

UNWOMEN. (2020). Press release: UN Women raises awareness of the shadow pandemic of violence against women during COVID-19. Available at: https://www.unwomen.org/ en/news/stories/2020/5/press-release-the-shadow-pandemic-of-violence-against-women-during-covid-19

Valeriani, G., Sarajlic Vukovic, I., & Mollica, R. (2020). Unconventional Answers to Unprecedented Challenges: The Swedish Experience During the COVID-19 Outbreak, *Journal of Preventive Medicine and Public Health, 53*(4), 233-235.

Vespa, E., Pugliese, N., Colapietro, F., & Aghemo, A. (2021). Stay (GI) Healthy: COVID-19 and Gastrointestinal Manifestations, Techniques and Innovations. *Journal of Techniques and Innovations in Gastrointestinal Endoscopy, 23*(2), 179-189. https://doi.org/10.1016/ j.tige.2021.01.006

Villapol, S. (2020). Gastrointestinal symptoms associated with COVID-19: impact on the gut microbiome. *Translational Research, The Journal of Laboratory and Clinical Medicine, 226*, 57-69. https://doi.org/10.1016/j.trsl.2020.08.004

Webb Hooper, M., Nápoles, AM., & Pérez-Stable, EJ. (2020). COVID-19 and racial/ethnic disparities. *JAMA, 323*(24), 2466-2467. https://doi.org/10.1001/jama.2020.8598

World Health Organisation. (2020). ApartTogether survey: preliminary overview of refugees and migrants self-reported impact of COVID-19. Available at: https://apps.who.int/ iris/bitstream/handle/10665/337931/9789240017924-eng.pdf?sequence=1&isAllowed=y

Zdravkovic, S., Carlzén, K., Grahn, M., & Mangrio, E. (2020). Kartläggning av hälsa, levnadsvanor, sociala relationer, arbetsmarknad och boendemiljö bland arabisktalande nyanlända inom etableringen Delrapport från MILSA 2.0.

IMPROVING THE DELIVERY OF IMMIGRATION AND REFUGEE HEALTHCARE IN THE USA: EXPERIENCES FROM ACADEMIC AND COMMUNİTY HOSPITALS

Benjamin Levy[1], Augustina Mensa-Kwao[2], Keng-Yu Chuang[3], Yasmin Hernandez-Barco[4]

Introduction

Over the past 250 years, the United States has welcomed immigrants and refugees from around the world – creating a melting pot of diversity that has disproportionally influenced American inventions, culture, music, and food. US refugees and immigrants to the United States have produced some of the most important inventions in modern history – Sergey Brin (the co-founder of Google) (Redding, 2018), Jawed Karim and Steve Chen (YouTube), Jacob Davis and Levi Strauss (Blue jeans), David Lindquist (Elevator) (Semuels, 2017), and Albert Einstein (photoelectric effect, nuclear energy (Isaacson, 2007). Between 1880 and 1940, immigrants produced 19.6% of inventions in the United States. Today, immigrants make an incredible impact on modern-day technology and account for 30% of all inventions (Akcigit et al., 2017).

Since World War II, American healthcare has continuously adapted to provide important medical services to recent immigrants and refugees. Over the past 20 years, a new generation of physicians and public health leaders in the United States are leading a movement to revolutionize healthcare for these vulnerable patient populations with an emphasis on preventive medicine, emotional well-being, medical literacy, social services, and job placement. Many American medical schools and residency programs have successfully created a new generation of empathetic physicians and public health leaders who understand the importance of health communication and cater to cultural differences to make immigrant patient populations feel comfortable.

Approximately 750,000 refugees have resettled to the United States from

[1] Benjamin Levy, University of Chicago, United States.
[2] Augustina Mensa-Kwao, University of Washington Department of Global Health, United States.
[3] Keng-Yu Chuang, University of Arizona College of Medicine-Phoenix; Creighton University School of Medicine, United States.
[4] Yasmin Hernandez-Barco, Massachusetts General Hospital; Harvard Medical School, United States.

2008-2019 (CDC, 2021a). The U.S. government-funded refugee program provides a medical exam within 90 days (including screening for HIV, Hepatitis, and TB) and important short-term health insurance for up to 8 months. This affords refugees important age-appropriate medical screening such as colonoscopies (where pre-cancerous polyps can be removed), mammography, skin cancer exams, and gynaecologic care. From our experiences, HIV, Hepatitis B, Hepatitis C, and Tuberculosis testing has been particularly important – many asymptomatic refugee patients are diagnosed during their initial medical exam. Frequently, refugees have not had access to modern-day preventive medicine in their former countries due to discrimination, domestic violence, war, lack of resources, or lack of medical providers.

As Gastroenterologists in different parts of the United States, we actively participate in colon cancer screening programs, Hepatitis B and Hepatitis C treatment, and anaemia work-up for both immigrants and refugees. Asymptomatic hepatitis B is particularly endemic in many countries from vertical transmission during childbirth. Young Gastroenterologists have had a profound impact on hepatitis B among immigrant communities too. Between 2011-2013, a Tulane University Gastroenterology Fellow developed a novel Hepatitis B screening program that teamed up with Vietnamese churches in New Orleans and Louisiana to encourage screening after church services and subsequently provide affordable treatment and liver management to those who tested positive. Asian and Pacific Islanders comprise more than 5% of the U.S. population but make up more than 50 percent of Americans living with chronic Hepatitis B. Approximately 20,000-30,000 Vietnamese live in the New Orleans metro area, so this was an important public health campaign organised by a Vietnamese American Gastroenterologist still in training[5]. Dr. Nguyen's campaign gained traction because he was trusted in the immigrant community. The program was particularly empowering to the Vietnamese population because 1) A Vietnamese American Gastroenterologist was given a platform in a church, 2) the health information was provided by a fluent speaker in the target patient population's first language, 3) and because of the continuity of care, Dr. Son Nguyen provided ongoing medical management in Tulane's Gastroenterology clinic.

This innovative outreach program combated many potential challenges in

---

[5]   https://www.beckersasc.com/gastroenterology-and-endoscopy/gastroenterologist-dr-son-nguyen-brings-attention-to-dangers-of-hbv-to-vietnamese-community.html

immigration healthcare, including "language barriers, culturally discordant health beliefs, issues with education access, limited knowledge of host cultures, and difficulties with healthcare access" (Hawkins et al., 2021).

Immigrants and refugees share similar struggles living in a foreign country and attempting to navigate the healthcare system and running into difficulties, such as understanding health insurance jargon. Augustina Mensa-Kwao[6] (MPH) realised from an early age the importance of access to health care resources and knowledge as well as social capital, as key factors in ameliorating mental and physical health issues. "It was not until years later as a college student that I realized that my families' experience navigating the US health care system is not unique".

Experiences such as these are often more prominent for refugee families, who are forced to flee their country because of a well-founded fear of persecution for race, religion, nationality, or political opinion. For more than 50 years, refugees have comprised a sizeable portion of new immigrants to the US (UNHCR, 2021). Since 1975, the United States has resettled approximately 3 million refugees (Filler, 2021). It has become increasingly necessary to meet the diverse needs of refugee communities in the US— many of whose experiences are further compounded by social, political, and structural determinants that influence their health outcomes.

Some immigrants and refugees may have a biased "mistrust of the healthcare system" (Clarke et al., 2021) due to previous experiences in their native country. The American healthcare system is very different than those around the world. With each healthcare communication experience, building rapport and trust with patients is important. This can be established by always using interpretation services, explaining the idea of preventive medicine, and carefully answering questions nonjudgmentally. We recommend asking patients open-ended questions and spending extended amounts of time with patients so they do not feel rushed. It is important to allocate longer time for refugee and immigrant clinic visits as the interpretation and explanations require patience and time.

Meeting refugees' health care and everyday needs — especially during public health emergencies — is necessary to keep communities healthy and safe, as demonstrated by the COVID-19 pandemic. Studies suggest that primary care physicians are well positioned to offer essential services for refugees and

---

[6] One of the authors who immigrated from Ghana to New Jersey at the age of 3. Currently in the Doctoral Public Health program studying Global Health at the University of Washington. She served for 1.5 years on the CDC's Global COVID-19 Task Force.

respond to their ongoing physical, psychological, behavioural, and social needs, given that many already work with multicultural, underserved, and vulnerable patient populations (Walden et al., 2017). Recent studies have also demonstrated the growing need for strengthening community-based healthcare as a valuable strategy to reduce health inequalities and improve the integration of migrants and refugees into local communities (Filler, 2021). As evidenced by community-based participatory research (CBPR) studies, involving refugees as partners in all stages of addressing their health needs is vital to ensuring that the diverse needs of refugee communities are met (Filler, 2021).

We strongly advocate for community-based approaches, employing an equity lens focused on inequities in healthcare delivery and involving primary beneficiaries in their health solutions. Our goal is to prioritise equity in immigrant and refugee health care so that all people are treated fairly by the systems of care based on their needs.

Helping Victims of Violence

Studies have also shown that refugee and immigrant women are particularly susceptible to violence during migration and frequently have higher rates of PTSD from these stressful transition periods (Hawkins et al., 2021). Physicians and medical providers can have a huge impact by providing social support, which reduces isolation (Hawkins et al., 2021). We recommend communicating health instructions that are easily understood and implemented. It is important to involve the help of therapists, psychiatrists, and/or social workers whenever needed. Providing a list of domestic violence centres can be helpful. Medical providers should look for signs of domestic violence – whether emotional, verbal, or physical – and help patients find safety quickly. Discussing these situations in a supportive environment (preferably with the patient separated from family members) is recommended.

Medical Literacy and Healthcare Navigation

Healthcare providers can improve adherence and "bridge gaps in medical literacy" by spending more time with patients, discussing rationale, answering patient questions, and clarifying medical instructions (Hawkins et al., 2021). Empowering patients to stay involved with English language courses can also be helpful. We also recommend keeping a list of local organizations with refugee services that can be easily provided to patients (Hawkins et al., 2021).

We also recommend providing patients with a navigator who can help steer patients through America's complicated health insurance landscape, facilitate referrals, and arrange patient transportation. It is our responsibility to help immigrants and refugee patients navigate "complex, unfamiliar healthcare systems" (Clarke et al., 2021). In Gastroenterology practices, patient call-back reminders need to be performed in appropriate patient-specific languages for effective communication. We recommend constantly utilising interpreting services and employing medical staff fluent in common patient languages whenever possible.

One effective strategy has been to keep a list of immigrants and refugees coming into the clinic who used to be doctors and nurses in their former countries – and after they become fluent in English through language courses, recruiting these patients to become medical assistants and facilitating their enrolment in the required medical certificate courses. However, we also encourage physicians to take the USMLE[7] Board Exams and complete an American residency program to practice medicine in the United States. It is important to empower immigrants and refugees to stay within the healthcare field as there continue to be shortages of doctors, nurses, and medical assistants around the country.

Recruiting former doctors and nurses to work as medical assistants in high-volume refugee and immigration-focused clinics has several advantages: 1) these employees are passionate about caring for migration populations, 2) they can serve as interpreters, 3) they have huge medical knowledge, and 4) have the ability to connect with and teach patients uniquely.

Helping Immigrants and Refugees Navigate the COVID-19 Pandemic

The COVID-19 pandemic has been an especially stressful time for immigrants and refugees. Immigrants and refugees who have recently moved to the United States are at greater risk of acquiring COVID-19 due to crowded living arrangements and working conditions (CDC, 2021a). Fortunately, primary care doctors and medical subspecialists (including Gastroenterologists) have successfully implemented social work into our practices throughout the pandemic. As directed by the CDC, we have helped immigrants and refugees identify free or low-cost COVID-19 testing (CDC, 2021a). We have provided patients with information about rent deferral assistance programs and food services and educated our patients about COVID-19 vaccines. We recommend that providers ask directed questions

---

[7] The United States Medical Licensing Examination.

to ensure patients work in safe environments from a COVID-19 and occupational health perspective. It is also important to establish a patient-specific "outreach plan that includes contact information, the preferred method of communication, and a plan for frequency of communication once someone tests positive for SARS-CoV-2" (Clarke et al., 2021).

Physicians and public health researchers have documented that many immigrant and refugee patients have experienced "restricted access to routine but critical healthcare services, including visits for primary care-responsive conditions (for example, asthma, hypertension, failure, and diabetes)" (Saifee et al., 2021). During various lockdowns, elective colonoscopies had to be cancelled at hospitals and endoscopy centres around the country due to COVID-19 transmissibility, lack of SARS-CoV-2 testing (especially true early during the pandemic), and a periodic decrease in medical staffing (when medical personnel got sick with COVID-19 or had to quarantine). Unfortunately, this caused many of our immigrants and refugees to postpone their screening of colonoscopies. Many patients cancelled their diagnostic colonoscopies (originally scheduled for work-ups concerning anaemia or rectal bleeding), especially our migrant patients who were already hesitant to have diagnostic procedures performed in the first place.

Several Gastroenterology societies, including the American College of Gastroenterology and the American Gastroenterological Association, formulated expert opinions on how to make endoscopy safer during COVID-19 rises to minimize any disruptions to important diagnostic and screening Gastroenterology procedures. Our goal was to maintain high colon cancer screening rates and prevent delays in diagnosis, especially for patients with alarm symptoms that would prompt urgent endoscopic evaluation. Many Gastroenterologists successfully advocated for hospitals and endoscopy centres to purchase Powered Air-Purifying Respirators (PAPRs) to make esophagogastroduodenoscopy and colonoscopy procedures safer when we needed to evaluate patients who had recently tested positive for SARS-CoV-2. Previously, PAPRs were uncommon in medical care facilities except occasionally stocked for managing tuberculosis patients (when N-95 masks did not fit) or in emergency departments to have on hand for biohazard emergencies.

Some states have developed COVID-19 task forces to facilitate communication between government public health leaders, the governor, physicians, and patients. For example, the Illinois Department of Public Health selected a Gastroenterologist to serve as a COVID-19 Ambassador to help promote vaccine and booster adherence, to educate the public about prevention (wearing a mask and physically distancing), and to encourage patients around the state to continue age-appropriate cancer screening. The Illinois Department of Public Health continues to produce social media graphic design messages (in many diverse languages) that their COVID-19 Ambassadors can promote. Monthly meetings have facilitated outstanding public health communications throughout the pandemic, as the messaging had to be tweaked to stay current as variants emerged. Public health officials can spread messages via social media and reach healthcare systems more easily by including physician leaders across Illinois. The Illinois Department of Public Health COVID-19 Ambassador program has also given Gastroenterologists a platform to communicate directly with policymakers and to better serve as advocates for our refugee and immigrant patients.

One silver lining of the pandemic has been our transition to telemedicine services, which allows immigrants to see physicians during clinic visits (pre-endoscopy and post-endoscopy appointments to review pathology) without taking off a day of work. This is especially important for immigrants and refugees who often have jobs requiring shift work or transportation issues. As Gastroenterologists, we advocate that medical clinics continue to use telemedicine whenever possible to decrease patient "apprehension of being absent from work, lack of transportation and/or inaccessibility" (Hill et al., 2021).

Overcoming Barriers to the Delivery of Good Medicine

We recommend that medical systems provide free or low-cost transportation to help patients attend clinic appointments, obtain labs/imaging, and come in for procedures (with a responsible adult for the post-op ride home). Whenever possible, provide immigrants and refugees with a lanyard or paper form indicating their name and the medical destination so that drivers and medical staff can help these patients every step of the way. Hospitals are notoriously difficult to navigate for any patient, especially those with language barriers who may be reticent to ask for help.

Over the past ten years, Gastroenterologists and medical subspecialists have increasingly tried to minimize insurance barriers to care. "Immigrants who are 'qualified non-citizens' are generally eligible for coverage through Medicaid and the Children's Health Insurance Program (CHIP) if they meet their state's income and residency rules"[8]. Patients whose "annual income is

---

[8] https://www.healthcare.gov/immigrants/lawfully-present-immigrants/

between 100% and 400% of the federal poverty level" are often eligible "for premium tax credits and other savings on Marketplace insurance"[9]. These "qualified non-citizens" include refugees, green card holders (lawful permanent residents), asylees, Cuban or Haitian entrants, non-citizen victims of domestic violence (including spouses, children, or parents), plus federally recognized Native-American tribes or American Indians born in Canada[10]. It should be noted that "Medicaid provides payment for treatment of an emergency medical condition for people who meet all Medicaid eligibility criteria in the state (such as income and state residency) but do not have an eligible immigration status"[11]. These health insurance provisions have been critical to allowing Gastroenterologists, Emergency Medicine physicians, and critical care ICU physicians to quickly treat several emergency conditions, including hepatic failure, hepatic, renal syndrome, oesophageal varices (banding via upper endoscopy), pancreatic cancer, cholecystitis, choledocholithiasis, foreign body ingestion, pancreatitis, and ascending cholangitis.

However primary care physicians and social workers need to educate their immigrant patients about federal assistance programs when they are healthy (preferably during the first visit) to minimize any delay in care due to patient hesitancy when immigrants become seriously ill. We recommend reviewing health insurance coverage and future options at each patient visit. It should be emphasized that applying for (or receiving) "Medicaid or CHIP benefits does not make someone a public charge." In other words, immigrants and refugees "will not affect their chances of becoming a Lawful Permanent Resident or U.S. citizen" by receiving Medicaid or CHIP benefits[12].

This has been especially important for our refugee and immigrant patients with Hepatitis B (usually acquired via vertical transmission at birth) who come to the United States from endemic countries such as Burma (CDC, 2021c) and African countries such as Somalia (CDC, 2021b), Zimbabwe, Eritrea, Sudan, Nigeria, and Liberia (CDC, 2021d). This includes "people born in any country with medium-to-high prevalence of hepatitis B (>2%). This includes all countries in Asia, the Pacific Islands, and most African countries, especially countries in Sub-Saharan Africa." (CDC, 2021d)

It is also important that we vaccinate our patients against hepatitis B to prevent sexually transmitted infections and vertical transmission within the

---

[9] Ibid.
[10] Ibid.
[11] Ibid.
[12] https://www.healthcare.gov/immigrants/lawfully-present-immigrants/

United State (Abara et al., 2017). Gastroenterologists, Hepatologists, the American Association for the Study of Liver Diseases, and the Centres for Disease Control and Prevention continue to work together on public health campaigns to teach the public about both Hepatitis B (preventable with a vaccine) and Hepatitis C (now easily treatable) (Terrault et al., 2018). We aim to prevent cirrhosis, liver cancer, liver failure, and early mortality. This is extremely important since many of our immigrants and refugees come from countries where Hepatitis B is endemic.

Ways to Help Patients Feel More Comfortable

When immigrants are matched with doctors of a similar cultural background who speak their native language, they frequently feel more comfortable and have improved health outcomes. Having accessible patient navigators and translators is critical to help navigate health care.

A notable example of patient-directed guidance is Massachusetts General Hospital's Centre for Immigrant Health, which "provides outreach and guidance to help immigrant patients, staff, and their families navigate access to hospital and community resources, including medical, dental, insurance, legal, educational, housing, nutrition, and interpretation services. All resources are vetted to ensure patients can access them without undue fear of repercussions for their immigration status."[13]

Another great exemplary immigration program with a strong Gastroenterology presence is Valleywise Health, formerly Maricopa Integrated Health System (MIHS), the only public safety net hospital in Phoenix, Arizona. Through Valleywise Health, immigrants and refugees are provided with complete primary care as well as specialty medical services. It also houses the only Women's Refugee Services in the state where full spectrum gynaecological services, as well as full maternity, ante- and postpartum care, are provided.

Phoenix, the capital of Arizona, is the 5th most populated city in the United States (United States Census, 2021). In 2018, 13% of the Arizona population comprised of immigrants, of which at least 50% originated from Arizona's neighbouring country, Mexico. Arizona also historically provided one of the highest numbers of refugee settlements of any state. According to data from the Arizona Department of Economic Security, Arizona has regularly resettled 3-6% of national refugee admissions since 1997. In recent years,

---

[13] https://www.massgeneral.org/children/immigrant-health

refugees from countries such as Iran, Iraq, Syria, Bosnia, Burma, Cuba, Somalia, and Sudan have found homes in the Grand Canyon state (DES, 2021).

To provide affordable care for the immigrants or refugees who do not qualify for the Arizona version of Medicaid, the Arizona Health Care Cost Containment System (AHCCCS), Valleywise Health has established a sliding scale system to provide uninsured patients discounted pricing for their medical care. A patient will be placed on a sliding scale based on multiple factors, including income level, family size, and pre-existing conditions.

The Interpreter Services at Valleywise Health comprise a large team of primarily Spanish interpreters to provide 24/7 in-person interpretation for physicians, nurses, medical assistants, and patients to ensure accurate and culturally sensitive communications are conducted regardless of the complexity of the care. For other languages, including American Sign Language, qualified interpreters can be obtained using telephone or video conferencing services. This is similar to most hospitals around the United States, catering to Spanish-speaking immigrants from Mexico, Central America, and South America.

Each city in the United States has its unique combination of immigrant communities. We encourage hospitals to continue providing as much in-person interpretation as possible. For instance, many hospitals in Chicago provide in-person Spanish, Russian, Polish, Serbian, and Chinese interpreters reflective of the vibrant communities that have emigrated.

Opportunities to pay for medical services with "sliding scale" is a commonly used payment system in safety net hospitals across the country, including Los Angeles, Chicago, New York City, and Phoenix, that helps immigrants obtain healthcare when they cannot afford private insurance or insurance programs through the Affordable Care Act. Many centres offer colonoscopies at discounted rates this way.

It should be noted that "health care inequities among immigrants and US-born residents" have decreased after the Affordable Care Act took effect;" however, there is still important work that the younger generation of physicians and public health leaders must do to help our vulnerable patient populations. "Unremitting inequities remain," especially "among noncitizen immigrants" (Bustamante & Chen, 2021). Hopefully, the recommendations in this chapter will help medical providers excel when organizing medical management for immigrants and refugees. Over the next few years, we aim to help 100% of patients receive age-appropriate medical screening, including colonoscopies, mammography, and pap smears. Improving medical literacy, facilitating communication, providing easy transportation, decreasing financial barriers, and helping patients navigate our complicated healthcare system are the keys to welcoming a diverse and wonderful patient population to the United States of America.

References

Abara W. E., Qaseem. A., Schillie, S., ... & Harris, A. M. (2017). Hepatitis B vaccination, screening, and linkage to care: best practice advice from the American College of Physicians and the Centers for Disease Control and Prevention. *Annals of Internal Medicine* , 794–804.

Akcigit, U., Grigsby, J., & Nicholas, T. (2017, April 2017). *Research: Immigrants Played an Outsize Role in America's Age of Innovation*. Retrieved from Harvard Business Review: https://hbr.org/2017/04/research-immigrants-played-an-outsize-role-in-americas-age-of-innovation

Bustamante, A., & Chen, J. O. (2021). Health Policy Challenges Posted By Shifting Demographics and Health Trends Among Immigrants To The United States. *Borders, Immigrants & Health*, 1-2.

CDC (2021a, July 8). *Refugee Populations*. Retrieved from CDC: https://www.cdc.gov/immigrantrefugeehealth/resources/refugee-populations.html

CDC (2021b, December 3). *Somali Refugee Health Profile*. Retrieved from Centers for Disease Control and Prevention: https://www.cdc.gov/immigrantrefugeehealth/ profiles/somali/index.html

CDC (2021c, December 3). *Burmese Refugee Health Profile*. Retrieved from Centers for Disease Control and Prevention: https://www.cdc.gov/immigrantrefugeehealth/ profiles/burmese/index.html

CDC (2021d, December 15). *People Born Outside of the United States and Viral Hepatitis*. Retrieved from Centers for Disease Control and Prevention: https://www.cdc.gov/hepatitis/populations/Born-Outside-United-States.htm

Clarke, S., Kumar, G., & Zaaeed, N. E. (2021). Potential Impact of COVID-19 on Recently Resettled Refugee Populations in the United States and Canada: Pespectives of Refugee Healthcare Providers. *Journal of Immigrant and Minority Health* , 184-189.

DES (2021, October 19). *Refugees Arrivals Report*. Retrieved from Arizona Department of Economic Security: https://des.az.gov/sites/default/files/Refugee_Arrivals_Report.pdf

Filler, T. B. (2021). A chair at the table: a scoping review of theparticipation of refugees in community-based participatory research in healthcare. *Global Health*, 103.

Hawkins, M., Schmitt, M., & Mkandawire-Valhmu, L. e. (2021). Promoting the health of refugee women: a scoping literature review incorporating the social ecological model. *International Journal for Equity in Health*, 1-10.

Hill, J., Rodriguez, D., & McDaniel, P. (2021). Immigration status as a health care barrier in the USA during COVID-19. *Journal of Migration and Health*, 1-7.

Isaacson, W. (2007). *Einstein: His Life and University* . New York: Simon & Schuster.

Redding, A. C. (2018). *Google It: A History of Google*. New York City: Feiwel & Friends.

Saifee, J., Franco-Paredes, C., & Lowenstein, S. (2021). Refugee Health During COVID-19 and Future Pandemics. *Current Tropical Medicine Reports*, 160-163.

Semuels, A. (2017, February). *How Immigrants Have Contributed to American Inventiveness*. Retrieved from The Atlantic: https://www.theatlantic.com/business/archive/2017/02/immigrants-american-inventiveness/515928/

Terrault, N., Lok, A., ... & Wong, J. B. (2018). Update on Prevention, Diagnosis, and treatment of chronic hepatitis B: AASLD 2018 hepatitis B guidance. *Hepatology*, 1560-1599.

UNHCR (2021, December 18). *Figures At A Glance*, Retrieved from UNHCR: https://www.unhcr.org/ph/figures-at-a-glance

United States Census (2021, December 19). Retrieved from Quick Facts Phoenix Arizona: https://www.census.gov/quickfacts/fact/table/phoenixcityarizona/PST045219

Walden, J., Valdman, O., Mishori, R., Carlough, M. (2017). Building Capacity to Care for Refugees. *Family Practice Management*, 21-27.

www.ingramcontent.com/pod-product-compliance
Lightning Source LLC
Chambersburg PA
CBHW030333270326
41926CB00010B/1606